THE NORTON
ENCYCLOPEDIC
DICTIONARY OF
NAVIGATION

THE NORTON ENCYCLOPEDIC DICTIONARY OF NAVIGATION

by

DAVID F. TVER

EDITED BY HEWITT SCHLERETH

A Stonesong Press Book

W · W · NORTON & COMPANY

New York   London

Copyright © 1987 by David F. Tver and The Stonesong Press, Inc.

Published simultaneously in Canada by Penguin Books Canada Ltd.,
2801 John Street, Markham, Ontario L3R 1B4.
Printed in the United States of America.

The text of this book is composed in Bembo, with
display type set in Centaur Titling. Composition by Com-Com
Manufacturing by Haddon-Craftsmen
Book design by Jacques Chazaud

First Edition

Library of Congress Cataloging-in-Publication Data
Tver, David F.
The Norton encyclopedic dictionary of navigation.

"A Stonesong Press book."
1. Navigation—Dictionaries.   I. Schlereth, Hewitt.
II. Title.
VK555.T88   1987   623.89′03′21   87-5659

ISBN 0-393-02406-7

W. W. Norton & Company, Inc., 500 Fifth Avenue, New York, N. Y. 10110
W. W. Norton & Company Ltd., 37 Great Russell Street, London WC1B 3NU

1 2 3 4 5 6 7 8 9 0

CONTENTS

PREFACE

The Norton Encyclopedic Dictionary of Navigation has been designed to simplify, as much as possible, navigational terms, methods, and procedures. The explanations have been placed in dictionary format so that each term is easily found for quick reference.

The information has been gathered through research in books on navigation, including such sources as U.S. Coast Guard manuals, the U.S. Department of Commerce, U.S. Army Engineers Office, National Weather Service, U.S. Naval Oceanographic Office, Defense Mapping Agency Hydrographic Center, and *The American Practical Navigator* and other sources written by experts in the field of navigation.

Presented here are essential, sound navigational procedures used by every mariner. These are the standard procedures used by navigators of both large and small vessels, pleasure and commercial craft.

Marine navigation is the process of conducting a vessel from one point to another. The navigator has to know his position at all times so that he can establish a safe and accurate direction to his destination and solve the related problems of distance, speed, and time. Position in coastal waters is found by reference to landmarks and manmade aids to navigation and by sounding the bottom; at sea, position is determined by observation of celestial bodies. Deduction of approximate position [DR] is obtained by applying distance and direction run from previously determined or deduced position.

None of the techniques a navigator uses is particularly difficult to master. Anyone who can perform basic arithmetic can become proficient in navigational methods and confident in passages on any of the earth's navigable waters. Anyone can master the instruments, prepare the charts, and become proficient in navigation. However, the ability to navigate is predicated on a thorough understanding of navigational mathematics, mariner's charts, and the magnetic compass.

Much of navigational mathematics involves measurement of an angle (the intersection of two straight lines that meet in a point). Measurement may be obtained visually, by computation, or by consultation of prepared tables of values. A chart is a flat representation of a portion of the earth's curved surface, intended primarily for navigational purposes, normally using the Mercator and gnomonic principles.

The primary purpose of a compass is to provide a means of determining the direction of magnetic north (the north geographic pole), from which any other direction may be obtained.

The Norton Encyclopedic Dictionary of Navigation defines and clarifies the most important areas of knowledge essential to good navigation. The book has been divided into four sections:

In the first section are navigational terms used by all mariners.

The second section covers weather terms and the understanding of weather characteristics.

The third section concerns navigational astronomy, that part of astronomy of direct use to a navigator, comprising principal stars, celestial coordinates, time, and the apparent motions of celestial bodies with respect to the earth.

The fourth section is an alphabet of navigation and sailing.

I

NAVIGATION

A

aclinic line—A line through those points on the earth's surface at which magnetic inclination (dip) is zero. In South America the aclinic line (magnetic equator) lies about 15°S; from central Africa to about Vietnam it coincides approximately with parallel 10°N. An irregular, variable line encircling the earth near the equator, where a magnetic needle has no dip; the magnetic equator.

acoustic Doppler navigation—A form of motion sensor, making it possible to measure speed with respect to the bottom, distance traveled, and drift angle, which when added to true heading provides the true course made good over the bottom. It makes use of the phenomenon of Doppler shift, as in satellite navigation. Unlike inertial navigation, acoustic Doppler is limited by signal attenuation to depths under the keel of less than 100 fathoms. However, echoes from thermal gradients and marine life can be used in Doppler navigation, provided such reverberations produce a signal level greater than the noise level.

Ageton tables—A volume entitled *Dead Reckoning Altitude and Azimuth Table,* formerly published as H.O. 211 and now included in DMAHC publication no. 9 (Bowditch), vol. 2, as table 35; referred to as the Ageton tables, after their original designer. They are also available from two commercial publishers in a small volume of roughly fifty pages. There is a single table of log secants and log cosecants, stated for each 0.5's of arc. Suitable for worldwide use with any declination and for any altitude, they are intended for use from a Dead Reckoning (see entry) position. In this method, two right triangles are formed by dropping a perpendicular from the celestial body to the celestial meridian of the observer. The right angle falls on the celestial meridian at a point that may lie either inside or outside of the navigational triangle. The right triangles are then solved for altitude and azimuth from equations derived from Napier's rules.

alidade—Gyro repeater with a telescopic sight mounted over it. If the telescopic sight is mounted so that it remains pointed in the same gyro direction regardless of the motion of the vessel, it is called a self-synchronous alidade and will retain its setting until oriented to a new gyro direction.

Almanac, Air—Presents celestial and related data for a period of four consecutive months; published three times a year. The daily pages begin with the front cover, with all data for one day contained on both sides of a single sheet; when the daily pages are removed at the end of the day, current information is always on the first page. Each daily page lists, at ten-minute intervals, GMT, GHA of Aries, and GHA of the sun, moon, and three navigational planets. Declination is given every ten minutes for the moon and every hour for the sun and planets. The inside front cover supplies the SHA and declinations of the fifty-seven selected navigational stars. Also on the inside front cover are the incremental corrections to be added for minutes and seconds between the ten-minute intervals of GHA given on the daily pages. The almanac includes altitude corrections, sky diagrams, time of twilight tables, a table for interconversion of arc and time, and other data of interest.

Almanac, Nautical—The coordinates of celestial bodies are tabulated in the *Nautical Almanac* with respect to Greenwich mean time. Using the GMT (or, in practical terms, UTC) of an observation, the navigator extracts the GHA and declination (Dec.) of the body observed. The position of the body establishes one vertex of the navigational triangle; the navigator solves this triangle to obtain a line of position. The GHAs of the sun, moon, planets, and Aries are tabulated in the *Nautical Almanac* for each hour of GMT, and tables of increments permit interpolation for the minutes and seconds of an observation. A small "v" correction factor applying to the GHA is also shown on the daily pages. The sum of the tabulated GHA, together with the increment for excess minutes and seconds, and the value of the "v" correction for these minutes and seconds, is the GHA of the body at the time of observation. The SHA of a star is added to the GHA of Aries to obtain the star's GHA. The SHA of the star is taken from the almanac without interpolation. The declinations of the sun, moon, and planets are tabulated in the daily pages of the *Nautical Almanac* for GMT, as is a "d" factor. The correction of the declination for "d" is obtained from the table of increments for the excess minutes and seconds over the tabulated value. The declination of a star is taken from the *Nautical*

Almanac without any correction. In practice, the navigator always obtains all values of GHA and Dec., plus associated data, from the daily pages during one book opening. He then turns to the increments and corrections tables for the remaining data. This procedure materially shortens the time required to reduce observations.

altitude correction tables *(Nautical Almanac)*—The altitude correction tables of the *Nautical Almanac* are based on the assumption that near-normal atmospheric conditions of temperature and barometric pressure prevail; the assumed temperature is 50°F (10°C) and the assumed pressure is 29.83 inches (1,010 millibars) of mercury. If actual atmospheric conditions differ markedly from these values, the atmospheric density and therefore its refractive characteristics are affected. Under these conditions, it is necessary to apply an additional refraction correction to the apparent altitude (Ha), especially when the Ha is 10° or less. To use the combined correction table for nonstandard air temperature and nonstandard atmospheric pressure of the *Nautical Almanac,* one first enters the top half, using as a vertical argument the temperature and, as a horizontal argument, the pressure. The point at which imaginary lines from these arguments cross locates a zone letter. Using as arguments this zone letter and the apparent altitude, one then finds a correction; interpolation to the nearest tenth is necessary for apparent altitude between tabulated values. The resulting correction is entered in the "add 1" space on the sight form and applied to the Ha along with the correction for standard conditions to obtain the observed altitude (Ho). In practice, corrections for unusual temperatures and barometric-pressure conditions are generally not applied to apparent altitudes greater than 10°, as the amount of the correction for higher altitudes is so small as to be considered insignificant for most applications.

amplitudes—An amplitude is defined, for navigational purposes, as the arc of the horizon between the prime vertical (azimuth 90° or 270°) and a body at rising or setting. When a body is on the horizon, its amplitude may be used to check compass accuracy by comparing the deviation card with the actual deviation observed. Amplitudes are designated E or W according to whether the declination is rising (E) or setting (W), and N or S according to the declination of the body. Two coordinates are required, as E x N, W x S, etc. The bearing is measured through the compass vane at the moment of rising or setting, and Bowditch table 28 is consulted to obtain the correction to be applied to the compass observation. Comparison of this finding with the amplitude contained in Bowditch table 27 furnishes the correct deviation (after the variation has been applied).

anemometer—Measures wind velocity; consists of a metal cross having a small hemisphere at each extremity which rotates in the horizontal plane as a result of wind force. It is mounted in an exposed location on the mast or yardarm and is equipped with an electrically operated indicating device, which is calibrated in knots. When the ship is underway, the wind speed measured is that of the apparent wind, which is the resultant force of the following components: (1) the true wind, and (2) ship's course and speed. Knowing the resultant and the second component, one may compute the first component (true wind speed).

angles (math)—An angle is the inclination to each other of two straight lines that meet at a point. It is measured by the arc of a circle intercepted between the two lines forming the angle, the center of the circle being the point of intersection. An acute angle is one less than a right angle (90°). A right angle is one whose sides are perpendicular (90°). An obtuse angle is one greater than a right angle (90°) but less than a straight angle (180°), one whose sides form a continuous straight line. A reflex angle is one greater than a straight angle (180°) but less than a circle (360°). An oblique angle is any angle not a multiple of 90°. Two angles whose sum is a right angle (90°) are complementary angles, and either is the complement of the other. Two angles whose sum is a straight angle (180°) are supplementary angles, and either is the supplement of the other. Two angles whose sum is a circle (360°) are explementary angles, and either is the explement of the other. Two angles formed when any two lines terminate at a common point are explementary. When two straight lines intersect, forming four angles, the two opposite angles, called vertical angles, are equal. A transversal is a line that intersects two or more other lines. If two or more parallel lines are cut by a transversal, groups of adjacent and vertical angles are formed. A dihedral angle is the angle between two intersecting planes.

Antarctic convergence—The Southern Hemisphere polar convergence. It is the best-defined convergence line in the oceans, being recognized by a relatively rapid northward increase in the surface temperature. It can be traced around the world in the broad belt of open water between Antarctica to the south and Africa, Australia, and South America to the north.

apparent time—Apparent time utilizes the apparent (real) sun as its celestial reference, and a meridian as the terrestrial reference. Local apparent time (LAT) uses the local meridian. The LAT at the 0°

meridian is called Greenwich apparent time (GAT). The LAT at one meridian differs from that at any other by the difference in longitude of the two places, the place to the east having the later time. Use of the real sun as a celestial reference point for time results in time of nonconstant rate for at least three reasons. First, revolution of the earth in its orbit is not constant. Second, motion of the apparent sun is along the ecliptic, which is tilted with respect to the celestial equator, along which time is measured. Third, rotation of the earth on its axis is not constant. The effect of this third cause is extremely small. For mean time, the apparent sun is replaced by a fictitious (mean) sun conceived as moving westward along the celestial equator at a uniform speed equal to the average speed of the apparent sun along the ecliptic, thus providing a nearly uniform measure of time equal to the approximate average apparent time. At any moment the accumulated difference between LAT and LMT (local mean time) is indicated by the equation of time (Eq. T), which reaches a maximum value of about 16^{m}4 in November. Apparent time can be found by converting hour angle to time units and adding or subtracting twelve hours. The navigator has little use for apparent time, as such. However, it can be used for finding the time of local apparent noon (LAN) when the apparent sun is on the celestial meridian.

artificial horizon—Measurement of altitude requires a horizontal reference. In the case of the marine sextant this is commonly provided by the visible sea horizon. If this is not clearly visible, reliable altitudes cannot be measured unless a different horizontal reference is available. Such a reference is commonly called an artificial horizon. If it is attached to or is part of the sextant, altitudes can be measured at sea in calm conditions, on land, or in the air, wherever celestial bodies are available for observation. On land, where the visible horizon is not a reliable indication of the horizontal, an external artificial horizon can be devised. To use an external artificial horizon, the observer stands or sits in such a position that the celestial body to be observed is reflected in the surface of a dish of liquid and is also visible by direct view. By means of the sextant, the double-reflected image is brought into coincidence with the image appearing in the liquid. In the case of the sun or moon, the bottom of the double-reflected image is brought into coincidence with the top of the image of the liquid, if a lower-limb observation is desired. For an upper-limb observation, the opposite sides are brought into coincidence. If one image is made to cover the other, the observation is of the center of the body. When the observation has been made, apply the index correction and any other instrumental correction. Take half the remaining angle and apply all other corrections except dip (height of the eye) correction, since there is no dip. If the center of the sun or moon is observed, omit the correction for semidiameter.

assumed position (AP)—An assumed position (AP) is employed for convenience in using tables for celestial navigation; usually it is a point on the parallel of latitude nearest to the DR position; its longitude is also assumed to suit the tables in use.

astronomic latitude (geodesy)—The angle between the plumb line at a station and the plane of the celestial equator. It is the latitude that results directly from observations of celestial bodies, uncorrected for deflection of the vertical, which in the United States may amount to as much as 25″ (seconds of arc). Astronomic latitude applies only to positions on the earth and is reckoned from the astronomic equator (0°), north and south through 90°.

astronomic longitude—The angle between the plane of the celestial meridian at a station and the plane of the celestial meridian at Greenwich. It is the longitude that results directly from observations of celestial bodies, uncorrected for deflection of the vertical, the prime vertical component of which in the United States may amount to more than 18″. Astronomic observations are made by optical instruments, theodolite, zenith camera, and prismatic astrolabe, which all contain leveling devices. When the instrument is properly adjusted, its vertical axis coincides with the direction of gravity and is therefore perpendicular to the geoid (real earth as opposed to ideal sphere). Thus astronomic positions are referenced to the geoid. Since the geoid is an irregular, nonmathematical surface, astronomic positions are wholly independent of each other.

astronomic triangle (nautical astronomy)—Combining the celestial-sphere concept and the horizon system of coordinates, a triangle is derived on the surface of the celestial sphere known as the astronomic triangle. This triangle projected back to the earth's surface is the navigational triangle; in practice, the terms "astronomic" and "navigational" as applied to triangles are synonymous. In the astronomic (or navigational) triangle, two sides and the included angle are given (co-lat, t, co-dec), and the opposite side (co-alt) and one angle (Z) are solved for. Actually, latitude of the observer (equal to co-lat) is not known exactly but is assumed, as is longitude, in arriving at it. The actual altitude is measured by sextant, and by its comparison with the computed altitude, the discrepancy in the assumption of latitude and longitude is determined. Solutions of the astronomic triangle may be accomplished by using the cosine-haversine law, or Agetan. However, practical navigators no longer resort to spherical trigonometry for the solution of the triangle. Instead, they make use of such tables as H.O. 214, which are tabulations of solutions of thousands of triangles.

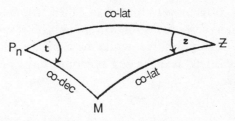

Astronomic triangle

astronomic unit (AU)—The mean distance between the earth and the sun, approximately 92,900,000 statute miles. The astronomic unit is often used as a unit of measurement of distance within the solar system.

atmospheric pressure units (weather)—The pressure exerted by the entire atmosphere on one square centimeter is approximately one bar (a bar being defined as a force of one million dynes per square centimeter). Since fluctuations of atmospheric pressure are very small compared to this large value, the millibar, which is a thousandth of a bar, is used in meteorology, thus avoiding pressure expressions involving many decimal places. Although atmospheric pressure varies continuously over a relatively small range, the average of these fluctuations is very close to a value adopted for certain standard conditions, defined as the standard atmosphere. At a temperature of 15°C and a latitude of 45° the normal pressure is given as 1,013.32 millibars. This latter value is equivalent to 29.92 inches and 760 millimeters. Thus 1 inch is equal to 33.86 millibars and 0.75 millimeter; 1 millibar is about the same as 0.03 inch and 1.33 millimeters.

atmospheric refraction—Light from a celestial body travels through the vacuum of space in a relatively straight line until it encounters the earth's atmosphere. Being a denser medium, the atmosphere has the effect of bending incoming light rays toward the earth's surface. Since the atmosphere itself is not uniform but increases in density as the earth's surface is approached, a light ray emanating from a celestial body striking the atmosphere at an oblique angle is bent on a gradual curving path. This gradual bending of an incoming light ray in the earth's atmosphere is called atmospheric refraction. The greater the angle of incidence of the ray with the atmosphere, the greater will be the angle of refraction toward the surface. The effect of atmospheric refraction is always to cause the celestial body observed to appear to have a greater altitude. Thus, the refraction correction for all celestial observations is always negative. In practice, the refraction correction for the sun and moon is combined in the *Nautical Almanac* with certain other positive corrections to form a so-called altitude correction. The resulting altitude corrections for lower-limb observations of the sun and moon are usually positive, while the basic altitude corrections for the stars and planets, being based predominantly on refraction, are always negative.

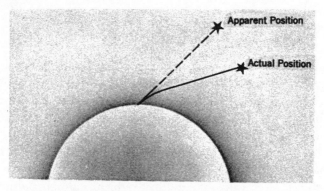

Effect of atmospheric refraction

atmospheric refraction (fata morgana)—Some very remarkable, complicated multiple mirages have been observed frequently in high latitudes along the coasts of the Atlantic and Pacific. These mirages, produced by atmospheric zones of varying densities and thicknesses, transform the appearance of coastline features into strange and often grotesque sights. Shore cliffs and buildings may be seen as tremendous, swelling towers and castles or depressed and flattened into other strange shapes. Observers likened this phenomenon to the legendary castles of Morgan le Fay. The term "fata morgana" has since been applied to any complicated mirage system.

atmospheric refraction (green flash)—The green flash is a strange and beautiful example of refraction that requires an unobstructed horizon and relatively clear atmosphere, two requirements fulfilled at sea. On rare occasions, the last beams of the setting sun (or rising sun) and the surrounding sky flash out in a deep green or blue-green, which lasts but a short time. Since the hued components of white light are refracted differently (violet the most and red the least), conditions can occur, when only a small slice of the sun is above the horizon, such that the red, orange, and yellow portions of sunlight are not refracted. The green parts are, and this results in the flash.

atmospheric refraction (halos)—Halos about the sun or moon are optical results of the refraction of sunlight by ice crystals in high, thin, cirrus, or cirrostratus clouds. The angles of refraction within the ice spicules determine the type of halo that forms, although the halo of 22° radius is the most commonly observed. Mild dispersion usually occurs with this refraction; and the red light, being bent the least, appears on the inner portion of the curve, with the other spectral colors following outward. The green and blue are usually too weak to be seen. For the production of halos, the ice crystals in the cloud must have a heterogeneous arrangement. In this case the refracted light forms a circle completely around the sun. Sometimes, instead of a circle, only two bright spots on either side of the sun result. These images have nearly the same radius as the halos would have if the crystals were situated randomly. They are known as parhelia, or sun dogs.

atmospheric refraction (inferior image)—The deceptive inferior (lower) mirage is rarely seen over the oceans but is common over highly heated land surfaces, particularly deserts. The mirage derives its name from the fact that it always appears below the actual object inverted in position. The mirage is normally manifested by the inverted image of distant objects that are often beyond the range of vision; by the inversion of the blue sky, it gives the appearance of a lake or water surface. The presence of a distant inverted image, shimmering in the sky mirage, creates the appearance of reflection from water. This mirage is the result of a thin, rarefied layer of air caused by the heating of the land surface. The observer's eye must be above this zone, in the denser overlying air. Light rays from the sky, or distant objects, instead of being bent downward in passing through the rarefied layer, as in the case of a looming or superior image, are refracted upward to the observer's eye. The observer's line of sight, being a straight line, projects this image back toward the earth in the direction from which the refracted rays came and creates this inferior mirage.

atmospheric refraction (looming and towering)—Looming and towering are phenomena in which objects actually below the horizon are brought to appear above the horizon (looming) and visible objects are stretched or elongated upward, with an apparent increase in their height (towering). These effects occur frequently in high middle latitudes or Arctic waters, when a marked increase in the density of the air exists near the surface (the density of the surface may be normal, but a marked decrease in density with altitude would have the same effect). In this case, the altitude of terrestrial objects is increased in much the same fashion as that of astronomical bodies. Owing to this effect, lights well below the horizon are often visible to the mariner. With close approach the refracted rays may no longer be intercepted, and the light disappears. When the actual light is seen, the effect of towering may greatly increase its apparent height. Hulls, masts, and stacks of ships are similarly affected.

atmospheric refraction (optical or refraction haze)—Frequently, visibility becomes very restricted even though the air is perfectly free of both dust and water droplets. A definite white haze obstructs the vision, resembling very closely a thin fog or mist, despite the actual clarity of the air. Tongues and layers of air of different densities may be superimposed on each other or intermingled generally, producing a pronounced optical heterogeneity of the air. Irregular refraction is then so great that little light can travel any distance without suffering marked distortion, yielding the resulting poor visibility. Coastlines are frequently shrouded in this haze, being invisible from a short distance offshore as a result of marked temperature inequalities prevailing along shore boundaries.

atmospheric refraction (rainbow)—The formation of rainbows involves refraction, reflection, and dispersion of light. Rainbows are visible on occasions when the sun is shining and the air contains water spray or raindrops. This condition is frequent during or immediately following local showers. The bow is always observed in that portion of the sky opposite the sun. The sun, the observer's eye, and the center of the rainbow arc are always on a straight line; thus a rainbow formed at sunrise or sunset can appear as a complete semicircle on the horizon opposite the sun. In the formation of the rainbow, light entering a waterdrop is refracted toward the rear of it. Some light strikes the rear surface at such an angle as to be totally reflected and then passed out of the front portion. This process, repeated in identical manner for myriads of drops, produces the primary rainbow, which has a radius of nearly 42°. The color bands forming the rainbow differ from those of the halo in that the red is on the outer, and blue on the inner, edge.

atmospheric refraction (superior image)—The superior image requires much the same conditions as looming, again with a rapid decrease in density of the air with increase in altitude. By virtue of the strong resulting refraction, the image of a ship or any object below the horizon may appear in the sky above the horizon in an inverted position. Such conditions may develop when a pronounced inversion occurs some distance above a relatively cold surface. At times the object itself may appear, together with its inverted counterpart directly above, almost as though a reflecting-mirror surface were present. Occasionally, the density stratification of the air is such as to produce still a second mirage above the first, but this time in a normal, upright position. Thus, ships have been seen near the horizon with an inverted image floating above them and a second, upright image above that. Owing to the appearance of the mirage above the actual object, the name "superior" is given to this type.

augmentation effects—The increase in apparent size of the sun and moon as a result of increase in the apparent altitude of these bodies is called augmentation. If the celestial body is near the visible horizon of the observer on the earth's surface, its distance is about the same as it would be if viewed from the center of the earth. If the body is near the zenith, however, its distance is decreased by the radius of the earth.

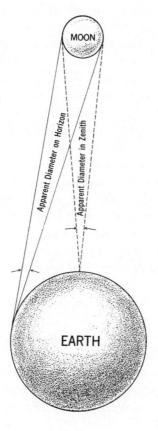

The augmentation effect

Hence the body appears larger than it should when it is near the zenith of the observer, assuming its mean distance from the earth is always the same. The augmentation correction for the sun is so small (a maximum of 1/24 of one second of arc) that it can be ignored, while the augmentation correction for the moon is indicated in the moon altitude correction tables on the inside back cover of the *Nautical Almanac.*

Automated Mutual-Assistance Vessel Rescue System (AMVER) —AMVER, operated by the U.S. Coast Guard, is a maritime mutual-assistance program that provides important aid to the development and coordination of SAR (search and rescue) efforts in the oceans of the world. Masters of merchant vessels of all nations making offshore passages of more than twenty-four hours are encouraged to send route plans and periodic position reports to the AMVER Center, in New York. This information is entered into an electronic computer that generates and maintains dead-reckoning positions of participating vessels throughout their voyages. The predicted locations and SAR characteristics of all vessels known to be within a given area are furnished upon request to recognized SAR agencies of any nation for use during emergency. AMVER is a free and voluntary program. An extensive radio-communications network supports the AMVER system and provides two routes for assistance messages as well as for AMVER messages, coast radio stations, and ocean station vessel radio facilities. The *AMVER Bulletin,* published bimonthly by Commander, Atlantic Area, U.S. Coast Guard, Governors Island, New York, provides information on the operations of the AMVER system.

axis of rotation—The axis of rotation, or polar axis, of the earth is the line connecting the North Pole and the South Pole.

azimuth (Zn)—An azimuth is the horizontal direction of a celestial body from a point on earth, measured from 000° at true north (the north celestial pole, an extension of earth's polar axis), clockwise through 360°. An azimuth (Zn) is a true direction, similar in all respects but nomenclature to true bearing. The azimuth of a celestial body is a true line of position.

azimuth, true—The horizontal angle measured along the celestial horizon in a clockwise direction from 000°T to 360°T from the principal vertical circle to the vertical circle passing through a given point or body on the celestial sphere.

azimuthal equidistant projection—A map projection in which the distance scale along any great circle through the point of tangency (of map with globe) is constant is called an azimuthal equidistant projec-

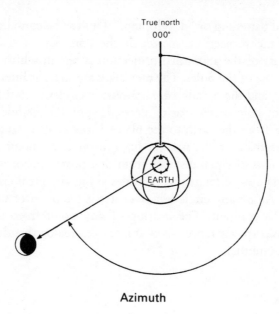

Azimuth

tion. If a pole is the point of tangency, the meridians appear as straight radial lines, and the parallels as concentric circles, equally spaced. If the plane is tangent at some point other than a pole, the concentric circles represent distance from the point of tangency. In this case meridians and parallels appear as curves. The projections can be used to portray the entire earth, the point 180° from the point of tangency appearing as the largest of the concentric circles. Near the point of tangency the distortion is small, but it increases with distance until shapes near the opposite side of the earth are unrecognizable. The projection is useful because it combines the three features of being azimuthal (showing direction), having a constant scale from the point of tangency, and permitting the entire earth to be shown on one map. Thus, if an important harbor or airport is selected as the point of tangency, the great-circle course, distance, and track from that point to any other point on the earth are quickly and accurately determined.

azimuthal projection—Map projection on which directions of all lines radiating from a central point or poles are the same as directions of corresponding lines on the spheres. When centered on one of the poles, it is sometimes called a polar projection. If points on the earth are projected directly to a plane surface, a map is formed at once, without cutting and flattening or "developing." This can be considered a special case of conic projection, in which the cone has zero height. The simplest case of the azimuthal projection is one in which the plane is tangent at one of the poles. The meridians are straight lines intersecting at the pole, and the parallels are concentric circles with their common center at the pole. Their spacing depends upon the method of transferring points from the earth to the plane. If the plane is tangent at some point other than a pole, straight lines through the point of tangency connect points of equal distance from that point. Distortion, which is zero at the point of tangency, increases along any great circle through the point. Along any circle whose center is the point of tangency, the distortion is constant. The bearing of any point from the point of tangency is correctly represented. It is for this reason that the projection is called azimuthal.

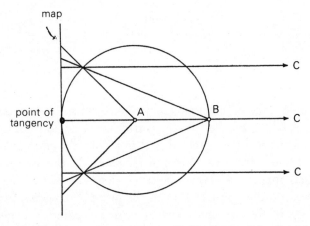

Azimuthal projections: A, gnomonic; B, stereographic; C (at infinity), orthographic. What the map is called depends upon the point from which the light rays originate. A = center of globe; B = opposite side from tangent; C = infinity.

azimuth angle (Z)—The angle between the local celestial meridian and the vertical circle; the arc of the horizon measured from either the north or south points of the horizon (depending upon which pole is elevated) right or left to the vertical circle and expressed in degrees from 0 to 180. Azimuth angle must be prefixed by N or S to indicate which is the elevated pole, and suffixed by E or W to indicate the direction of measurement. If the meridian angle is east, the suffix will be E; if the meridian angle is west, the suffix will be W.

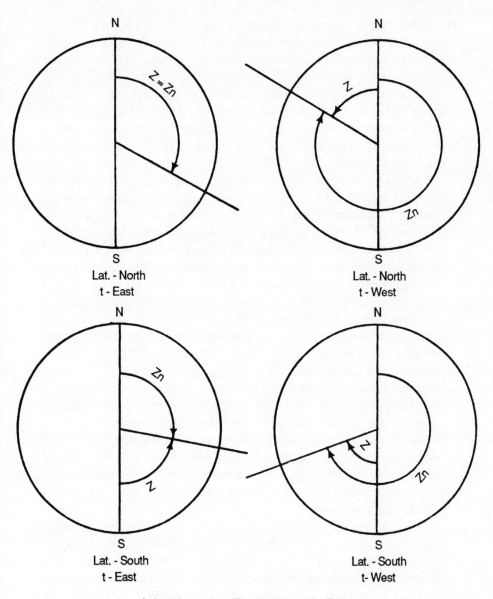

Lat. - North
t - East

Lat. - North
t - West

Lat. - South
t - East

Lat. - South
t- West

Azimuth angles (Z) and azimuth (Zm)

azimuth circle—A nonmagnetic metal ring sized to fit upon a 7.5-inch compass bowl or upon a gyro repeater. The inner lip is graduated in degrees from 0 to 360 in a counterclockwise direction for the purpose of taking relative bearings. Two sighting vanes—the forward, or far, vane, containing a vertical wire; and the after, or near, vane, containing a peep sight—facilitate the observations of bearings and azimuths. Two finger lugs are used to position the instrument exactly while the vanes are aligned. A hinged reflector vane mounted at the base and beyond the forward vane is used for reflecting stars and planets while azimuths are observed. Beneath the forward vane a reflecting mirror and the extended vertical wire are mounted, enabling the navigator to read the bearing, or azimuth, from the reflected portion of the compass card. For observing azimuths of the sun, an additional reflecting mirror and housing are mounted on the ring, each midway between the forward and after vanes. The sun's rays are reflected by the mirror to the housing, where a vertical slit admits a line of sight. This admitted light passes through a 45° reflecting prism and is projected on the compass card, from which the azimuth is read directly. In the observation of both bearings and azimuths, two spirit levels, which are attached, must be used to level the instrument. An azimuth circle without the housing parts is called a bearing circle.

azimuth of Polaris; of the sun (observation)—To observe the azimuth of Polaris, the sun, or any other celestial body, one uses the azimuth circle. When the azimuth of the star Polaris (North Star) is to be recorded, the procedure used is somewhat similar to that for the observation of the bearing of a terrestrial object. The star is first aligned on the black-coated reflector incorporated in the far sight vane; then the gyro azimuth is read from the portion of the compass card directly beneath the sight vane.

To observe the azimuth of the sun, one uses the mirror and prism assemblies at right angles to the sight vanes. A narrow reflected beam of sunlight is cast across the proper portion of the compass card, and the bearing illuminated on the card is the gyro azimuth of the sun recorded. Because of the construction of the azimuth circle, azimuths of celestial bodies are most accurately read when the body under observation is less than 20° in altitude; the most accurate observations possible occur when the body is located on the celestial horizon of the observer. Hence, when the sun is to be used to determine gyro error, the optimal time of observation is near the time of sunrise and sunset.

B

ballistic deflection error—When the north–south component of the speed changes, an accelerating force acts upon the syno compass, causing a surge of mercury from one part of the system to the other, or a deflection (along the meridian) of the mass of a perpendicular compass. In either case, this is called ballistic deflection. It results in a precessing force that introduces a temporary ballistic deflection error in the reading of the compass unless it is corrected. A change of course or speed also results in a change in the speed error, and unless the correcting mechanism responds promptly to this change, a temporary error from this source is also introduced. The sign of this error is that of the ballistic deflection, and so the two tend to cancel each other. If they are of equal magnitude and equal duration, the cancellation is complete and the compass responds immediately and automatically to changes of speed error.

bank—An elevation of the sea floor located on a continental (or island) shelf and over which the depth of water is relatively shallow but sufficient for safe surface navigation. It may support shoals or bars on its surface that are dangerous to navigation.

bar—A submerged embankment of sand, gravel, or mud built on the sea floor in shallow water by waves and currents. A bar may also be composed of mollusk shells. When it is a ridge generally parallel to shore and submerged by high tides it is a longshore bar. Offshore bars or barrier bars or beaches are built principally by wave action on sand or gravel at a distance from the shore and separated from it by a lagoon. When a bar extends partly or completely across the entrance to a bay it is called a baymouth bar. A crescentic bar commonly found off the entrance to a harbor is also called a lunate bar.

barograph—A recording barometer in which the effect of changes of atmospheric pressure on the vacuum chamber is communicated to a long pen arm, which exaggerates this movement. The pen rests on a rotating drum similar to that of the thermograph and yields a continuous trace on coordinate paper wrapped around the drum. This sheet is calibrated vertically in pressure units and horizontally in time, with a line for every two hours. The barograph requires the same corrections as the aneroid: elevation and instrument corrections.

barometer, aneroid—An instrument for measuring atmospheric pressure. It is constructed on the following principles: an aneroid capsule (a thin corrugated hollow disk) is partially evacuated of gas and is restrained from collapsing by an external or internal spring. The deflection of the spring will be nearly proportional to the difference between the internal and external pressures. Magnification of the spring deflection is obtained both by connecting capsules in series and by mechanical linkages. The aneroid barometer is temperature compensated at a given pressure level by adjusting the residual gas in the aneroid or by the bimetallic link arrangement. The instrument is subject to uncertainties, owing to variation in the elastic properties of the spring and capsules, and because of wear in the mechanical linkages. They are ideal pressure instruments for use on board smaller seagoing vessels.

barometer, aneroid (elevation correction)—Unless a barometer is located at sea level, it will naturally show a lower reading than at that level, since pressure decreases with elevation. All barometer readings should be reduced to mean level by adding the proper correction for elevation. Normal pressure is approximately 30 inches. At 900 feet it would be 1/30 less, or approximately 29 inches. A barometer in a ship's bridge 30 feet above sea level would thus have a correction of 0.03 inch. Since the barometer is read to a hundredth of an inch, this is a significant difference. This correction is always positive. Complete corrections are given on page 24.

barometer, mercurial—The most accurate of barometers, used by almost all weather stations and many large ships. There are basically two types: (a) the glass tube containing the mercury, U-shaped, with one end sealed and the other end open to the atmosphere. This is known as the siphon-type barometer. The mercury column is supported by the pressure of the air in the open end. When the air pressure is high on the open end of the tube, the mercury column is also high. As the pressure of the atmosphere decreases on the open end, the mercury column lowers. Pressure readings are made either in inches or in millibars. (b) a mercurial barometer with a long glass tube, a little over a yard long, with one end sealed and the other end open, filled completely with mercury. The open end is then temporarily sealed, inverted, and placed in a cistern partly filled with mercury. When the cork or finger is removed, the mercury in the tube will sink and come to rest at a level of about 30.0 inches above the level of the mercury in the cistern. There is, then, a vacuum above the mercury in the tube and no atmospheric pressure above the mercury within the tube. Since the atmospheric pressure acts on the free surface of the mercury in the cistern, it is clear that the weight of the mercury column above the free surface of the mercury in the cistern must be equal to the weight of the air column above the same surface. The length of the mercury column at any moment indicates the atmospheric pressure, and it is measured by means of a scale placed alongside the glass tube. This is called the cistern-type barometer.

Barometer Scales Comparison (°Normal Atmospheric Pressure)

Inches	Millibars	Millimeters
31.00	1050.0	787.0
30.50	1032.9	774.7
30.00	1015.9	762.0
29.92	10.3.2	760.0
29.50	999.0	749.3
29.00	982.0	736.6
28.50	965.1	723.9
28.00	948.2	711.2
27.50	931.3	698.5
27.00	914.3	685.8
26.50	897.4	673.1
26.00	880.5	660.4

1 inch = 33.86 millibars = 25.4 millimeters

barometer, mercurial (elevation correction)—Unless a barometer is located at sea level, it will naturally show a lower reading than at that level, since pressure decreases with elevation. All barometer readings should be reduced to mean sea level by adding the proper correction for elevation. Normal pressure is approximately 30 inches. At 900 feet it would be 1/30 less, or approximately 29 inches. A barometer on a ship's bridge 30 feet above sea level would thus have a correction of 0.03 inch.

Correction of Barometer Reading for Height Above Sea Level

All barometers.   All values positive.

Height in feet	Outside temperature in degrees Fahrenheit													Height in feet
	−20°	−10°	0°	10°	20°	30°	40°	50°	60°	70°	80°	90°	100°	
	Inches	*Inches*	*Inches*	*Inches*	*Inches*	*Inches*	*Inches*	*Inches*	*Inches*	*Inches*	*Inches*	*Inches*	*Inches*	
5	0.01	0.01	0.01	0.01	0.01	0.01	0.01	0.01	0.01	0.01	0.01	0.01	0.01	5
10	0.01	0.01	0.01	0.01	0.01	0.01	0.01	0.01	0.01	0.01	0.01	0.01	0.01	10
15	0.02	0.02	0.02	0.02	0.02	0.02	0.02	0.02	0.02	0.02	0.02	0.02	0.02	15
20	0.03	0.02	0.02	0.02	0.02	0.02	0.02	0.02	0.02	0.02	0.02	0.02	0.02	20
25	0.03	0.03	0.03	0.03	0.03	0.03	0.03	0.03	0.03	0.03	0.03	0.03	0.03	25
30	0.04	0.04	0.04	0.04	0.04	0.03	0.03	0.03	0.03	0.03	0.03	0.03	0.03	30
35	0.04	0.04	0.04	0.04	0.04	0.04	0.04	0.04	0.04	0.04	0.04	0.04	0.04	35
40	0.05	0.05	0.05	0.05	0.05	0.05	0.04	0.04	0.04	0.04	0.04	0.04	0.04	40
45	0.06	0.06	0.05	0.05	0.05	0.05	0.05	0.05	0.05	0.05	0.05	0.05	0.05	45
50	0.06	0.06	0.06	0.06	0.06	0.06	0.06	0.06	0.05	0.05	0.05	0.05	0.05	50
55	0.07	0.07	0.07	0.07	0.06	0.06	0.06	0.06	0.06	0.06	0.06	0.06	0.06	55
60	0.08	0.07	0.07	0.07	0.07	0.07	0.07	0.07	0.06	0.06	0.06	0.06	0.06	60
65	0.08	0.08	0.08	0.08	0.08	0.07	0.07	0.07	0.07	0.07	0.07	0.07	0.07	65
70	0.09	0.09	0.09	0.08	0.08	0.08	0.08	0.08	0.08	0.08	0.07	0.07	0.07	70
75	0.10	0.09	0.09	0.09	0.09	0.09	0.08	0.08	0.08	0.08	0.08	0.08	0.08	75
80	0.10	0.10	0.10	0.10	0.09	0.09	0.09	0.09	0.09	0.08	0.08	0.08	0.08	80
85	0.11	0.11	0.10	0.10	0.10	0.10	0.10	0.09	0.09	0.09	0.09	0.09	0.09	85
90	0.11	0.11	0.11	0.11	0.10	0.10	0.10	0.10	0.10	0.10	0.09	0.09	0.09	90
95	0.12	0.12	0.12	0.11	0.11	0.11	0.11	0.10	0.10	0.10	0.10	0.10	0.10	95
100	0.13	0.12	0.12	0.12	0.12	0.11	0.11	0.11	0.11	0.11	0.11	0.10	0.10	100
105	0.13	0.13	0.13	0.13	0.12	0.12	0.12	0.12	0.11	0.11	0.11	0.11	0.11	105
110	0.14	0.14	0.13	0.13	0.13	0.13	0.12	0.12	0.12	0.12	0.11	0.11	0.11	110
115	0.15	0.14	0.14	0.14	0.13	0.13	0.13	0.13	0.12	0.12	0.12	0.12	0.12	115
120	0.15	0.15	0.15	0.14	0.14	0.14	0.13	0.13	0.13	0.13	0.13	0.12	0.12	120
125	0.16	0.16	0.15	0.15	0.15	0.14	0.14	0.14	0.13	0.13	0.13	0.13	0.12	125

barometer, mercurial (latitude or gravity correction)—Since the earth is flattened at the poles and bulges at the equator, there will be a greater pull on a mercury column near the poles and a lesser pull at the equator, producing increased and decreased density, respectively. This correction is therefore positive above 45° latitude, negative below, and zero at 45°.

barometer, mercurial (temperature correction)—The mercury in a barometer will expand or contract just as in a thermometer. Thus, an arbitrary reference level must be taken; for the mercurial barometer this is 32°F or 0°C. Hence, when the temperature is above freezing, the mercury stands too high in the tube and the correction is negative and must be subtracted to lower the reading of the mercury column to normal. If it is below freezing, the correction is added in order to raise

Conversion Tables for Thermometer Scales

F = Fahrenheit, C = Celsius (centigrade), K = Kelvin

F	C	K	F	C	K	C	F	K	K	F	C
-20	-28.9	244.3	+40	+4.4	277.6	-25	-13.0	248.2	250	-9.7	-23.2
19	28.3	244.8	41	5.0	278.2	24	11.2	249.2	251	7.9	22.2
18	27.8	245.4	42	5.6	278.7	23	9.4	250.2	252	6.1	21.2
17	27.2	245.9	43	6.1	279.3	22	7.6	251.2	253	4.3	20.2
16	26.7	246.5	44	6.7	279.8	21	5.8	252.2	254	2.5	19.2
-15	-26.1	247.0	+45	+7.2	280.4	-20	-4.0	253.2	255	-0.7	-18.2
14	25.6	247.6	46	7.8	280.9	19	2.2	254.2	256	+1.1	17.2
13	25.0	248.2	47	8.3	281.5	18	-0.4	255.2	257	2.9	16.2
12	24.4	248.7	48	8.9	282.0	17	+1.4	256.2	258	4.7	15.2
11	23.9	249.3	49	9.4	282.6	16	3.2	257.2	259	6.5	14.2
-10	-23.3	249.8	+50	+10.0	283.2	-15	+5.0	258.2	260	+8.3	-13.2
9	22.8	250.4	51	10.6	283.7	14	6.8	259.2	261	10.1	12.2
8	22.2	250.9	52	11.1	284.3	13	8.6	260.2	262	11.9	11.2
7	21.7	251.5	53	11.7	284.8	12	10.4	261.2	263	13.7	10.2
6	21.1	252.0	54	12.2	285.4	11	12.2	262.2	264	15.5	9.2
-5	-20.6	252.6	+55	+12.8	285.9	-10	+14.0	263.2	265	+17.3	-8.2
4	20.0	253.2	56	13.3	286.5	9	15.8	264.2	266	19.1	7.2
3	19.4	253.7	57	13.9	287.0	8	17.6	265.2	267	20.9	6.2
2	18.9	254.3	58	14.4	287.6	7	19.4	266.2	268	22.7	5.2
-1	18.3	254.8	59	15.0	288.2	6	21.2	267.2	269	24.5	4.2
0	-17.8	255.4	+60	+15.6	288.7	-5	+23.0	268.2	270	+26.3	-3.2
+1	17.2	255.9	61	16.1	289.3	4	24.8	269.2	271	28.1	2.2
2	16.7	256.5	62	16.7	289.8	3	26.6	270.2	272	29.9	1.2
3	16.1	257.0	63	17.2	290.4	2	28.4	271.2	273	31.7	-0.2
4	15.6	257.6	64	17.8	290.9	-1	30.2	272.2	274	33.5	+0.8
+5	-15.0	258.2	+65	+18.3	291.5	0	+32.0	273.2	275	+35.3	+1.8
6	14.4	258.7	66	18.9	292.0	+1	33.8	274.2	276	37.1	2.8
7	13.9	259.3	67	19.4	292.6	2	35.6	275.2	277	38.9	3.8
8	13.3	259.8	68	20.0	293.2	3	37.4	276.2	278	40.7	4.8
9	12.8	260.4	69	20.6	293.7	4	39.2	277.2	279	42.5	5.8
+10	-12.2	260.9	+70	+21.1	294.3	+5	+41.0	278.2	280	+44.3	+6.8
11	11.7	261.5	71	21.7	294.8	6	42.8	279.2	281	46.1	7.8
12	11.1	262.0	72	22.2	295.4	7	44.6	280.2	282	47.9	8.8
13	10.6	262.6	73	22.8	295.9	8	46.4	281.2	283	49.7	9.8
14	10.0	263.2	74	23.3	296.5	9	48.2	282.2	284	51.5	10.8
+15	-9.4	263.7	+75	+23.9	297.0	+10	+50.0	283.2	285	+53.3	+11.8
16	8.9	264.3	76	24.4	297.6	11	51.8	284.2	286	55.1	12.8
17	8.3	264.8	77	25.0	298.2	12	53.6	285.2	287	56.9	13.8
18	7.8	265.4	78	25.6	298.7	13	55.4	286.2	288	58.7	14.8
19	7.2	265.9	79	26.1	299.3	14	57.2	287.2	289	60.5	15.8
+20	-6.7	266.5	+80	+26.7	299.8	+15	+59.0	288.2	290	+62.3	+16.8
21	6.1	267.0	81	27.2	300.4	16	60.8	289.2	291	64.1	17.8
22	5.6	267.6	82	27.8	300.9	17	62.6	290.2	292	65.9	18.8
23	5.0	268.2	83	28.3	301.5	18	64.4	291.2	293	67.7	19.8
24	4.4	268.7	84	28.9	302.0	19	66.2	292.2	294	69.5	20.8
+25	-3.9	269.3	+85	+29.4	302.6	+20	+68.0	293.2	295	+71.3	+21.8
26	3.3	269.8	86	30.0	303.2	21	69.8	294.2	296	73.1	22.8
27	2.8	270.4	87	30.6	303.7	22	71.6	295.2	297	74.9	23.8
28	2.2	270.9	88	31.1	304.3	23	73.4	296.2	298	76.7	24.8
29	1.7	271.5	89	31.7	304.8	24	75.2	297.2	299	78.5	25.8
+30	-1.1	272.0	+90	+32.2	305.4	+25	+77.0	298.2	300	+80.3	+26.8
31	0.6	272.6	91	32.8	305.9	26	78.8	299.2	301	82.1	27.8
32	0.0	273.2	92	33.3	306.5	27	80.6	300.2	302	83.9	28.8
33	+0.6	273.7	93	33.9	307.0	28	82.4	301.2	303	85.7	29.8
34	1.1	274.3	94	34.4	307.6	29	84.2	302.2	304	87.5	30.8
+35	+1.7	274.8	+95	+35.0	308.2	+30	+86.0	303.2	305	+89.3	+31.8
36	2.2	275.4	96	35.6	308.7	31	87.8	304.2	306	91.1	32.8
37	2.8	275.9	97	36.1	309.3	32	89.6	305.2	307	92.9	33.8
38	3.3	276.5	98	36.7	309.8	33	91.4	306.2	308	94.7	34.8
39	3.9	277.0	99	37.2	310.4	34	93.2	307.2	309	96.5	35.8
+40	+4.4	277.6	+100	+37.8	310.9	+35	+95.0	308.2	310	+98.3	+36.8

Courtesy of Bowditch/American Practical Navigator

the reading of the now contracted mercury column to normal. At freezing, the correction is zero. All mercurial barometers have an attached thermometer to indicate the temperature.

Reduction of the Mercurial Barometer to Standard Gravity (45°)

Lat.,°	Corr., in.	Lat.,°	Corr., in.
0	−0.08	45	0.00
5	−.08	50	+.01
10	−.08	55	+.03
15	−.07	60	+.04
20	−.06	65	+.05
25	−.05	70	+.06
30	−.04	75	+.07
35	−.03	80	+.08
40	−.01	85	+.08
45	−.00	90	+.08

bathymetric navigation—The art of establishing a geographic position on the open sea by utilization of geological features of the ocean floor. These features are located by means of an instrument called the echo sounder; in practice this device is more commonly known as the fathometer. In order to utilize information received from the fathometer in an intelligent manner, the navigator must first be aware of the basic characteristics of the geological features present on the ocean floor. In general, ocean-bottom features are equivalent to topographical features seen on land, with the difference that undersea geology is usually more subdued and gentle than land geology, owing to the more subtle erosion forces present within oceans. The ocean-bottom areas contiguous to the continents are generally devoid of any distinguishing features, but they are nevertheless useful for navigation by means of their depth contours, which are lines on a chart representing points of equal depth with respect to the surface datum. The zone between the emergence of a continent from the sea and the deep-sea bottom is called continental margin. Within this margin three different subdivisions can generally be identified: (1) The continental shelf is the bottom zone immediately adjacent to a continent or island extending from the low-water shoreline and sloping gently to an area of steeper slope. Its depth ranges from 10 to 20 fathoms down to 300 fathoms and may extend seaward from beyond the shoreline for widely varying distances. (2) The continental slope is the area extending from the edge of the continental shelf into greater depth. (3) The continental rise is a gentle slope with a generally smooth surface, rising from the deep-sea floor to the foot of the continental slope.

beam sea—Waves moving in a direction approximately 90° from the heading. Those moving in a direction approximately opposite to the heading are called head seas; those moving in the general direction of the heading are called following seas; and those moving in a direction approximately 45° from the heading (striking the quarter) are called quartering seas.

beam tide—In navigational usage, a tidal current setting in a direction approximately 90° from the heading of a ship. One setting in a direction approximately 90° from the course is called a cross tide. In common usage these two expressions are usually synonymous. One setting in a direction approximately opposite to the heading is called a head tide; from behind, a fair tide.

bearing—A bearing is the direction of one point on the earth's surface to another, measured from a reference direction clockwise through 360°, and is a means of finding a line of position. True bearings use the reference point true north. Magnetic bearings use the reference point magentic north and must be corrected for variation if true bearing is wanted. Compass bearings are read from the compass with the aid of a sighting vane positioned over the bowl; the method is not always feasible and depends on the height of the compass in relation to superstructure in line with the object of the bearing observation. A compass bearing must be corrected for deviation according to the ship's heading to convert it to a magnetic bearing. A relative bearing is the angular direction relative to the ship's bow, that is, the angle between the keel and the line of sight to the object, measured clockwise from a reference point of 0° at the bow. Reciprocal bearings are those taken from the object to the ship and differ by 180° (+ or −) from those taken from the ship to the object. Below is an example of some bearings. Bearings are measured clockwise from a reference point: true bearings from true north, magnetic bearings from magnetic north, relative bearings from the ship's bow.

bearing, magnetic—Magnetic or compass bearings are taken in exactly the same manner as true bearings, the pelorus card being set beforehand to the magnetic or compass course, respectively. By applying to such bearings the variation or the compass error, as appropriate, one can convert them to true bearings for plotting on a chart.

bearing, relative—A straight line between two objects expressed directionally clockwise through 360°. The difference is that where the normal bearing is expressed in degrees of the magnetic compass, the relative bearing is expressed in degrees relative to the bow of the craft. The bow is zero or 360°. A relative bearing directly to starboard will be 90°; a relative bearing directly to port will be 270°. Before plotting a relative bearing it is first necessary to add it to the magnetic direction of the craft, at the time the bearing is taken. Should the sum exceed 360, it is necessary to subtract 360 to obtain a plottable bearing.

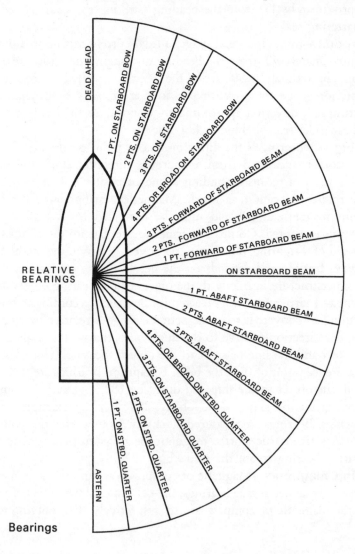

Bearings

bearing, true—Obtained as follows: Set the pelorus to the ship's true course by turning the card until its true-course graduation coincides with the lubber's line. Secure the card. Line up the sighting vanes approximately on the object to be observed. Direct the steersman to say "Mark! Mark! Mark!" when he is steady on his steering–compass course, and when he does so, take the bearing and read the degree on the card indicated by the sighting vanes. As an alternative method of obtaining a true bearing the navigator can give the steersman a warning "Stand by!" followed by a "Mark!" at the instant of the observation. If the steersman was on his course, the bearing was true. If not, one may correct it by applying the number of degrees the steersman was off, being careful to apply the correction in the right direction.

bearing, turning—During conditions when precise piloting is required the navigator must know at what point the rudder must be put over, so that when allowance has been made for the advance and transfer of the ship, she will steady on the desired heading at the time the desired track or point is reached. When he has determined this point, his next task is to establish a means by which he will know when that point

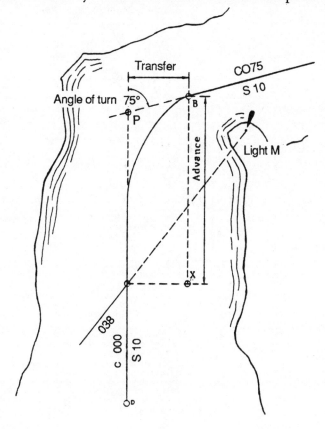

A turning bearing

is reached. This he does by selecting a prominent mark, such as an aid to navigation or a landmark ashore, and predetermining its bearing. This is the turning bearing, and the appropriate rudder angle is ordered when it is reached. Ideally, the object upon which the turning bearing is taken should be abeam at the time of starting the turn; this will give the greatest rate of change of bearing, and hence the most precisely determined point. In actual practice, relative bearings from roughly 30° to 160°, port or starboard, can be used if care is exercised at the extremes of this range; such bearings are usually true bearings.

Beaufort wind scale—A system of estimating and reporting wind speeds, devised in the early nineteenth century (1806) by Admiral Beaufort of the British navy. It was originally based on the effects of various wind speeds on the amount of canvas that a full-rigged frigate of the period could carry but has since been modified and modernized. In its present form for international meteorological use it equates *(a)* Beaufort force (or Beaufort number), *(b)* wind speed, *(c)* descriptive terms, and *(d)* visible effects upon land objects or sea surfaces.

Beaufort Scale of Wind Force

Beaufort No.	Knots (mph)	Description	Effect at Sea	Effect Ashore
0	Less than 1	Calm	Sea like a mirror.	Smoke rises vertically.
1	1–3 (1–3)	Light air	Ripples with the appearance of a scale are formed but without foam crests.	Does not move wind vanes, but wind direction shown by smoke drift.
2	4–6 (4–7)	Light breeze	Small wavelets, still short but more pronounced; crests have a glassy appearance and do not break.	Wind felt on face; leaves rustle; ordinary vane moved by wind.
3	7–10 (8–12)	Gentle breeze	Large wavelets. Crests begin to break. Foam of glassy appearance. Perhaps scattered white horses.	Leaves and small twigs in constant motion; wind extends light flag.
4	11–16 (13–18)	Moderate breeze	Small waves, becoming longer; fairly frequent white horses.	Raises dust and loose paper; small branches are moved.
5	17–21 (18–24)	Fresh breeze	Moderate waves, taking a more pronounced long form; many white horses are formed. (Chance of some spray.)	Small trees in leaf begin to sway; crested wavelets form on inland waters.
6	22–27 (25–31)	Strong breeze	Large waves begin to form; the white foam crests are more extensive everywhere. (Probably some spray.)	Large branches in motion; whistling heard in telegraph wires; umbrellas used with difficulty.
7	28–33 (32–38)	Moderate gale (high wind)	Sea heaps up and white foam from breaking waves begins to be blown in streaks along the direction of the wind. Spindrift begins.	Whole trees in motion; inconvenience felt in walking against wind.
8	34–40 (39–46)	Fresh gale	Moderately high waves of greater length; edges of crests break into spindrift. The foam is blown in well-marked streaks along the direction of the wind.	Breaks twigs off trees; generally impedes progress.
9	41–47 (47–54)	Strong gale	High waves. Dense streaks of foam along the direction of the wind. Sea begins to roll. Spray may affect visibility.	Slight structural damage occurs (chimney pots and slate removed).
10	48–55 (55–63)	Storm	Very high waves with long overhanging crests. The resulting foam in great patches is blown in dense white streaks along the direction of the wind. On the whole the surface of the sea takes a white appearance. The rolling of the sea becomes heavy and shocklike. Visibility is affected.	Seldom experienced inland; trees uprooted; considerable structural damage occurs.

Beau-fort No.	Knots (mph)	Description	Effect at Sea	Effect Ashore
11	56–63 (64–73)	Violent storm	Exceptionally high waves. (Small and medium-sized ships might for a long time be lost to view behind the waves.) The sea is completely covered with long white patches of foam lying along the direction of the wind. Everywhere the edges of the wave crests are blown into froth. Visibility affected.	Very rarely experienced; accompanied by widespread damage.
12	Above 63 (73)	Hurricane	The air is filled with foam and spray. Sea completely white with driving spray; visibility very seriously affected.	

Beaufort Scale of Wind Force *(Cont.)*

Wind Speed (knots)	Wind and Sea Scale for Fully Arisen Sea[a]			Average Period	Average Wave Length	Minimum Fetch (nautical miles)	Minimum Duration (hours)	Average Wave Height[b] (maximum)
	Wave Height–Feet							
	Average	Significant Average 1/3 Highest	Average 1/10 Highest					
0	0	0	0	—	—	—	—	—
2	0.05	0.08	0.10	0.5	10 in.	5	18 min	
5	0.18	0.29	0.37	1.4	6.7 ft	8	39 min	
8.5	0.6	1.0	1.2	2.4	20	9.8	1.7 hrs	2(3)
10	0.88	1.4	1.8	2.9	27	10	2.4	
13.5	1.8	2.9	3.7	3.9	52	24	4.8	3½(5)
16	2.9	4.6	5.8	4.6	71	40	6.6	
18	3.8	6.1	7.8	5.1	90	55	8.3	6(8½)
19	4.3	6.9	8.7	5.4	99	65	9.2	
20	5.0	8.0	10	5.7	111	75	10	
22	6.4	10	13	6.3	134	100	12	9½(13)
24.5	8.2	13	17	7.0	164	140	15	
26	9.6	15	20	7.4	188	180	17	
28	11	18	23	7.9	212	230	20	13½(19)
30.5	14	23	29	8.7	258	290	24	
32	16	26	33	9.1	285	340	27	
34	19	30	38	9.7	322	420	30	18(25)
37	23	37	46.7	10.5	376	530	37	
40	28	45	58	11.4	444	710	42	
42	31	50	64	12.0	492	830	47	23(32)
44	36	58	73	12.5	534	960	52	
46	40	64	81	13.1	590	1110	57	
48	44	71	90	13.8	650	1250	63	29(41)
50	49	78	99	14.3	700	1420	69	
51.5	52	83	106	14.7	736	1560	73	
54	59	95	121	15.4	810	1800	81	
56	64	103	130	16.3	910	2100	88	37(52)
59.5	73	116	148	17.0	985	2500	101	
>64	>80	>128	>164	18	~	~	~	45(–)

[a] To attain a fully arisen sea for a certain wind speed, the wind must blow at that speed over a minimum distance (fetch) for a minimum time (duration). When winds are 50 knots or more, the required fetch and duration for a fully arisen sea rarely occur. The wave heights shown in the last column, "Average Wave Height" represent what will be found on the average at given wind speeds.
    Wave heights refer only to wind waves, and swells from distant or old storms are nearly always superimposed on the wind-wave pattern.
    Practical Methods of Observing and Forecasting Ocean Waves, Pierson, Neuman, James, H.O. Pub. 603, 1955.
[b] H.O. 118A.

binnacle—The compass is housed in a binnacle, which may vary from a simple wooden box to an elaborate device of bronze or other nonmagnetic material. Most binnacles provide means for housing or supporting the various objects used for compass adjustment, as well as the equipment for compensating for deviation caused by degaussing.

boxing the compass—The naming of the various graduations of the compass in order. (*See* compass card.)

buoy—Aid to navigation most commonly encountered. Some are simple metal cylinders moored to the bottom; others, particularly those located offshore, are complex mechanisms that carry special devices for calling attention to their locations at night or in bad weather. Lighted buoys commonly carry a blinking white light or may emit coded signals of various colors or patterns. Others use bells, gongs, horns, or whistles to send out distinctive sound signals. Like the lighted signals, these noisemakers are identified on charts and in U.S. government publications called light lists, which help the mariner to locate buoy positions and his own position in times of poor visibility. Sound buoys are operated in the main by wave action; the motion of the sea causes their bells and gongs to ring, or air to flow through carefully designed chambers to blow whistles. Though the noisemakers are of great value to the navigator, especially along a fogbound coast, they have limited range; the loudest of them usually can be heard no farther off than half a mile. A lighted buoy may be seen for distances of up to seven miles.

buoy, bell—A bell buoy produces an erratic pattern of sounds of a single tone as wave action causes its four tappers, hinged atop the buoy's frame, to strike the lip of the bell. The tappers are equipped with governing devices that limit their swing in order to prevent them from doing damage to the buoy.

buoy, day mark—Day marks are without either lights or audible signals, being intended for daylight use only. In general, these aids are located to mark minor hazards in areas where the water is shallow enough to permit the erection of a fixed structure at small expense. Day marks may also be constructed along the shoreline and may sometimes be paired to form a range. Day marks are now standardized as buoys. For craft entering from seaward, day marks on the portside are square, exhibiting odd numbers on either a white or a black background edged with green. On the starboard, triangular markers show even numbers on a red or orange field. Day marks establishing a range are rectangular, with simple geometric patterns displayed in white, black, or orange. On the western rivers, crossing and passing areas are indicated by day marks.

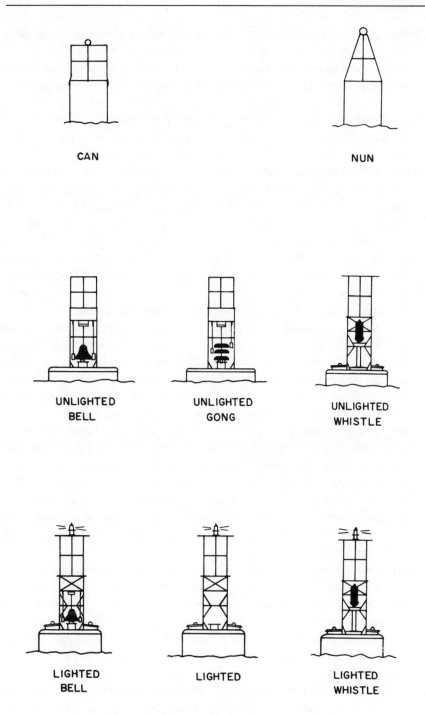

CAN   NUN

UNLIGHTED   UNLIGHTED   UNLIGHTED
BELL   GONG   WHISTLE

LIGHTED   LIGHTED   LIGHTED
BELL   WHISTLE

Principal types of buoys in U.S. waters

buoy, gong—A gong buoy contains a stack of either three or four gongs, each one sounding a different note as it is struck by one of the buoy's hinged rappers. This chime effect enables the mariner to differentiate between gong and bell buoys where two exist in close proximity.

buoy, horn—A horn buoy emits blasts of predetermined lengths and intervals toward all points of the compass. The power comes from the same type of battery system that works a light buoy.

buoy, Intracoastal Waterway (ICW)—Yellow color indicates a navigational aid on the Intracoastal Waterway. On the waterway, any can, nun, or lighted buoy will thus bear a yellow band near the top. Black odd-numbered cans will be left to port by anyone entering the waterway from the north and east traveling south and west, while red even-numbered nuns will be left to starboard. Lettered, banded junction buoys have the usual significance. Vertically stripped midchannel buoys are not used on the waterway. Where the Intracoastal Waterway coincides with another type of navigable water, the standard buoy types for the latter are used, the top yellow band is omitted, and each can or nun is marked with either a yellow square or a yellow triangle. Vessels traversing the waterway must treat the square as a black can and the triangle as a red nun, no matter what type of buoy is bearing the mark. Day marks or range markers on the waterway follow the regular inland conventions, but each is edged or top-banded with yellow.

buoy, navigational (large)—Light towers were developed as a more economical means than a lightship for maintaining a light in an offshore location. The present trend is toward the use of large navigational buoys, which provide a platform for a light, a fog signal, and a radio beacon, plus sensors for sea and weather conditions which can be sent ashore over a radio link. Such buoys can be put on station at only a small fraction of the cost of a light tower and require no on-board crews.

buoy, "red, right, returning"—Of the four buoyage systems employed in the United States, the most important one is that used in waters officially termed navigable waters by the Coast Guard. This system of aids to navigation serves as the basis for the other three. Essentially, the system depends upon the observance of one basic rule. When returning to the land from seaward, a boat must leave all red marks to starboard and black to port, following a traditional mariner's dictum: "red, right, returning." Such marks are coded not only by color but by number and sometimes by shape; and this code is matched to a system of chart symbols. Floating red marks with a conical outline, commonly known as nuns, carry even numbers. Floating black (green) marks, or cans, are cylindrical in shape and bear odd numbers. Day marks are affixed to stakes or pilings driven into the bottom and convey similar messages. Other marks in the system convey other messages: which of two channels is preferable, or where to anchor.

buoy, river—The western rivers buoyage system employs certain aids for dealing with the peculiarities of river navigation. Notable among these are passing and "crossing" day marks. The passing day marks are set down where the river channel runs along one of its banks. As with other aids used in all the systems, their colors, shapes, and lights indicate on which side they are to be passed. Crossing day marks are positioned in places where the channel crosses to the opposite bank. In addition, the system frequently employs aids called ranges. These are two marks used together. A skipper positions his boat to line up the range nearer him with another range farther away, and follows an imaginary line drawn through them to keep on course. Such ranges are also used in other systems, but they are seen most often on western rivers. Western rivers have a few additional distinctions. Since the changing velocity of river currents causes buoys to vary position more than elsewhere, most western rivers are not charted. Aids are not numbered or lettered. Occasionally a mark, however, will show the distance from one point to another.

buoy, special-purpose—Special buoys are not part of the lateral system. Their meaning is indicated by their colors as follows: White buoys mark anchorage areas. Yellow buoys mark quarantine anchorage areas. White buoys with green tops are used in connection with dredging and surveying operations. White and black horizontally banded buoys mark fishnet areas. White and international orange buoys, alternately banded, either horizontally or vertically, are for special purposes to which neither the lateral-system colors nor the other, special-purpose colors apply. Yellow and black vertically striped buoys are used for seadrome markings and have no marine significance.

buoy, station—Buoys do not always maintain exact position; therefore they should always be regarded as warnings and not as fixed navigational marks, especially during the winter months or when moored in exposed waters. A smaller nun or can buoy, called a station buoy, is sometimes placed in close proximity to a major aid, such as a sea buoy, to mark the station in case the regular aid is accidentally shifted from station. Station buoys are colored and numbered the same as the major aids to navigation. Lightship station buoys bear the letters "LS" above the initials of the station.

buoy, whistle—As a whistle buoy rises and falls with the action of the waves, water is forced in and out of a tube in the center of the buoy. When the water enters, it pushes the air within the tube, forcing it under pressure through an aperture in the top, producing a "whistle," which usually sounds more like a low moan.

buoyage system—Buoys are navigational aids, placed to mark dangers or obstructions and to indicate channels in which vessels may be safely operated. U.S. buoys are deployed according to the lateral system, under which a buoy, by its shape, color, number (odd or even), and light characteristics, indicates to the navigator the need to direct his course laterally, either to the right or the left of the buoy, to operate safely. The U.S. system prescribes distinguishing characteristics for the right or left sides of a channel as seen from aboard a vessel proceeding from the open sea toward the head of navigation, a port or harbor. The buoyage system adopted by the Coast Guard is based on this rule: "Proceeding from seaward toward harbor, red buoys shall be kept on the right side of the vessel, black or green buoys on the left." To aid in identification, red buoys are given even numbers; black or green buoys, odd. Several distinct shapes are used as a further aid in buoy identification. A can buoy is a watertight steel cylinder with parallel sides with heavy lugs projecting from the top for lifting. A nun buoy is also made of steel with a cylindrical submerged portion and a typical conical shape above the water line. Skeleton structures are made of steel frames rising above a buoyant steel cylinder. Nun and can buoys are used in a variety of sizes, primarily depending on the weight of mooring chain each must support.

Navigational hazards are too complex to be completely handled by a simple two-color system, so color variations are used. At a junction of two channels where there is a choice of routes, or a point at which there is an obstruction near the center of an otherwise clear channel, the point will be marked by a buoy with black and red horizontal bands, the color of the top band showing the preferred channel. The can having an upper black band indicates that a vessel may pass well clear on either side but that the preferred course is to starboard (buoy to port) for a vessel entering the harbor. A junction or middle-ground buoy will usually have a shape associated with the color of the top band, black or green for cans, red for nuns. Lighted junction buoys have the typical skeleton structure with color banding. Junction buoys may be lettered but are unnumbered. A midchannel buoy has vertical black and white stripes. It may be a nun or a can, either of which is denoted on charts by the divided diamond.

The characteristics of buoys and other aids to navigation along the coasts, in the Intracoastal Waterways and on the Great Lakes, are as if a vessel were returning from seaward when she is proceeding in a westerly and southerly direction along the Maine coast and in a southerly direction along the remainder of the Atlantic coast; in a northerly and westerly direction along the Gulf coast; in a northerly direction on the Pacific coast; and in a northerly and westerly direction on the Great Lakes (southerly in Lake Michigan). Canada maintains a buoage system in general accord with that of the U.S. lateral system.

buoyage system, cardinal—In some waters, particularly those of foreign nations, the cardinal system of buoyage is used. The location of each mark indicates its direction from the danger. There are four quadrants (north, east, south, and west), bounded by the true bearings NW-NE, NE-SE, SE-SW, and SW-NW, respectively, from the danger. A distinctive shape, color, and light characteristic (and "topmark" if one is used) is assigned to each quadrant. A cardinal mark is named after the quadrant in which it is placed, and it should be passed on the named side of the mark. A cardinal mark may be used to indicate that the deepest water is on the named side of the mark, or it may be used to indicate the safe side on which to pass a danger. Such a mark may also be used to draw attention to a feature in a channel such as a bend, a junction, or the end of a shoal. Closely related to the cardinal system are two other types of aids to navigation. An isolated danger mark is one erected on or moored over an isolated hazard that has navigable water all around it and thus may be passed on any side. Somewhat similarly, a safe-water mark also has navigable water all around it, but it does not mark a danger at or beneath it; these include buoys marking midchannel or the centerline of a fairway. A safe-water mark may also be used as an alternative to a cardinal or lateral mark to indicate a landfall.

buoyage system, Western Rivers—Aids to navigation on the "Western Rivers" of the United States, the Mississippi River and its tributaries are generally similar to those on other U.S. waters, but there are a few differences that should be noted. Buoys are not numbered; their color system conforms to the U.S. lateral system, or red–right–returning from sea, with white tops added for improved visibility. (The descriptions "right side" and "left side" are sometimes used, but in terms of a person on a vessel proceeding downstream toward the sea.) Lights and day beacons are numbered, but not in the even–odd style of the lateral system; numbers related to the distance upstream in statute miles from some arbitrary point of origin. Lights and lighted buoys

IALA MARITIME BUOYAGE SYSTEM 'A'
CARDINAL MARKS

Topmarks are always fitted (when practicable)

Buoy shapes are pillar or spar

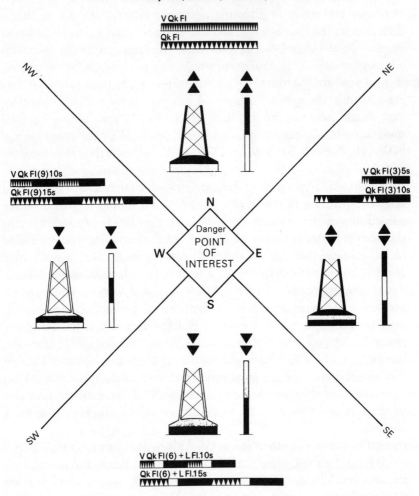

Lights, when fitted, are **white**, Very Quick Flashing
or Quick Flashing; a South mark also has a Long
Flash immediately following the quick flashes.

The cardinal system of buoyage

on the starboard side proceeding downriver show a single green or white flash; those on the portside show a double red or white flash. Special "crossing" day marks are used at bends where the deeper-water channel crosses from one side of the river to the other.

buoy, identification colors—Each maritime country has developed and, in most cases, standardized by law the colors for its own particular buoyage system. These systems are described in appropriate Oceanographic Office Sailing Directions. The following colors represent U.S. buoys and, with the exception of white and yellow, indicate lateral significance: RED identifies buoys on the starboard hand of a channel entering from seaward. A rule to remember is "3 R's," meaning "red, right, returning." These buoys are usually of any type except can, and bear even numbers commencing with 2 at the seaward end of a channel. They may carry a red or white light. BLACK or GREEN identifies buoys on the port hand of a channel entering from seaward. These buoys are usually of any type except nun, and bear odd numbers commencing at the seaward end of the channel with 1. They may carry a green or white light. RED AND BLACK HORIZONTAL STRIPED identifies an obstruction or junction and may be passed on either side. If the topmost band is black, the preferred channel will be followed by keeping the buoy on the port hand, as if the whole buoy were black. If the topmost band is red, the preferred channel will be followed by keeping the buoy to starboard. However, in some instances it may not be feasible for larger vessels to pass on either side of such a buoy, and the chart should always be consulted. Black and white vertically striped buoys mark the fairway, or midchannel. Such buoys are also used in vessel traffic separation schemes at the entrance to busy ports or in narrow passages congested with heavy traffic. BLACK AND WHITE VERTICALLY STRIPED identifies a fairway or midchannel buoy, which should be passed close aboard. Only white lights are carried by this type of buoy. WHITE identifies anchorage. YELLOW identifies quarantine anchorage. Beacons, stakes, and spindles may be erected in shallow water. Their color is in accord with the buoyage system but usually also provides a contrast with the background. These are fixed landmarks and are generally more reliable than buoys.

buoy lights—Buoys of the U.S. lateral system may be lighted as well as unlighted; the colors used and the light-phase characteristics aid in their proper identification at night.

COLOR OF LIGHTS. The three standard light colors used for lighted aids to navigation are white, red, and green. Red lights on buoys are used only on red buoys, or on red and black horizontally banded buoys with the topmost band red. Green lights on buoys are used only on black or green buoys, or red and black horizontally banded buoys with the topmost band black. White lights are used on any-color buoys when required to distinguish them from other buoys in the vicinity or because of the greater intensity of a white light. Since white lights may be shown on buoys of any color, the color of the light has no lateral significance; and the purpose of the buoy must be found in its body color, number, or light-phase characteristics. Lights shown from buoys and other aids to navigation have distinct characteristics to assist in their identification. Lights are described as flashing when the time on is less than the time off. Lights are termed occulting when they are on more than they are off. If the times on and off are equal, the light is designated as equal-interval or isophase. The period of a light is the time it takes for it to complete one full cycle of on-and-off changes. By varying the lengths of the periods and the elements of a cycle, one can obtain a considerable variety of light-phase characteristics. Advantage is taken of this to provide the necessary distinction between aids in the same area and to aid in the recognition of a primary seacoast light by the navigator of a vessel making landfall. The emission patterns are made up of variations of the following types:

FIXED. Abbreviated F; a continuous, steady light showing no change in color or intensity.

FIXED AND FLASHING. F Fl; a fixed light varied at regular intervals by a flash of greater brilliance of the same color.

FIXED AND GROUP FLASHING. F Gp Fl; a fixed light varied at regular intervals by groups of two or more flashes of greater brilliance of the same color.

FLASHING. Fl; a single light flash with no change in color, repeated at regular intervals, with no more than thirty flashes per minute. The duration of each flash will always be less than the intervening dark time.

GROUP FLASHING. Gp Fl; a closely spaced group of two or more flashes, repeated at regular intervals.

OCCULTING. Occ; a light totally eclipsed at regular intervals, with the duration of the light always equal to or greater than the duration of the darkness

GROUP OCCULTING. Gp Occ; a light of a single color subjected to groups of two or more eclipses repeated at regular intervals.

ALTERNATING. Alt; a continuous light that alternates between two colors, with very little change in intensity between the colors.

ALTERNATING FLASHING. Alt Fl; a single flash repeated at regular intervals, with two colors alternating, with not more than thirty flashes per minute. The duration of each flash will always be less than the intervening dark time.

ALTERNATING FIXED AND FLASHING. Alt F Fl; a fixed light of one color, varied at regular intervals by a flash of a different color.

GROUP FLASHING (_____). Gp Fl (_____); a group flashing light in which the flashes are emitted in alternating groups of different numbers. The numbers are shown in the parentheses. Thus, a light emitting a single flash alternating with three flashes will be designated by Gp Fl (1 3).

MORSE CODE. Mo ( ); a group flashing light by which flashes of different duration are grouped so as to produce a character or characters in Morse code. The characters formed will be shown in the parentheses. Thus a light flashing the group "dot, dash" would be shown on a chart or in the light list as Mo (A).

QUICK FLASHING. Qk Fl; a light flash with no change in color, repeated at least sixty times per minute.

INTERRUPTED QUICK FLASHING. I Qk Fl; shows a series of flashes of a single color at the quick flashing rate for a period of about four seconds. This will be followed by a dark period of about four seconds.

EQUAL INTERVAL. E Int; a light with exactly equal periods of light and darkness.

ALTERNATING FIXED AND GROUP FLASHING. Alt F Gp Fl; a fixed light of one color, varied at regular intervals by groups of two or more flashes of a different color.

ALTERNATING OCCULTING. Alt Occ; a light totally eclipsed at regular intervals, with each light duration equal to or greater than the duration of the dark periods, with alternate flashes of different colors.

Color and Lighting Assignments

Buoy	Light Color	Light Character
Black (Green)	White or Green	F, Fl, Qk Fl, Occ
Red	White or Red	F, Fl, Qk Fl, Occ
Junction	White, Red, or Green	1 Qk Fl
Midchannel	White only	Mo
Miscellaneous	White only	F, Fl, Occ

buoy numbers—Most buoys are given numbers, letters, or combinations of numbers and letters, which are painted conspicuously upon them. These markings facilitate identification and location of the buoys on the charts. All solid-colored red or black buoys are given numbers or combinations of numbers and letters. Other-colored buoys may be given letters. Numbers increase sequentially from seaward; numbers are sometimes omitted when there are more buoys of one type than another. Odd numbers are used only on solid black or green buoys. Even numbers are used only on solid red buoys. Numbers followed by letters are used on solid-colored red or black (green) buoys when a letter is required so as not to disturb the sequence of numbers, such as when an additional buoy is placed after the numbering system has been established. Letters may also be used on certain important buoys, particularly those marking isolated offshore dangers. An example of the latter case would be a buoy marked "6 WQS." In this instance the number has the usual significance, while the letters "WQS" indicate the place as winter quarter shoal. Letters without numbers are applied in some cases to black and white vertically striped buoys, red and black horizontally banded buoys, solid yellow or white buoys, and other buoys not solid-colored red or black (or green). The numbers and letters (as well as portions of the buoy) are of reflective material, for better visibility at night.

buoy shapes—In order to provide easier identification under certain light conditions where the color may not be readily discerned, certain unlighted buoys are differentiated by their shape. Nun buoys are used for red buoys or for red and black horizontally banded buoys where the topmost band is red. Can buoys are used for black or green buoys or red and black horizontally banded buoys where the topmost band is black. In the case of other unlighted buoys and non–lateral-system special-purpose buoys, shape has no significance; for example, an unlighted black and white vertically striped buoy may be either a can or a nun buoy. Full reliance should not be placed on the shape alone of an unlighted buoy. Charts and light lists should be consulted to ascertain the significance of unlighted buoys as determined by their colors. Lighted buoys and sound buoys are not differentiated by shape to indicate the side on which they should be passed. Since no special significance is attached to the shapes of these buoys, their purpose is indicated by the coloring, numbering, or light characteristics.

Buys Ballot's law—A law describing the relation of the horizontal wind direction in the atmosphere to the pressure distribution; if one stands with one's face to the wind, the pressure to the right is lower than to the left in the Northern Hemisphere. In the Southern Hemisphere, the relation is reversed. The law was formulated in 1857 by the

Dutch meteorologist Buys Ballot. Buys Ballot's law is also known as the Law of Storms and enables the observer to obtain a fairly accurate approximation of the bearing of the lowest pressure, or storm center. Owing to surface friction, the wind blows at a slight angle with the isobars in an area of low pressure (cyclone). Thus, when facing the wind, the observer in the Northern Hemisphere will have the low or storm-center bearing 90° to 120° on his right, and in the Southern Hemisphere, 90° to 120° on his left. Since the winds at higher altitudes are unhampered by surface friction, they are more nearly parallel to the isobars. Consequently, a discrepancy usually exists between the surface wind direction and the direction exhibited by the movement of the lower clouds. The storm center will be very nearly 90° to the right when the observer faces into the cloud motion.

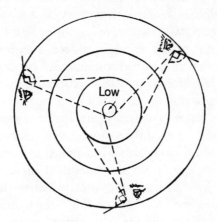

Buys Ballot's law in the Northern Hemisphere

C

carrier waves (electronic navigation)—A series of electromagnetic waves transmitted at constant frequency and amplitude is called a continuous wave (CW). This wave cannot be heard except at the very lowest frequencies, where it may produce a high-pitched hum in a receiver. Because an unmodified continuous wave cannot convey much information in electronic navigation, the wave is often modified or modulated in some way. When this is done, the basic continuous wave is referred to as a carrier wave. There are three methods by which a carrier wave may be modulated to convey information: amplitude, frequency, and pulse modulation. In amplitude modulation (AM), the amplitude of the carrier wave is modified in accordance with the amplitude of a modulating wave, usually but not always an audible frequency. In frequency modulation (FM), the frequency of the carrier wave instead of the amplitude is altered in accordance with the frequency of the modulating wave. This type of modulation is used for FM commercial radio and the sound portion of television broadcasts. Pulse modulation is different from either amplitude or frequency modulation in that there is usually no impressed modulating wave employed. In this form of modification, the continuous wave is actually broken up into very short bursts of "pulses" separated by relatively long periods of silence during which no wave is transmitted. This is the transmission used in most types of radar; it is also used in some common long-range radio navigational aids, most notable of which is loran.

celestial computations (twilight)—The navigator utilizes morning and evening twilight for star observations because during twilight the stars become visible, yet there is sufficient light to define the horizon. Both conditions are necessary if an accurate Hs (sextant altitude) is to be

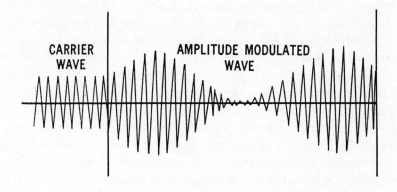

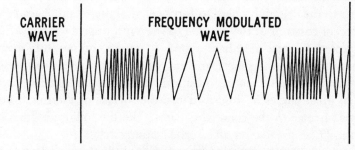

SAME INFORMATION TRANSMITTED BY
AMPLITUDE AND FREQUENCY MODULATED WAVES

Amplitude, frequency, and pulse modulation of a carrier wave

obtained. There are four stages of twilight, based upon the position of the sun with respect to the horizon. They are: (1) Astronomical twilight: sun 18° below the horizon, too dark for observations; (2) Nautical twilight: sun 12° below the horizon, marginal for observations, recorded in *Nautical Almanac;* (3) Observational twilight: sun 10° below the horizon, best for observations; and (4) Civil twilight: sun 6° below the horizon, usually too light for observations, also recorded in *Nautical Almanac.* In practice the navigator should be ready to make observations during the span between civil and nautical twilights.

celestial coordinate system—Just as any position on the earth can be located by specifying its terrestrial coordinates, any heavenly body can be located by specifying its celestial coordinates. To form the celestial coordinate system, the terrestrial equator is projected outward to form a celestial equator, an imaginary celestial sphere. The celestial equator is the reference for north–south angular measurement on the celestial sphere. In similar fashion, terrestrial meridians can be projected outward to the celestial sphere to form celestial meridians. Because of the apparent rotation of the celestial sphere with respect to the earth, these projected celestial meridians appear to sweep continuously across the inner surface of the sphere, making them inconvenient to use as bases for lateral measurements of position on the celestial sphere. A separate set of great circles is "inscribed" on the surface of the celestial sphere perpendicular to the celestial equator, like the longitude lines on the earth. These great circles are called hour circles.

celestial equator system of coordinates—If the terrestrial graticule of latitude and longitude lines is expanded until it reaches the celestial sphere, it forms the basis of the celestial equator system of coordinates. On the celestial sphere, latitude becomes declination (Dec.), north or south; but longitude is measured through 360° toward the west from the vernal equinox and becomes the sidereal hour angle (SHA), which has no east or west tag.

DECLINATION (Dec.) is the angular distance north or south of the celestial equator. It is measured along an hour circle from 0° at the celestial equator through 90° at the celestial poles and is labeled N or S to indicate the direction of measurement. All points having the same declination lie along a parallel of declination.

LOCAL HOUR ANGLE (LHA) is the angular distance between the upper branch of a local celestial meridian and an hour circle on the celestial sphere, measured westward from the local celestial meridian. If the Greenwich (0°) meridian is used instead of a local meridian, the expression Greenwich hour angle (GHA) applies. Because of the apparent daily rotation of the celestial sphere, hour angles continually increase; but meridian angle (t) is defined to increase from 0° at a local meridian to 180°W, which is also 180°E, and then decrease to 0° again. As the celestial sphere rotates, each body crosses each branch of the celestial meridian approximately once a day. This crossing is called meridian transit. It may be called upper transit to indicate crossing of the upper branch (i.e., that part above the equator) of the celestial meridian, and lower transit to indicate crossing of the lower branch.

POLAR DISTANCE is the angular distance from a celestial pole, or the arc of an hour circle between the celestial pole and a point on the celestial sphere. It is measured along an hour circle and may vary from 0° to 180°, since either pole may be used as the origin of measurement. It is usually considered the complement of declination, though it may be either 90° − d or 90° + d, depending on the pole used.

celestial fix—In piloting, a navigator can fix his position by taking bearings of two or more landmarks or other aids to navigation in rapid succession. For practical purposes, it is assumed that these bearings are taken simultaneously, and no adjustment of the lines of position is required. In celestial navigation, observations cannot be taken as rapidly as in piloting, with the result that the lines of position obtained must usually be adjusted for the travel of the ship between sights. This means that what is termed a fix in celestial navigation is actually constructed using the principles of the running fix used in piloting, since lines of position (LOPs) are advanced or retired to a common time. It is customary to consider the position resulting from observations obtained during a single round of sights as a fix, with the term "running fix" being reserved for a position obtained from observations separated by a considerable period of time, typically more than thirty minutes.

celestial fix (running)—When the times of the observations used are separated by a considerable interval (more than thirty minutes) the result is a celestial running fix (R fix). The observations may be of different bodies, or successive sights of the same body. Since the time between observations is usually an hour or more, the LOP obtained from the earlier observation is plotted for the information it provides. This LOP is then advanced to the time of the later observation to establish the running fix, using the same methods employed in establishing an R fix in piloting. There is no absolute limit on the maximum time interval between observations used for a celestial running fix. This must be left to the navigator, who will have to consider how accurately he can determine course and speed during the interval. In most instances, three hours might be considered a practical limit. It should be noted that in summer, when the sun transits at high altitudes, it changes azimuth very rapidly before and after transit; excellent running fixes may thus be obtained within reasonable periods of time.

celestial horizon—A great circle on the surface of the celestial sphere everywhere 90° from the zenith. The visual horizon is the line at which the earth appears to meet the sky. If a plane is passed through the observer's eye and perpendicular to the zenith–nadir axis, we have the sensible horizon. The visual horizon is corrected to the sensible horizon by application of a correction for height of observer's eye. If a plane is passed through the center of the earth perpendicular to the zenith–nadir axis, we have the national horizon. When projected to the celestial sphere, both the sensible and the rational horizon meet at the celestial horizon. This occurs because the planes of the sensible and rational horizons are parallel, and parallel lines meet at infinity (the radius of the celestial sphere).

celestial meridian—A great circle on the surface of the celestial sphere which passes through the celestial poles over a given position on the earth. There are an infinite number of celestial positions or meridians. Each meridian has an upper branch (180° of arc passing over a position and terminating at the celestial poles) and a lower branch (remaining 180° of arc). In common usage the term "celestial meridian" refers to the upper branch.

celestial observations:

LATITUDE BY POLARIS—The latitude of a place is equal to the altitude of the elevated pole. If a star were located exactly over each celestial pole, the altitude of the star would equal the observer's latitude. No star is located exactly at either pole, but Polaris (North Star) is less than a degree from the north celestial pole. Twice during every twenty-four hours, as it moves in its so-called diurnal circle, Polaris is at an altitude at which no correction is required to its observed altitude (Ho) to obtain latitude. At all other times a correction, constantly changing in value, must be applied. The value at any instant is obtained from the tables in the *Nautical Almanac,* the entering argument being LHA (local hour angle of Aries). ♈

LOCAL APPARENT NOON (LAN)—To determine the time of LAN accurately, the navigator, while the sun is still well to the east, enters the *Nautical Almanac* for the appropriate day and finds the tabulated Greenwich hour angle (GHA) of the sun that is nearest to, but east of, the DR longitude, and notes the Greenwich mean time (GMT) of this entry. He then turns to his chart, and for this GMT he determines difference of longitude between the sun's GHA and the ship's longitude at the hour of GMT found in the *Nautical Almanac*. This difference is meridian angle (t) east. The next step is to determine the instant when the sun's hour circle (celestial longitude) will coincide with the ship's terrestrial longitude; this establishes the time of LAN and is accomplished by combining the rate of the sun's change of longitude with that of the ship. The sun changes longitude at an almost uniform rate of 15° (900' of arc) per hour. The rate of the ship's change of longitude per hour is usually determined by measurement on the chart. If the ship is steaming toward the east, its hourly rate of change of longitude is added to that of the sun; if it is steaming west, the rate of change is subtracted from that of the sun. All that remains is to divide the meridian angle east, expressed in minutes of arc, by the combined rate of change of longitude.

MOON—When observing the moon, the navigator measures the sextant altitude of either the upper or lower limb of the body and records the time and date of the observation. He also checks the index error of the instrument. He then converts time to GMT and Greenwich date and enters the appropriate daily pages of the *Nautical Almanac* to obtain GHA, "v", which for the moon is always (+), declination, "d" (noting the sign by inspection), and HP (horizontal parallax). Turning to the appropriate increments and corrections table, he obtains the increments of GHA for minutes and seconds, and the corrections to GHA and declination for the "v" and "d" values. Applying these values to those obtained from the daily pages, he obtains the GHA and Dec. of the moon at the time of the observation. The navigator records the IC (sextant index correction) on his form. Using the *Nautical Almanac,* he determines the dip correction for his height of eye; he records this value and the corrections for altitude and HP from the altitude correction tables for the moon. The latter two corrections are always additive, but if the upper limb is observed, an additional correction of −30' is made. These corrections are combined with Hs (sextant altitude) to obtain Ha (apparent altitude) and then Ho (observed altitude). The navigator then selects an AP (assumed position), based on the best estimate of his position, and uses an a λ (assumed longitude) to determine LHA (local hour angle) in whole degrees. Entering publication no. 229 with integral degrees of LHA, AL (assumed latitude), and Dec., he obtains the tabulated altitude, "d" and its sign, and Z. Z is corrected by visual interpolation for the actual declination at the time of the sight. The correction to the tabulated altitude for the actual declination is then taken from a multiplication table inside the cover of publication no. 229 and applied to Ht (tabulated altitude) to obtain Hc (computed altitude). Hc is then compared with Ho to find the difference of intercept (a). By converting Z to Zn, the navigator can then use Zn and (a) to plot the LOP (line of position) from the AP.

STAR—When observing a star, the navigator measures the sextant altitude of the body and records the time and date of the observation. He also checks the index error of the instrument. The navigator enters the IC on the form and then the dip correction as determined from the *Nautical Almanac* for his height of eye. He applies these to Hs to obtain Ha. The altitude correction is found in the stars and planets column of table A2 or the bookmark; this is added to Ha to give Ho. He then converts the time to GMT and Greenwich date and enters the appropriate daily pages of the *Nautical Almanac* to obtain the GHA of Aries at the whole hour of GMT, and the SHA (sidereal hour angle) and declination of the star. Turning to the appropriate increments and corrections table, he obtains the increments of GHA of Aries for minutes and seconds. Adding this value to the GHA of Aries and SHA of the star obtained from the daily pages, he obtains the star's GHA at the time of the observation. The Dec. is the value tabulated on the daily page. From here he proceeds to "reduce the sight" as described above under *moon*.

SUN—When observing the sun, the navigator measures the sextant altitude of either the upper or lower limb of the body and records the time and date of the observation. He also records the index error of the sextant. This, with its appropriate sign, would be entered in the form, as would the correction for dip, obtained from the *Nautical Almanac*. These would be combined with Hs to obtain Ha. He then converts the time to GMT and Greenwich date and enters the appropriate daily pages of the *Nautical Almanac* to obtain the GHA and declination at the whole hour of GMT and the "d" value for the period (noting the sign of "d" by inspection). If maximal accuracy were desired, he would also note the SD (semidiameter) of the sun from the daily pages. Ordinarily, the Ha is corrected by means of the sun altitude-correction tables, on the inside front cover of the *Nautical Almanac*, which include corrections for average values of semidiameter, refraction, and parallax. Alternatively, the value of the semidiameter, found at the bottom of the sun column in the daily pages of the *Nautical Almanac*, may be used together with the refraction corrections, found under the heading "Stars and Planets" and an additional correction of $+0.1'$ for parallax to be used for altitudes of 65° and less.

These corrections are applied to Ha to obtain Ho. Having entered the GHA and declination for the whole hour of GMT, the navigator now turns to the appropriate page of the increments and corrections table and obtains the increments of GHA for minutes and seconds and the correction to the declination for the "d" value. Applying these values to those obtained from the daily pages, he obtains the GHA and Dec. of the sun at the time of the observation. With the *Nautical Almanac* still open, the navigator notes the value of IC (as determined from the sextant) and extracts the appropriate value of D (dip). These are combined with Hs to obtain Ha. The appropriate correction for ☉ (lower limb) or ☉ (upper limb), taken from the sun table, is then applied to Ha to obtain Ho. The navigator then selects an AP as outlined above under *moon*.

celestial poles—Points on the surface of the celestial sphere which mark the points of intersection of the celestial sphere and the earth's extended axis. The north celestial pole is abbreviated Pn, and the south celestial pole is abbreviated Ps.

celestial running fix—The procedure for plotting a running fix using a celestial line of position at sea is virtually identical to the procedure

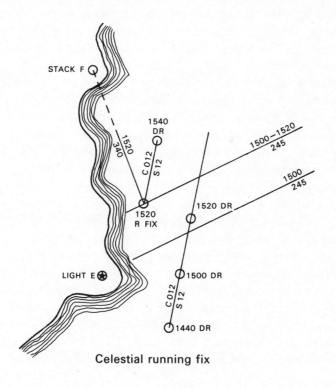

Celestial running fix

used during piloting along shore. A celestial LOP may be advanced for any reasonable time interval to be crossed with a subsequent LOP derived from any source, or an earlier LOP may be advanced and crossed with a later celestial LOP to determine a running fix. No arbitrary time limit exists for the advancement of an LOP at sea, because of the less stringent positioning requirement in this environment as opposed to piloting waters. The only criteria that should be applied are the angles of intersection of the advanced and subsequent LOPs. As in piloting, the distance and direction through which the LOP is advanced is based on the DR plot. It is the normal procedure at sea to obtain running fixes using sun LOPs every few hours during the day. The noon position at sea, for example, is normally obtained by advancing a morning-sun line to cross the LAN latitude line; a midafternoon running fix is normally plotted by advancing the LAN line to cross an afternoon-sun line.

celestial sphere—In celestial navigation, certain assumptions are made that, while astronomically incorrect, are practical because of the great distances involved. A celestial sphere is assumed, concentric with the earth, upon which all celestial bodies are located; the earth's center is the hub of this sphere. The celestial sphere slowly rotates around an immobile earth, causing heavenly bodies to rise in the east and set in the west. This is the apparent action upon which navigation tables are constructed. The components of the celestial sphere are extensions of the earth's navigational components. The axis around which the sphere apparently revolves and the north (Pn) and south (Ps) celestial poles of this sphere are extensions of the earth's axis. The celestial equator is formed by projecting the plane of the earth's equator to the celestial sphere. A celestial meridian is formed by the intersection of the plane of a terrestrial meridian extended and the celestial sphere. The point on the celestial sphere vertically over an observer is the zenith (Z), and the point on the opposite side of the sphere, vertically below him, is the nadir (Na). The zenith and nadir are the extremities of a diameter of the celestial sphere passing through the observer and the common center of the earth and the celestial sphere. The arc of a celestial meridian between the poles is called the upper branch if it contains the zenith and the lower branch if it contains the nadir. An hour circle is a great circle through the celestial poles and a point or body on the celestial sphere. It is similar to a celestial meridian but moves with the celestial sphere as it rotates about the earth, while a celestial meridian remains fixed with respect to the earth. The location of a body along its hour circle is defined by the body's angular distance from the

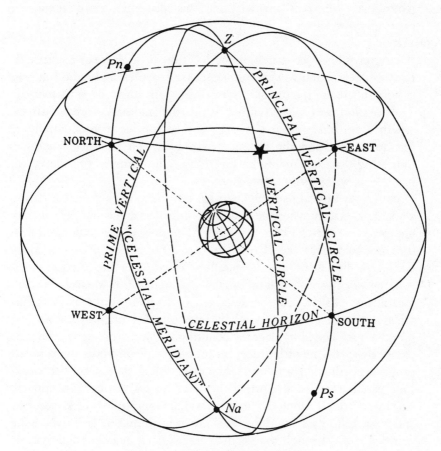

Elements of the celestial sphere

celestial equator. This distance, called declination, is measured north or south of the celestial equator in degrees, from 0° through 90°, similar to latitude on the earth. A circle parallel to the celestial equator is called a parallel of declination, since it connects all points of equal declination. The path of a celestial body during its daily apparent revolution around the earth is called its diurnal circle.

chart—A marine navigational map of the Mercator type on which latitude and longitude lines are at right angles to one another. Compass roses, both true and magnetic, will be found in strategic locations, one inside the other. Distances are measured either from printed scales or from bordering meridians, which are scaled in minutes of latitude or nautical miles.

chart:

CHECKPOINTS—To pinpoint the location of high, man-made landmarks such as water towers, smokestacks, flagpoles, and radio beacons, cartographers use the standard symbol of a dot surrounded by a circle. The notation next to the symbol defines the landmark's precise nature, whether, for example, it is a large domed roof or a small cupola. If the dot is omitted the notation will be given in lowercase type, indicating that the landmark's position is approximate. On the facing page are keys to prominent checkpoints.

GRIDS—A typical nautical chart has built into it a system for telling a boatman exactly where he is, and the direction and distance from any one place on the chart to any other. The principal element is a grid superimposed over the chart. The grid's horizontal lines run in an east–west direction and are parallels of latitude; the vertical lines, running north–south, are meridians of longitude. In this system, any location or position can be described or fixed in terms of the point where a parallel and a meridian intersect. All major parallels and meridians are coded by degrees, counting upward from zero. The zero parallel, or baseline of latitude, is the equator. From there the parallels progress north and south until they reach 90° at the poles. The longitude baseline, called the prime meridian, passes through Greenwich, England. From 0° along the prime meridian, longitude is reckoned, east and west, halfway around the world to a maximum of 180°, where the meridian runs through the Pacific Ocean. Each degree is subdivisible into 60 units called minutes ('), with each minute representing one nautical mile. Each minute further subdivides into 60 seconds ("), or multiples thereof. The basic reference point for calculating nautical directions is north; but a navigator has to contend with two norths. One is true north, that is, the chart direction to the North Pole, where on a globe the meridians converge. The other is magnetic north, the place to which magnetized compass needles point. These two locations are some distance apart; in making calculations, navigators must compensate for the variation. On the next page is an example of a grid of the latitude and longitude lines that overlie every chart. Longitude is reckoned by degrees east (E) or west (W) of the prime meridian, which runs through Greenwich, England, and latitudes are indicated as north (N) or south (S) of the equator. Thus, the coordinates 20°N 20°W mark a spot (✖) just off Africa's west coast.

⊙ CHY	The chimney of a building; the building is not charted, because the more visible chimney gives a navigator a better bearing.
⊙ GAB	A prominent gable on the roof of a building, providing a more precise bearing than would the building as a whole.
⊙ TR	A tower that is part of a larger building.
⊙ STACK	A tall industrial smokestack.
⊙ FP	A free-standing flagpole.
⊙ R TR	A radio tower—either a tall pole or a tall scaffolded structure for elevating radio antennas.
⊙ S'PIPE	A standpipe or a tall cylindrical structure, such as a water tower, whose height is greater than its diameter.
⊙ FS	A flagstaff attached to a building.
⊙ R MAST	A radio mast—a relatively short pole or scaffolded structure for elevating radio antennas.
⊙ TANK	A water tank that is elevated above the ground by means of a tall skeletal framework.
⊙ DOME	The dome of a building. If the building is well known, its name may appear in parentheses; e.g., DOME (STATE HOUSE).
⊙ LORAN TR	A loran tower—a tall, slender structure, braced with guy wires, for elevating loran antennas.
⊙ MON	A monument, such as an obelisk or statue.
⊙ CUP	A cupola—a small, dome-shaped turret atop a building.
⊙ TELEM ANT	The large dish-shaped antenna—known as a telemetry antenna—of a missile tracking station.

Key to prominent chart checkpoints

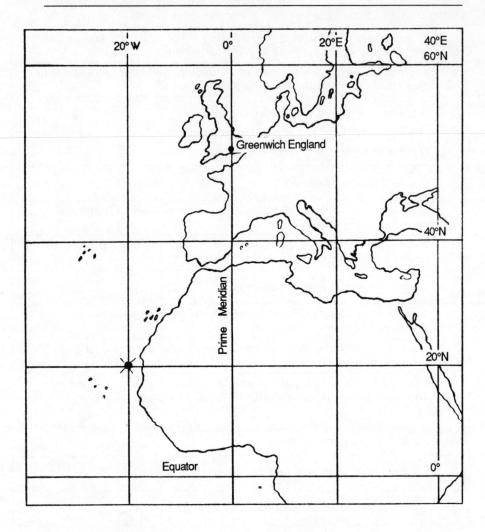

On the next page, the northern terminus of the lines of longitude represents true north, but the north magnetic pole, toward which compass needles generally point, is 1,000 miles away, at Tathurst Island, Canada. Navigators compensate for the variation between the two poles by using a device called a dual compass rose. The amount of variation differs with each locale.

LABELS AND SYMBOLS—Strict conformity to convention is required in identifying lines and points put on a chart if they are to be understood by all who may use them. Every line and point should be completely labeled as soon as it is plotted. The following conventions apply.

Magnetic north   True north

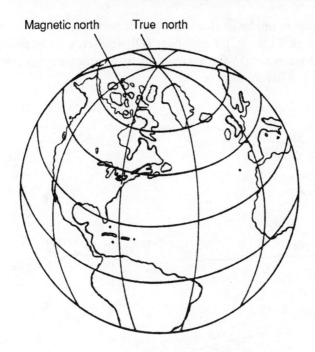

A. The course line is identified by the letter "C" with the true course in three figures above the line. The letter "S" and the speed in knots are placed below the line directly under the course label.

B. A bearing line is identified by the time of observation in four figures above the line, and the true direction of the bearing from the vessel in three figures below the line and directly under the time.

C. A range is identified by the time of observation in four figures above the line. Nothing is placed below the line.

D. A dead-reckoning point is identified on the course line by a small circle. It is labeled with the time in four figures followed by the letters "DR." The labels should be written at an angle to the course line to avoid any possible confusion with other data.

E. An estimated position is identified by a small square drawn around the point. It is labeled with the time in four figures and the letters "EP."

F. A fix is identified by a small circle drawn around the point. It is labeled with the time in four figures and the letters "Fix."

G. A running fix is identified by a small circle drawn around the point. It is labeled by the two times given in four figures and the term "R Fix."

Below are examples of chart-labeling conventions: (A) course line; (B) bearing, or LOP; (C) range line; (D) dead-reckoning point; (E) estimated position; (F) fix obtained by any means, in this case by cross bearings; (G) running fix.

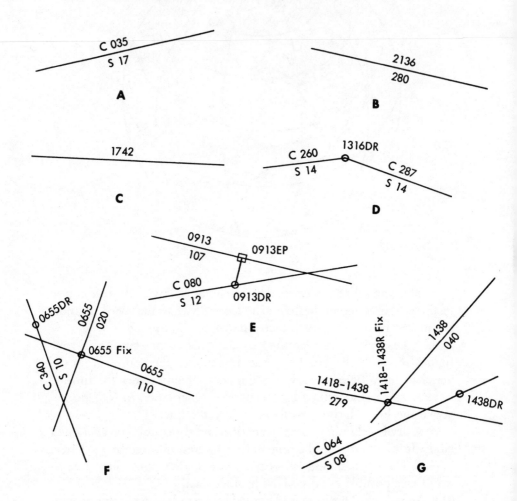

STRUCTURES DRAWN TO SCALE—For low-lying structures such as piers, ramps, bridges, buildings, and towns, cartographers have developed shorthand representations like the ones on the next page. Thus, various rectangular or triangular shapes may indicate streets with houses along them; old military forts are shown by an outline of their ramparts. Such symbols are drawn to scale and depict the landmarks as viewed from overhead.

Buildings and Structures

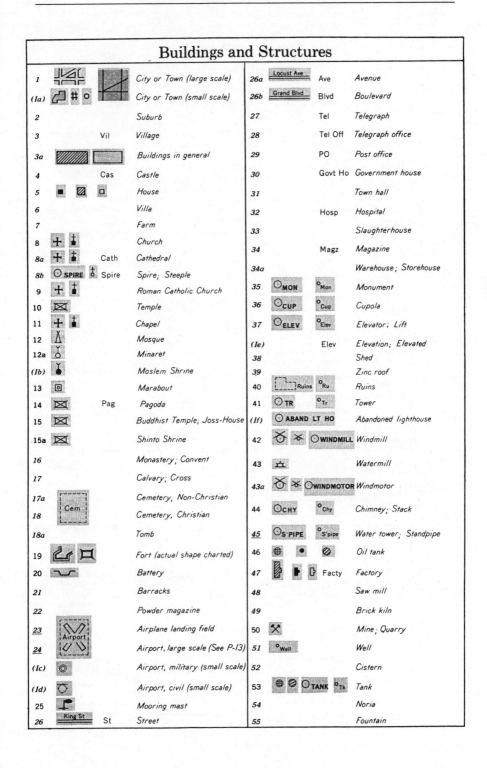

No.	Abbr.	Description	No.	Abbr.	Description
1		City or Town (large scale)	26a	Ave	Avenue
(1a)		City or Town (small scale)	26b	Blvd	Boulevard
2		Suburb	27	Tel	Telegraph
3	Vil	Village	28	Tel Off	Telegraph office
3a		Buildings in general	29	PO	Post office
4	Cas	Castle	30	Govt Ho	Government house
5		House	31		Town hall
6		Villa	32	Hosp	Hospital
7		Farm	33		Slaughterhouse
8		Church	34	Magz	Magazine
8a	Cath	Cathedral	34a		Warehouse; Storehouse
8b	Spire	Spire; Steeple	35	Mon	Monument
9		Roman Catholic Church	36	Cup	Cupola
10		Temple	37	Elev	Elevator; Lift
11		Chapel	(1e)	Elev	Elevation; Elevated
12		Mosque	38		Shed
12a		Minaret	39		Zinc roof
(1b)		Moslem Shrine	40	Ru	Ruins
13		Marabout	41	Tr	Tower
14	Pag	Pagoda	(1f)	ABAND LT HO	Abandoned lighthouse
15		Buddhist Temple; Joss-House	42	WINDMILL	Windmill
15a		Shinto Shrine	43		Watermill
16		Monastery; Convent	43a	WINDMOTOR	Windmotor
17		Calvary; Cross	44	Chy	Chimney; Stack
17a		Cemetery, Non-Christian	45	S'pipe	Water tower; Standpipe
18	Cem	Cemetery, Christian	46		Oil tank
18a		Tomb	47	Facty	Factory
19		Fort (actual shape charted)	48		Saw mill
20		Battery	49		Brick kiln
21		Barracks	50		Mine; Quarry
22		Powder magazine	51	Well	Well
23		Airplane landing field	52		Cistern
24		Airport, large scale (See P-13)	53	Tk	Tank
(1c)		Airport, military (small scale)	54		Noria
(1d)		Airport, civil (small scale)	55		Fountain
25		Mooring mast			
26	St	Street			

Ports and Harbors

#			#		
1	Anch	Anchorage (large vessels)	20		Berth
2	Anch	Anchorage (small vessels)			
3	Hbr	Harbor	20a	(14)	Anchoring berth
4	Hn	Haven			
5	P	Port	20b	3	Berth number
6	Bkw	Breakwater	21	Dol	Dolphin
6a		Dike	22		Bollard
			23		Mooring ring
7		Mole	24		Crane
			25		Landing stage
8		Jetty (partly below MHW)	25a		Landing stairs
			26	Quar	Quarantine
8a		Submerged jetty	27		Lazaret
			•28	Harbor Master	Harbormaster's office
(Ga)		Jetty (small scale)	29	Cus Ho	Customhouse
			30		Fishing harbor
9	Pier	Pier	31		Winter harbor
			32		Refuge harbor
10		Spit	33	B Hbr	Boat harbor
			34		Stranding harbor (uncovers at LW)
11		Groin (partly below MHW)	35		Dock
12	ANCH PROHIB	Anchorage prohibited (screen optional)(See P 25)	36		Drydock (actual shape on large-scale charts)
12a		Anchorage reserved	37		Floating dock (actual shape on large-scale charts)
12b	QUAR ANCH	Quarantine anchorage	38		Gridiron; Careening grid
			39		Patent slip; Slipway; Marine railway
13		Spoil ground	39a	Ramp	Ramp
(Gb)		Dumping ground	40	Lock	Lock (point upstream) (See H 13)
			41		Wetdock
(Gc)		Disposal area	42		Shipyard
			43		Lumber yard
(Gd)		Pump-out facilities	44	Health Office	Health officer's office
14	Fsh stks	Fisheries; Fishing stakes	45	Hk	Hulk (actual shape on large-scale charts) (See O 11)
14a		Fish trap; Fish weirs (actual shape charted)	46	PROHIB AREA	Prohibited area (screen optional)
14b		Duck blind	46a	(10)	Calling-in point for vessel traffic control
15		Tuna nets (See G 14a)	47		Anchorage for seaplanes
15a	Oys	Oyster bed	48		Seaplane landing area
16	Ldg	Landing place	49	Under construction	Work in progress
17		Watering place	50		Under construction
18	Whf	Wharf	51		Work projected
19		Quay	(Ge)	Subm ruins	Submerged ruins

SYMBOLS FOR LANDMARKS—In addition to a knowledge of underwater terrain, the mariner needs a clear representation of the coastal landscape; coastlines are depicted at both high tide and low, inland topography is defined, and any landmarks that might help a navigator fix his position are noted and labeled. Some of the drafting techniques used to portray the shape and character of coastal areas are shown below. Contour lines or hatch marks designate slopes and cliffs. Dots or speckles along the shoreline indicate a sandy or boulder-strewn beach. Green tints denote areas that are uncovered when the tide goes out. A variety of dots, circles, and other symbols give the location of prominent landmarks, and on some charts churches, temples, and mosques merit their own symbols.

chart datum:

DEPTHS—All depths indicated on charts are reckoned from some selected level of the water, called the chart datum. On charts made from surveys conducted by the United States, the chart datum is selected with regard to the tides of the region so that depths may be shown in their least favorable aspect. On charts based upon those of other nations the datum is that of the original authority. When it is known, the datum used is stated on the chart. For U.S. Coast and Geodetic Survey charts of the Atlantic and Gulf coasts of the United States and Puerto Rico, the chart datum is mean low water. For charts of the Pacific coast of the United States, including Alaska, it is mean lower low water. Most U.S. Navy Hydrographic Office charts are based upon mean low water, mean lower low water, or mean low-water springs. The chart datum of the largest-scale charts of an area is generally the same as the reference levels from which height of tide is tabulated in the tide tables. The height of a chart datum is usually only an approximation of the actual mean value specified, for determination of the actual mean height usually requires a longer series of tidal observations than is available to the cartographer, and the height changes somewhat over a period of time.

HEIGHTS—The shoreline shown on charts is the high-water line, generally the level of mean high water. The heights of lights, rocks, islets, and so on are generally reckoned from this level. However, heights of islands, especially those at some distance from the coast, are often taken from sources other than hydrographic surveys and may be reckoned from some other level, often mean sea level. The plane of reference for topographic detail is frequently not stated on the chart. Since heights are usually reckoned from high water and depth from some form of low water, the reference levels are seldom the same.

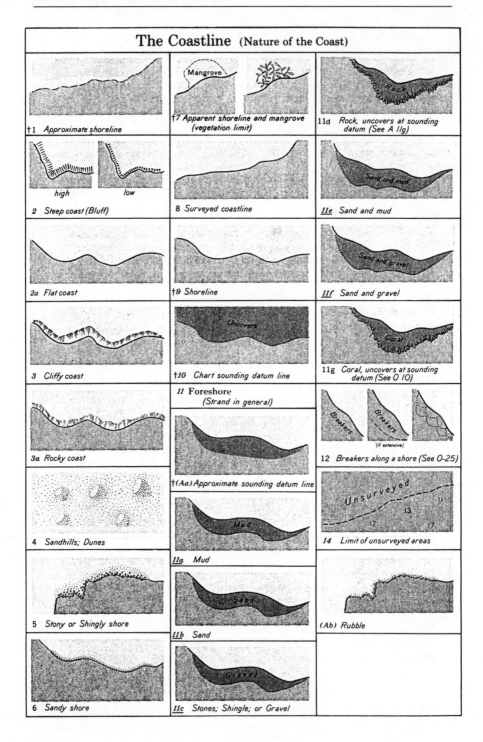

The Coastline (Nature of the Coast)

†1 Approximate shoreline

†7 Apparent shoreline and mangrove (vegetation limit)

11d Rock, uncovers at sounding datum (See A 11g)

2 Steep coast (Bluff)
high   low

8 Surveyed coastline

11e Sand and mud

2a Flat coast

†9 Shoreline

11f Sand and gravel

3 Cliffy coast

†10 Chart sounding datum line

11g Coral, uncovers at sounding datum (See O 10)

3a Rocky coast

11 Foreshore (Strand in general)

12 Breakers along a shore (See O-25)
(if extensive)

4 Sandhills; Dunes

†(Aa) Approximate sounding datum line

14 Limit of unsurveyed areas

5 Stony or Shingly shore

11a Mud

6 Sandy shore

11b Sand

(Ab) Rubble

11c Stones; Shingle; or Gravel

Coast Features

1	G	Gulf
2	B	Bay
(Ba)	B	Bayou
3	Fd	Fjord
4	L	Loch; Lough; Lake
5	Cr	Creek
5a	C	Cove
6	In	Inlet
7	Str	Strait
8	Sd	Sound
9	Pass	Passage; Pass
	Thoro	Thorofare
10	Chan	Channel
10a		Narrows
11	Entr	Entrance
12	Est	Estuary
12a		Delta
13	Mth	Mouth
14	Rd	Road; Roadstead
15	Anch	Anchorage
16	Hbr	Harbor
16a	Hn	Haven
17	P	Port
(Bb)	P	Pond
18	I	Island
19	It	Islet
20	Arch	Archipelago
21	Pen	Peninsula
22	C	Cape
23	Prom	Promontory
24	Hd	Head; Headland
25	Pt	Point
26	Mt	Mountain; Mount
27	Rge	Range
27a		Valley
28		Summit
29	Pk	Peak
30	Vol	Volcano
31		Hill
32	Bld	Boulder
33	Ldg	Landing
34		Tableland (Plateau)
35	Rk	Rock
36		Isolated rock
(Bc)	Str	Stream
(Bd)	R	River
(Be)	Slu .	Slough
(Bf)	Lag	Lagoon
(Bg)	Apprs	Approaches
(Bh)	Rky	Rocky
†(Bi)	Is	Islands
†(Bj)	Ma	Marsh
†(Bk)	Mg	Mangrove
†(Bl)	Sw	Swamp

The Land

1 Contour lines (Contours)

1a Contour lines, approximate (Contours)

2 Hachures

2a Form lines, no definite interval

2b Shading

3 Glacier

4 Saltpans

5 Isolated trees

5a Deciduous or of unknown or unspecified type

5b Coniferous

5c Palm tree

5d Nipa palm

5e Filao

5f Casuarina

5g Evergreen tree (other than coniferous)

6 Cultivated fields

6a Grass fields

7 Paddy (rice) fields

7a Park; Garden

8 Bushes

8a Tree plantation in general

9 Deciduous woodland

10 Coniferous woodland

10a Woods in general

11 Tree top height (above shoreline datum)

12 Lava flow

13 River; Stream

14 Intermittent stream

15 Lake; Pond

16 Lagoon (Lag)

Symbol used in small areas

17 Marsh; Swamp

18 Slough (Slu.)

19 Rapids

20 Waterfalls

21 Spring

chart numbering system—To provide an orderly system for the numbering of U.S. charts, a worldwide scheme has been adopted which generally identifies a chart by means of a scale range and geographic location. U.S. charts have numbers consisting of one to five digits as follows:

One digit	No scale involved
Two digits	1:9,000,001 and smaller
Three digits	1:2,000,001 to 1:9,000,000
Four digits	Various non-navigational items
Five digits	1:2,000,000 and larger

The one-digit category comprises the symbol and abbreviation sheets for the United States and some other nations. Also included is the chart of International code flags and pennants published by DMAHC. The two- and three-digit categories contain charts of very large areas, such as entire oceans or major portions thereof. For these numbers, the world's waters have been divided into nine ocean basins numbered as follows: The first digit of a two- or three-digit chart number (with limited exceptions) indicates the ocean basin concerned. (The small areas of the Mediterranean and Caribbean seas make very small-scale charts valueless; thus two-digit chart numbers beginning with 3 or 4 do not fit into the overall numbering scheme.) The four-digit category consists of a series of non-navigational, special-purpose charts. These are numbered by arbitrarily assigning blocks of new numbers to existing series and to new series when originated. The five-digit category includes those charts most often used by navigators. Except on bathymetric charts, the first of the five digits indicates one of the nine coastal regions of the world in which the chart is located. The second of the five digits identifies a subregion. The final three digits associate the chart with a specific location; they are assigned counterclockwise around the subregion. Many gaps are left in the assignment of numbers, so that any future charts may be smoothly fitted into the system.

chart projection types—Projections are classified primarily by the type of surface to which the spheroidal globe is transferred. The projection used most frequently by mariners is commonly called Mercator, after its inventor. Classified according to type, this is an equatorial cylindrical orthomorphic projection, the cylinder conceived as being tangent along the equator. A similar projection, based upon a cylinder tangent along a meridian, is called transverse Mercator or transverse cylindrical orthomorphic. If the cylinder is tangent along a great circle other than the equator or a meridian, the projection is called oblique Mercator or oblique cylindrical orthomorphic. In a simple conic projection, points on the surface of the earth are conceived as transferred to a tangent cone. In a Lambert conformal projection, the cone intersects the earth (a secant cone) at two small circles. In a polyconic projection, a series of tangent cones is used. An azimuthal or zenithal projection is one in which points on the earth are transferred directly to a plane. If the origin of the projecting rays is the center of the earth, a gnomonic projection results; if it is the point opposite the plane's point of tangency, a stereographic projection; and if at infinity (the projecting lines being parallel to each other), an orthographic projection. A graticule is the network of latitude and longitude lines laid out in accordance with the principle of any projection.

chart sources—There are two major chart-issuing agencies for U.S. vessels: the Naval Oceanographic Office and the National Ocean Survey; both are situated in Washington, D.C., and have numerous branches. The Naval Oceanographic Office, by its own surveys and through liaison with foreign oceanographic agencies, prepares and publishes both nautical and aeronautical charts of the high seas and foreign waters. The National Ocean Survey, within the Department of Commerce, prepares and publishes coastal and harbor charts of the United States and its possessions. Aeronautical charts of the United States are published by the National Ocean Survey. The U.S. Lake Survey Office, Army Engineer District, Detroit, Michigan, publishes charts of the Great Lakes (less Georgian Bay and Canadian harbors), Lake Champlain, and the St. Lawrence River above St. Regis and Cornwall, Canada. The Department of the Army, Corps of Engineers Army Map Service, Washington, D.C., does topographic maps.

chart types:

COAST CHARTS—Coast charts are plotted to scales of 1:50,000 or 1:100,000. These charts have sufficient detail to assist navigation into bays and sounds, inside of outlying reefs and shoals. Charts in this series necessarily cover a smaller area than do the general charts.

GENERAL CHARTS—General charts are plotted to scales of from 1:100,000 to 1:600,000. They are used primarily for coastwise navigation outside of reefs and shoals, but in water where positions can be determined from landmarks, lights, buoys, and depth soundings. These show more aids to navigation and much more coastal detail than do sailing charts.

GREAT LAKES—Charts prepared by the U.S. Army Corps of Engineers for use in the Great Lakes are based on polyconic projections rather than on the Mercator. Because of the small span of latitude covered by each chart, the convergence of the meridians is scarcely noticeable. Traffic on the lakes is so heavy that specific sailing courses are recommended and are plotted on the charts. Distances in the Great Lakes charts are given in statute rather than in nautical miles, and scales are given in feet, yards, meters, and statute miles.

HARBOR CHARTS—Scaled 1:500,000 or even larger. Show sufficient detail to permit navigation into harbors or other restricted areas; all pertinent details of land and water are included.

INTRACOASTAL WATERWAY (ICW)—The Intracoastal Waterway, running from Manasquan Inlet, New Jersey, to Brownsville, Texas, with interconnections, is covered by a special series of SC (small craft) charts. Each chart in this series is supplemented by descriptive material showing controlling depths of water, bridge clearances, and hours of operation; other pertinent information.

PILOT CHARTS—Pilot charts are used for planning long-distance voyages rather than for detailed navigation. Three pilot charts are published each month by the Oceanographic Office: North Atlantic Ocean; Greenland and Barents Sea; North Pacific Ocean. Some coastal details are included in these charts, but the emphasis is on oceanographic and meteorological data. Pilot charts depict, for the month issued, average prevailing winds, gales, calms, fog, ocean currents, air and water temperatures, limits of field ice, and icebergs. The location of ocean weather vessels and steamship routes are shown.

SAILING CHARTS—Small-scale charts covering large areas of ocean. They are used for planning and navigating offshore passages to distant ports, for plotting positions at sea, and for making approaches to the coast from the open ocean. Modern sailing charts show the hyperbolic position lines of the loran system. These lines permit a rapid and accurate determination of a ship's position from a pair of loran readings. Sailing charts are usually to a scale of 1:600,000, 1;1,200,000, or even smaller. Soundings within the sixty-feet line are omitted. Only principal lights and offshore buoys are charted.

SMALL-CRAFT CHARTS—The National Ocean Survey has recognized the needs of small-boat pilots by issuing small-craft charts, arranged to cover areas of intense boating activity. The special format of these charts makes for easy use on small-chart tables, or folded on the pilot's lap. Basic chart scales in this series are usually 1:40,000, although some harbor inserts are scaled to only 1:10,000. Charts in this series are designated by the letters "SC" followed by the chart identification number.

chinook winds—Warm, dry winds descending the leeward slopes of mountains. The air, in falling to the floor of an adjacent valley or plain after coming across the mountaintop, warms by compressing (adiabatically) at the rate of 1°F for each 185 feet of descent. Thus, if the wind descends the side of a mountain several thousands of feet high, it will be considerably warmer and hence drier than the air prevailing in that area. In the winter and early spring, such warm, dry winds are responsible for rapid melting of the snow, clearing the soil for spring farming. In Europe, the name foehn is applied to this wind, while in the United States and Canada along the eastern or lee slopes of the Rockies, the Indian name chinook is used. The chinook originates from winds that ascend the windward slopes and descend the leeward slopes of a mountain range.

chronometer—The navigator's most accurate timepiece. It is usually stowed so as to be protected against shock, electrical influence, and extreme changes in temperature. Most vessels carry three chronometers for purposes of comparison. The chronometer is set to GMT and never reset until returned to a chronometer pool for cleaning and adjustment; this is necessary every two or three years. The chronometer is wound daily at a regular time. Time signals for checking chronometers may be received from radio stations WWV and WWVH, of the National Bureau of Standards, Department of Commerce, transmitting from Colorado and Hawaii respectively, and from the naval radio station, NSS, Annapolis, Maryland. Upon receiving a radio time signal, the navigator checks the chronometer and establishes the chronometer error. There is nearly always a chronometer error (CE), either fast (F) or slow (S). The change in chronometer error in twenty-four hours is called chronometer rate, or daily rate, and is designated gaining or losing. With a consistent rate of 1s per day for three years, the chronometer error could be approximately 18^m. Since chronometer error is subject to change, it should be determined from time to time, preferably daily at sea. Chronometer error is found by radio time signal, by comparison with another timepiece of known error, or by applying chronometer rate to previous readings of the same instrument. It is recorded to the nearest whole or half second. Chronometer rate is recorded to the nearest 0^{s}1

chronometer, marine, quartz-crystal—Used as replacements for spring-driven aboard ships of the U.S. Navy. The accuracy of these instruments is such that the time can be read without resort to chronometer rate. The quartz-crystal chronometer designed for the U.S. Navy displays time using a twenty-four-hour dial. It indicates the day of the week. The basic element for time generation is a quartz–crystal oscillator. The quartz crystal is temperature compensated and sealed in a vacuum. Adjustment is provided for the aging of the crystal. The chronometer is designed to operate a minimum of one year on a set of batteries.

chronometer, spring-driven marine—A timepiece having a nearly constant rate. It is used aboard ship to provide accurate time, primarily for timing celestial observations for lines of position, and for setting the ship's other timepieces. It differs from a watch principally in that it contains a variable-level device to maintain even pressure on the mainspring and a special balance designed to compensate for temperature variations. A spring-driven chronometer is set approximately to Greenwich mean time (GMT) and is not reset until the instrument is overhauled and cleaned, usually at three-year intervals. A spring-driven chronometer is mounted in gimbals in a box. Principal maintenance requirement aboard ship is regular winding at about the same time each day.

circle (math)—A circle is a plane, closed curve, all points of which are equidistant from a point within called the center. The line forming the circle is called a circumference. The length of this line is the perimeter. An arc is part of a circumference. A major arc is more than a semicricle (180°); a minor arc is less than a semicircle (180°); a quadrant is a quarter of a circle (90°); a quintant is a fifth of a circle (60°); an octant is an eighth of a circle (45°). Concentric circles have a common center. A radius, or semidiameter, is a straight line connecting the center of a circle with any point in its circumference. A diameter of a circle is

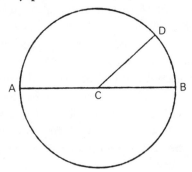

C: Center
AB: Diameter
CD: Radius (also CA, CB)

DB: Arc of angle DCB
AD: Arc of angle ACD

(Diameter AB is a straight angle dividing the circumference into two equal parts, each with 180° of arc.)

a straight line passing through its center and terminating at opposite sides of the circumference. It divides a circle into two equal parts. The ratio of the length of the circumference of any circle to the length of its diameter is 3.14159+. A sector is that part of a circle bounded by two radii and an arc. A chord is a straight line connecting any two points on the circumference of a circle. Chords equidistant from the center of a circle are equal in length. A segment is that part of a circle bounded by a chord and the intercepted arc. A chord divides a circle into two segments, one less than a semicircle (180°) and the other greater than a semicircle. An inscribed angle is one whose vertex is on the circumference of a circle and whose sides are chords. It has half as many degrees as the arc it intercepts. A secant of a circle is a line intersecting the circle, or a chord extended beyond the circumference. A tangent to a circle is a straight line in the plane of the circle which has only one point in common with the circumference. A tangent is perpendicular to the radius at the point of tangency.

For practical-navigation purposes, the earth is considered to be a perfect sphere, absolutely round, with all surface points equidistant from the center, and, because it is perfectly round, all circles lying on the earth's surface are also perfectly round. A cross section of the earth is therefore in the form of a perfect circle, with central angles formed by the radii creating arcs at the circumference. Great circles are those with planes bisecting the earth into two equal parts. The equator is a great circle, as are all other circles passing through the polar axis. Small circles do not divide the earth equally, because their planes do not pass through the earth's center; that is, any circle not a great circle is a small circle. When two circles are concentric (having a common center), the arc measurement of a central angle is identical on either circumference. The astronomical distances from earth to the multitudinous bodies in space allow the practical assumption that the distances are infinite and that all celestial bodies are therefore equidistant from the earth's center. Thus the arc formed by two bodies on the celestial sphere can be measured by the concentric arc on the earth's (terrestrial) sphere formed by their common central angle.

circle of equal angle—Used for plotting a three-point fix without a three-arm protractor. The procedure is to find the center of each circle of position, also called a circle of equal angle, and then, about such center, to strike an arc of radius equal to the distance on the chart from the circle center to one of the two objects through which the circle passes. The same procedure is applied to the other pairs of objects to establish the fix at the intersection of the two arcs. The center of the

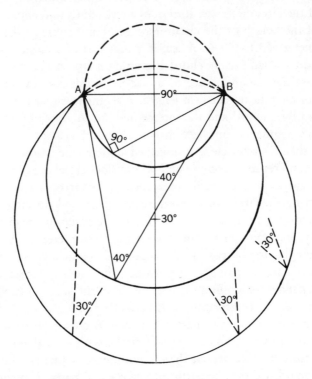

Circles of equal angle for 90°, 40°, 30°. The center for each circle is marked on the vertical bisector S; the baseline between objects ashore as A and B.

circle of equal angle lies on the perpendicular bisector of the baseline of the pair of objects. With the bisector properly graduated, one needs only to place one point of the compasses at the appropriate graduation, the other point at one of the observed objects, and then to strike the circle of equal angle or an arc of it in the vicinity of the DR. The bisector is graduated by calculation or by using a protractor.

circles of the earth—A great circle is the line of intersection of a sphere and a plane through the center of the sphere. This is the largest circle that can be drawn on a sphere. The shortest line between two points on a sphere is part of a great circle. On the slightly flattened earth, the shortest line is called a geodesic but a great circle is a near-enough approximation of a geodesic for most navigation. A small circle is the line of intersection of a sphere and a plane which does not pass through the center of the sphere.

coast charts—Intended for inshore navigation where the course may lie inside reefs and shoals, for entering or leaving bays and harbors, and for navigating large inland waterways. The scales range from about 1:50,000 to 1:100,000.

compass—A mariner's compass is designed to give a navigator his boat's correct heading relative to magnetic north. The compass card is plainly marked in degrees and usually illuminated for night steering by a light with a red filter, which preserves the helmsman's night vision. On most compasses, a vertical pin called a lubber's line is fixed to the compass housing and thus, in effect, to the boat itself, to indicate the direction in which the boat is heading. Some compasses have similar pins mounted at 90° intervals around the card, for use in determining when a landmark is directly abeam or astern. Another pin, centered on the compass card and taller than the others, is called the shadow pin. It is so named because navigators can use its shadow and a precalculated bearing of the sun to check magnetic heading. For most boatmen the shadow pin is used to determine position by taking bearings on fixed objects such as buoys, smokestacks, and lighthouses. Inside a compass, as shown in the cutaway drawing, are gimbals and a counterweight to keep the card level when the boat tilts. The card, and the attached magnets that align it with the earth's magnetic field, balance on a pivot. The housing is filled through an opening sealed by a plug with clear, highly refined kerosene. The fluid buoys up the card, reducing pivot friction, and damps oscillations and vibration. A flexible diaphragm beneath lets the fluid expand and contract with changes in temperature. Corrector magnets in the base aid in adjusting the compass after installation.

Compasses normally used by the mariner are magnetic and gyroscopic. The magnetic compass tends to align itself with the magnetic lines of force of the earth, while the gyro compass seeks the true (geographic) meridian. A compass may be designated to indicate its principal use, as a standard, steering, or boat compass. The compass designated "standard" is usually a magnetic compass installed in an exposed position having an unobstructed view in most directions, permitting determination of error.

compass, Flinders bar—On the magnetic equator there is no vertical component of the earth's magnetic field and consequently no induced magnetism in vertical soft iron. In higher latitudes, the vertical component can cause the compass to become unreliable. This statement represents an oversimplification of the problem, as the various coefficients are interrelated. To compensate for or neutralize any induced magnet-

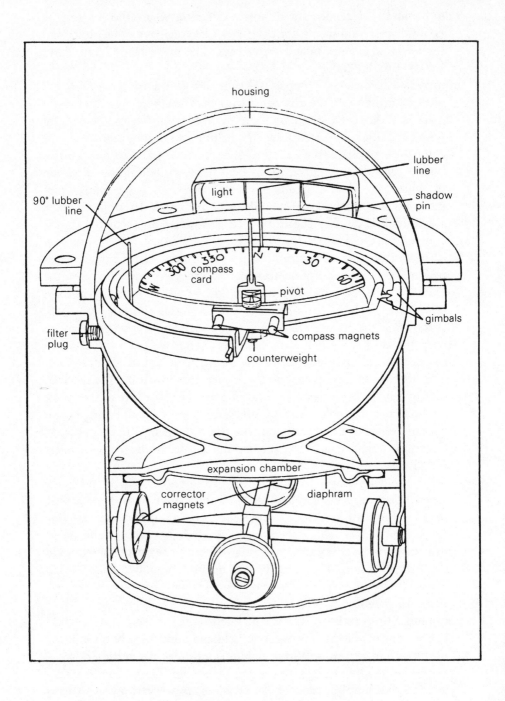

ism in vertical soft iron, a Flinders bar is used. This consists of soft iron rods having no permanent magnetism; as many sections as required are installed vertically in a tube on the side of the compass opposite the effective pole of the ship's field.

compass, hand—The hand-held compass is designed for taking bearings. Holding the device at eye level, the navigator centers an object in the sighting notch and reads the bearing from the compass card through a reflecting prism. Such a compass usually contains a battery-powered light for night use.

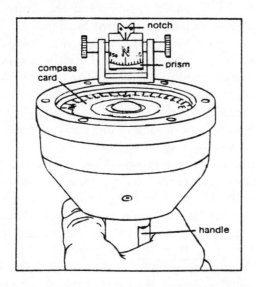

compass, magnetic, limitations of—The limitations of a magnetic compass are: (1) It is sensitive to any magnetic disturbance. It is useless at the magnetic poles and is sluggish and unreliable in areas near the poles. (2) Deviation changes as the ship's magnetic properties change. The magnetic properties change with changes in the induced magnetism, changes in the ship's structure, or changes in the magnetic cargo. Prolonged periods in dry dock or alongside a dock, riding out a heavy sea, or the vessel's being struck by lightning can alter the magnetic properties. (3) Deviation changes with heading. (4) It does not point to true north. (5) It requires adjustment annually.

compass, magnetic, principles of—Magnetism is a fundamental physical phenomenon that occurs both naturally, as in a lodestone, and artifically, by induction. It is the property of certain metals to attract or repel items of like materials or certain other metals; it is also an effect of electrical current. An object that exhibits the property of magnetism is called a magnet. It can be elongated, as in a bar magnet, shaled like a horseshoe, or take other forms. The space around each magnet in which its influence can be detected is called its field; this can be pictured as many lines of force. Each magnet always has two—no more, no fewer—areas of opposite polarity; one is termed north and the other south.

compass, spherical—A type of compass popular among yachtsmen and commercial operators, offering several advantages compared to the conventional flat-topped compass. These compasses are internally gimbaled and the compass card is pivoted at the center of the sphere, assuring maximum stability of the card in all directions of pitch, roll, and yaw. In addition, the transparent spherical dome of the compass acts as a powerful magnifying glass and greatly increases the apparent size of the compass card in the area of the lubber's line. In addition, a "dished" card, together with the spherical dome, permits such a compass to be read accurately from a distance of 10 feet (3 m) or more. When fitted with shock-absorbing mounts, a spherical compass gives excellent results in high-speed boats.

compass, standard and steering—Most vessels of any size carry at least two magnetic compasses; these are the standard compass and the steering compass. The standard compass, whenever possible, is located on the ship's center line, and on a weather deck near the bridge, at a point where it will be least affected by unfavorable magnetic influences. Headings read from this compass are termed "per standard compass." The steering compass in most ships is also located on the center line, just forward of the steering wheel, where it can be seen easily by the helmsman. Its headings are termed "per steering compass."

compass, swing ship—The navigator computes deviation and prepares the magnetic compass table by an operation called swinging ship. Briefly, swinging ship consists of recording compass bearings on different headings and comparing these compass bearings with true bearings obtained in some other manner, thus finding compass error. By applying variation to compass error one determines deviation. Five techniques for determining deviation are: (1) comparison with gyrocompass; (2) comparison with other magnetic compass of known deviation; (3) reciprocal bearings from shore; (4) known direction of distant objects; and (5) ranges—any two objects onshore, when in line, provide direction and are referred to as a range.

compass card—Composed of light, nonmagnetic material, the compass card is graduated through 360°, increasing clockwise from north through east, south, and west. Some compass cards are graduated in "points" in addition to the degree graduations. There are thirty-two points of the compass, 11.25° apart. The four cardinal points are north, east, south, and west. Midway between these are four intercardinal points, at northeast, southeast, southwest, and northwest. The eight points between cardinal and intercardinal points are named for the two directions between which they lie, the cardinal name being given first, as north northeast, east northeast, east southeast, etc. The remaining sixteen points are named for the nearest cardinal or intercardinal point by the next cardinal point in the direction of measurement, as north by east, northeast by north, etc. Smaller graduations are provided by dividing each point into four "quarter points," thus producing 128 graduations altogether. The naming of the various graduations of the compass in order is called boxing the compass.

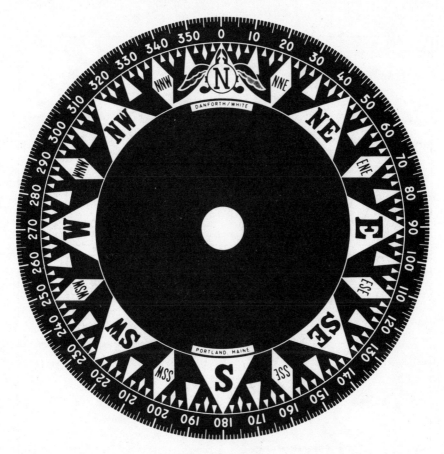

Compass card

compass conversions—Practical piloting requires the frequent conversions of angles from true to magnetic and from magnetic to true. For example, an aid to navigation may be sighted and a bearing taken on it. The bearing is usually taken in magnetic angles, which must be converted to the true system before the bearing can be plotted. Conversely, a navigator determines from the chart a true course that must be made good in order to reach the next objective. The true course must be converted to the magnetic system for the helmsman if his compass shows magnetic directions. The term "correcting" is sometimes used in connection with making conversions from true to magnetic and from magnetic to true.

compass corrector magnets—To reduce deviation in a mariner's compass to a minimum, a skipper uses two pairs of corrector magnets, mounted in the compass base on brass shafts; he changes their setting

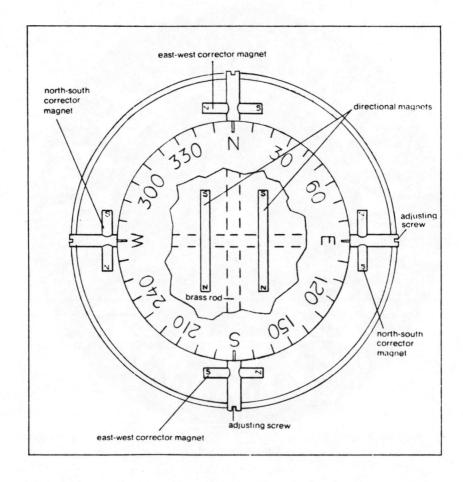

with adjusting screws. On a north–south heading, the north–south (a-thwartship) corrector magnets are used to correct the compass; on an east–west heading, the fore-and-aft magnets are employed.

compass deviation—A compass needle free to turn horizontally tends to align itself with the earth's magnetic lines of force. Unfortunately, it is not free to do so in a steel ship; such ships have marked magnetic properties of their own, and these tend to deflect the compass. The divergence thus caused between the north–south axis of the compass card and a magnetic meridian is called deviation (Dev. or D). Even in a vessel made of wood or fiberglass there is enough magnetic material on board—engines, fuel and water tanks, rigging, etc.—to cause deviation. Also, direct currents flowing in straight wires establish magnetic fields. Care must be taken that wiring in the vicinity of a compass is twisted to eliminate effects on the compass; checks should be made for deviation with the circuits turned on and off. Although deviation differs from variation in that the latter is caused by the earth's magnetism, the two are designated in the same manner. Thus, if no deviation is present, the compass card lines up with a magnetic merid-ian, and its north point indicates the direction of magnetic north. If deviation is present and the north point of the compass points eastward of magnetic north, the deviation is easterly and is marked E. If it points westward of magnetic north, the deviation is named westerly and is marked W. The navigator can easily find the correct variation by referring to the chart of his locality. Deviation, however, is not so simple to ascertain. It not only varies on different ships, but on any particular ship it varies with changes in the ship's heading. Also, it often changes with large changes in the ship's latitude.

compass error—Two magnetic influences, variation and deviation, affect compass direction, their combined total effect being termed the compass error. Variation changes with location and is published on charts. Deviation is caused by magnetic influences contained within the individual ship and the location of the ship's compass in relation to these influences and must be determined by observation.

compass error (azimuth by amplitude)—When one is using an azimuth to check a compass, a low altitude is most desirable, as it is both easy to observe and gives the most accurate results. An amplitude observation is one made when the center of the observed body is on either the celestial or the visible horizon; that is, it is rising or setting. In the latter case, a correction is applied to the observation in order to obtain the corresponding amplitude when the center of the body is on the celestial horizon. The sun is the body most frequently ob-

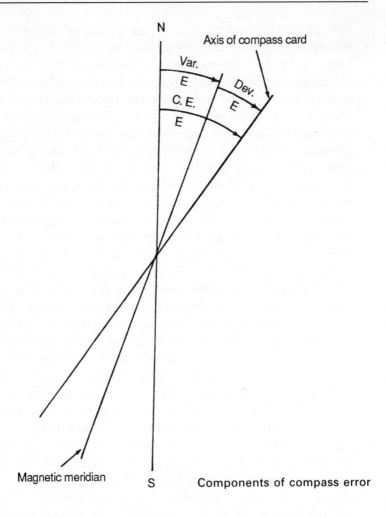

N

Axis of compass card

Var.

E

Dev.

C. E.

E

E

Magnetic meridian   S   Components of compass error

served in obtaining an amplitude. However, the moon, a planet, or a bright star having a declination not exceeding 24° may also be used. Amplitudes should be avoided in high latitudes. Amplitude may be defined as an angular distance measured north or south from the prime vertical to the body on the celestial horizon. It is given the prefix E (east) if the body is rising and W (west) if it is setting; the suffix is N if the body rises or sets north of the prime vertical, as it does with a northerly declination, and S if it rises or sets south of the prime vertical, having a southerly declination. If a body is observed when its center is on the celestial horizon, the amplitude may be taken directly from table 27 in Bowditch. When observing amplitudes with a height of eye typical of ships' bridges, one can make two assumptions that will yield results sufficiently accurate for practical purposes. The first is that when the sun's lower limb is about two-thirds of a diameter above the visible horizon, its center is on the celestial horizon. The second is that when the moon's upper limb is on the visible horizon, its center is on the celestial horizon. This apparent anomaly is due to the sun's parallax being very small (0.1') as compared to the refraction, which at this altitude amounts to about 34.5', whereas the moon's parallax is large (between 54.0' and 61.5', depending on the date), while the refraction is about 34.5'. When planets or stars are on the celestial horizon, they are about one sun diameter, or some 32.0', above the visible horizon. If a body is observed on the visible horizon, the observed value is corrected by a value from Bowditch table 28.

compass rose—The compass rose, imprinted on most charts, contains both true and magnetic directions. The outer circle is aligned with true north, its N–S axis parallel with the longitude meridians on a Mercator chart; the inner circle coincides with the local magnetic meridians and is oriented to magnetic north. In the center of the rose the variation and its annual change from a base date are given.

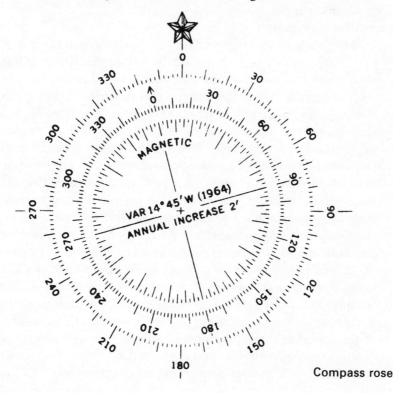

Compass rose

compass variation—The magnetic poles of the earth are large, slowly moving areas located within the Arctic and Antarctic circles several hundred miles from the geographic poles. Since the magnetic meridians converge fairly close to the geographic poles, there are a few places on the earth where a magnetic compass reads true. Variation at any point on the earth is the number of degrees measured from geographic north to magnetic north, that is, the number of degrees between the geographic and magnetic meridians at that point. When the magnetic meridian is west of the geographic meridian, variation is said to be west. A compass with no other displacement will then have its card pulled to the west of the geographic scale. A reverse situation leads to an easterly variation, where an otherwise undisplaced compass will have a card pulled to the east of true north. Values of variation have been obtained from measurements made over practically all land and sea areas of the globe. Charts published by the NOS (National Ocean Survey) carry double compass roses. The outer rose has a zero at true or geographic north; zero on the inner rose is at magnetic north. The two scales are offset by the amount of variation at that point on the earth, the value being given at the center of the rose. The annual change in variation is also given.

computer navigation

INTEGRATED NAVIGATION SYSTEM (INS)—Integrated navigation system (INS) consists of a ship's inertial navigation system (SINS), to which are added an automatic star tracker, a multispeed repeater, and instrumentation to provide accurate data on attitude (roll, pitch, and heading), for radar stabilization. The system also supplies velocity (north, east, or vertical), and latitude and longitude coordinates for ship control and navigation. The system is used aboard the NASA range-instrumentation ships, which supplement the range-tracking stations established ashore in various parts of the world. For effective space-vehicle tracking and control, the positions of the tracking stations must be established to the closest possible tolerance; the navigational-accuracy requirements for the range-instrumentation ships are therefore unusually stringent. The INS receives inputs from a number of sources, processes the data, positions the star tracker (for day and night observations), and gives an output of navigational data and heading. This enables the proper positioning of the tracking equipment (radar) for immediate acquisition of the spacecraft. INS is a subsystem of the complete ship's position and attitude measurement system.

MINIATURE INERTIAL NAVIGATION DIGITAL AUTOMATIC COMPUTER (MINDAC)—A general-purpose digital computer in a SINS system designed primarily to calculate present ship's position from heading and velocity data, and to provide appropriate corrections to the gyros in order to keep the SINS inertial platform aligned to the vertical. In addition, it provides periodic readout of the ship's velocity and position to the central data processor and resets the platforms to the correct position when necessary at the operator's command.

computers, navigation (analog)—The analog computer solves a particular physical problem instantaneously through the use of an electrical circuit which is mathematically analogous to the problem. The solution is instantaneous and continuous, but analog computers are not versatile. Analog computers are, therefore, usually designed to furnish repeated solutions for very specific problems. (Speed through the water, true wind from apparent, depth of the water under the boat, etc.) The limited versatility of analog computers has led to the development of digital computers.

computers, navigation (digital)—The digital computer may be defined as a machine that calculates the solution of a mathematical problem in any desired degree of accuracy through a prearranged sequence (algorithm) of arithmetic steps. A major advantage of digital over analog computers is versatility. Analog computers require a hardware change to solve new problems, but a digital computer may be reprogrammed to solve a new problem by the preparation of new instructions; in other words, a "software" change.

conformal projection—A map that preserves angles; that is, a map such that if two arcs on a globe intersect at a given angle, their images on the map also intersect at the same angle. On such a map, the scale is the same in every direction. Shapes of small regions are preserved, but areas are only approximate (accurate areas are shown on an equal-area map). The most commonly used conformal map is the Lambert projection, with standard latitude at 30° and 60°N. On the standard latitudes, the scale is exact; between them it is decreased by about 1 percent; outside them, distortion increases rapidly. The Mercator and stereographic projections are also conformal maps.

conic projection—A chart produced by transferring points from the surface of the earth to a cone or series of cones, which are then cut along a longitude and spread out flat. If the axis of the cone coincides with the axis of the earth—the usual situation—the parallels appear as arcs of circles and the meridians as either straight or curved lines converging toward the nearer pole. A parallel along which there is no distortion is called a standard parallel. Neither the transverse projection, in which the axis of the cone is in the equatorial plane, nor the

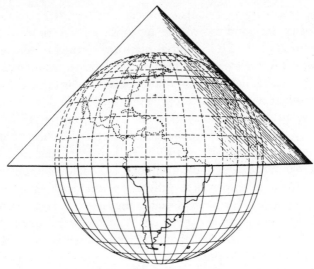

A simple conic projection

oblique conic projection, in which the axis of the cone is oblique to the plane of the equator, is ordinarily used for navigation, their chief use being for illustrative maps. The appearance and features of conic projections are varied by the use of cones tangent at various parallels, tangent at two parallels (secant), or nested within one another (polyconic).

conic sections—If a cone of indefinite extent is intersected by a plane perpendicular to the axis of the cone, the line of intersection of the plane and the surface of the cone is a circle. If the intersecting plane is tilted, the intersection is an ellipse, or flattened circle. The longest diameter of an ellipse is called its major axis, and half of this is its semi-major axis. The shortest diameter of an ellipse is called its minor axis, and half of this is its semi-minor axis. Two points (foci) on the major axis are so located that the sum of their distances from any point (P) on the ellipse is equal to the length of the major axis. If the intersecting plane is parallel to one side of the cone, the intersection is a parabola. Any point on a parabola is equidistant from a fixed point, called the focus or focal point, and a fixed straight line called the directrix. The point midway between the focus and the directrix is called the vertex. If the sides of the cone are extended to form a second cone having the same axis and apex but extending in the opposite direction, and the intersecting plane is tilted beyond the position forming a parabola, so that it intersects both curves, the intersections

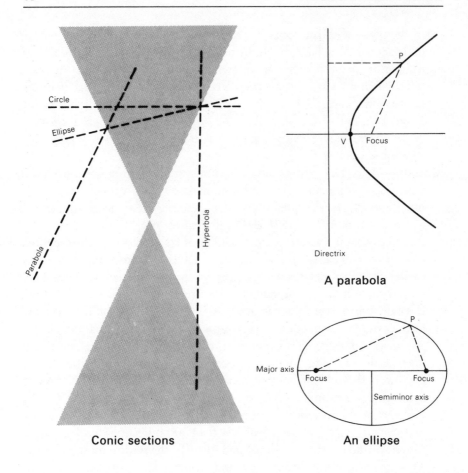

Conic sections

A parabola

An ellipse

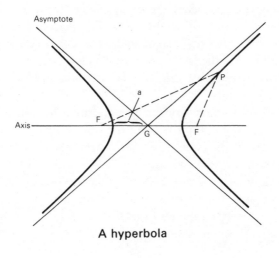

A hyperbola

of the plane with the cones is a hyperbola. There are two intersections or branches of a hyperbola. At any point (P) on either branch, the difference in the distance from two fixed points called foci or focal points, F and F′, is constant and equal to the shortest distance between the two branches. That is, PF − PF′ = 2a. The straight line through F and F′ is called the axis. Each side of a hyperbola approaches ever closer to, but never reaches, a pair of straight lines called asymptotes. These intersect at G.

Consol—A long-ranged radionavigation system that requires no special receiving equipment. There are stations in several European countries, but none in North America. Full characteristics of each station are given in chapter 7 of DMAHC publication no. 117A.

To obtain a bearing from a Consol station, tune to the desired beacon on any radio receiver capable of receiving medium-frequency carrier-wave transmissions on the appropriate frequency. Automatic gain control must be off, and the beat frequency oscillator turned on. If a radio direction finder is used, the loop antenna should be rotated to the position of maximum reception of the Consol signal during the period of counting. To suppress interference or for other reasons, it may be necessary to rotate the loop away from this position. If this is done it should not be rotated more than 45° from the position of maximum reception. When the loop is rotated to, or near to, the position of minimum reception, an error in the count may be introduced, particularly at ranges of less than 300 miles (555 km) at night. Listen for the continuous signal and identify the station by its call sign. Then count the number of dots and dashes which follow. A total of sixty dot and dash characters should be heard in each cycle. In practice this is rarely the case, since the exact change from dots to dashes (or from dashes to dots) is difficult to hear. This period is generally known as the "twilight zone." Consequently, the actual count must be corrected to allow for the last characters. The total observed count should be subtracted from sixty and half the difference added to each of the dot and dash counts.

Consolan—A long-range navigation aid, similar to Consol, giving lines of position up to 1,200 miles from the transmitter (but not within 50 miles) on any RDF equipment (or other radio receiver) capable of receiving frequencies in the range of 194–200 kHz. When the receiver is equipped with an internal beat frequency oscillator, the signal is heard as a sharp "beep," otherwise as a mushy hiss. Dots and dashes may also be read from the null meter if the RDF is so equipped. Like Consol, the Consolan station transmits a signal consisting of mixed dots and dashes, plus a three-letter call sign; the number of dots and dashes is counted, and from this count the bearing from the transmitter is determined by means of special tables found in DMAHC publication no. 117A, "Radio Navigational Aids."

constancy of the current—The ratio of the magnitude of the resultant velocity to the mean velocity of the current. It equals 100 percent if all observations indicate the current setting exactly in the same direction at the same speed; it equals zero if there are an equal number of observations from opposite directions and all show the same speed.

coordinates—Numbers used to define a position. If a position is known to be on a given line, a single number (coordinate) is needed to identify the position. If a position is known to be on a given surface, two numbers (coordinates) are needed to define the position. Thus, if a vessel is known to be on the surface of the earth, its position can be identified by means of latitude and longitude. If nothing is known regarding a position other than that it exists in space, three numbers (coordinates) are needed to define its position. Each coordinate requires an origin, either stated or implied. In addition to latitude–longitude, another system of plane coordinates in common use consists of stating a direction and distance from an origin called a pole. Direction and distance from a fixed point constitutes polar coordinates. Spherical coordinates are used to define a position on a sphere by indicating the angle between a primary and a secondary great circle. Examples of this system are altitude and azimuth; declination and hour angle.

course (C, Cn)—The intended direction of travel, expressed as angular distance from north, usually from 000° at north, clockwise through 360°. The term is applied to direction through the water, not the direction intended to be made good over the bottom. The course is designated true, magnetic, compass, or grid as the reference is true, magnetic, compass, or grid north, respectively. Course made good (CMG) is the actual track from the point of departure at any given time. Sometimes the expression course of advance (COA) is used to indicate the direction intended to be made good over the ground, and course over ground (COG) the direction of the actual track.

course recorder—A continuous graphic record of the heading of a vessel can be obtained by means of a course recorder. In its usual form, paper with both heading and time scales is slowly wound from one drum to another by a spring-powered mechanism. A pen traces a line to indicate the heading. The pen is attached to an arm controlled by a compass, usually the master gyro.

crepuscular rays—Beams of light from the sun passing through openings in the clouds and illuminating dust in their paths. The rays are virtually parallel but because of perspective appear to diverge. Those appearing to extend downward are popularly called "backstays of the sun." Those extending upward and across the sky, appearing to converge toward a point 180° from the sun, are called anticrepuscular rays.

cross sea—The confused, irregular state of the sea which occurs when waves from two or more different storms arrive in the same area.

crosswind—That wind component which is perpendicular to the course of an exposed moving object. Wind blowing in a direction approximately 90° from the heading is called a beam wind. One blowing from ahead is called a head wind. One blowing from astern is called a following wind.

current—May be any one of several types of horizontal water movement and may be categorized under two general headings of tidal or ocean current. The direction toward which a current flows is its set; speed, its drift. The effect of current is to push a vessel from its intended course if set and drift are not computed and compensated for.

current, permanent—The oceans contain well-defined permanent current systems that change periodically, but predictably, with seasonal changes in the wind systems that are their generators. At sea certain winds blow almost continuously in the same general direction over large areas with the result that their forces mainly determine the set, drift, and permanence of the current created. North–south currents are affected by the Coriolis force (the earth's rotation) as well, creating a deflection clockwise in the Northern Hemisphere, and counterclockwise below the equator. Contrary winds of long duration reduce the drift of a current substantially and, to a lesser degree, alter the set; when the wind again becomes normal for the area, the current returns to normal. Pilot charts and surface-current atlases delineate the known direction and velocity of permanent ocean currents.

current, polar—The waters of the North Atlantic enter the Arctic Ocean between Norway and Svalbard. The currents flow easterly north of Siberia to the region of the Novo Sibirskie Ostrova, where they turn northerly across the North Pole and continue down the Greenland coast to form the East Greenland current. On the American side of the Arctic basin there is a weak, continuous, clockwise flow centered in the vicinity of 80°N, 150°W. A current north through the Bering Strait along the American coast is balanced by an outward southerly flow along the Siberian coast.

current, reversing—In rivers, bays, and straights where the direction of flow is more or less restricted to certain channels, the tidal current is called a reversing current; that is, it flows alternately in approximately opposite directions, with a short period of little or no current (called slack water) between. During the flow, the speed varies from zero at slack water to maximum flood or ebb about midway between the slacks. The symmetry of reversing currents is affected in certain areas by the configuration of the land and/or the presence of rivers.

current, river—Unlike currents in tidal channels, which may reverse themselves as often as four times a day, a freshwater river flows in one main direction. Yet the internal dynamics of a river can be extremely complex. The flow of every stream, whether Mississippi or creek, varies from spot to spot, depending on the bends and twists of its banks and on the shape of its bed. The current is strongest where the water is deepest. In shallows the current is weak because the bottom drags against the water, slowing it down. Wherever the river curves, the main current is thrown by centrifugal force to the outside bank. There it erodes the bank and deepens the bottom just under it, and the current speeds up. Along the inside of the curve, however, the current slackens, leaving deposits of silt that build up into shoals. Because of this constant erosion and sedimentation, the river's bed continually changes.

current, rotary—Offshore, where the direction of flow under tidal influence is not restricted by land, the tidal current is rotary; that is, it flows continuously, with the direction changing through all points of the compass during the tidal period. Due to the effect of the earth's rotation (Coriolis), the change is generally clockwise in the Northern Hemisphere, and counterclockwise in the Southern Hemisphere. The speed usually varies throughout the tidal cycle, passing through two maximums in approximately opposite directions, and two minimums about halfway between the maximums. Rotary currents are depicted by a series of arrows representing the direction and speed of the current at each hour (a current rose). A distinguishing feature of a rotary current is that it has no time of slack water. Although the current varies in strength, the variation is from a maximum to a minimum and back without slack.

current, wind—In addition to prevailing winds generating permanent ocean currents, transient winds appear as a result of shifting pressure systems in the atmosphere (highs and lows). These winds cause the surface layer of water to move and form a temporary, or wind, current; twelve hours of steady wind usually produces a detectable current. The speed of the current (drift) depends on the velocity and constancy of the wind. Wind currents are generally influenced by Cariolis force; in deep water the difference between the wind and the current is frequently 35° to 45°. In northern latitudes the deflection is clockwise, that is, the current flows to the right of the wind flow. In southern latitudes current is deflected counterclockwise or left. Deflection decreases as the shoreline is approached and ultimately follows the bottom contours.

current profile—A graphic presentation of current flow from the surface to a specified depth. The speed of the current is generally represented horizontally and the depth vertically, from the surface (zero) downward.

current rose—A graphic presentation of currents for specified areas, utilizing arrows at the cardinal and intercardinal compass points to show the direction toward which the prevailing current flows and its speed.

current triangle—A vector triangle to find graphically the heading necessary to counter the effects of a known current. A tabulation of the parts of the triangle is given below.

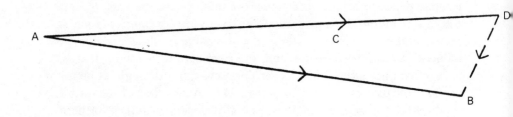

Current Triangle and Its Parts

Part	Using Estimated Current	Using Actual Current
Point A	Present position (fix) of ship	Previous position (fix) of ship
Point D	DR position of ship at future time	DR position of ship at present time
Point B	Estimated position at future time	Present position (fix) at present time
Side AD	Course and speed vector	Course and speed vector
Side AB	Track and speed of advance	Course and speed made good
Side DB	Anticipated or expected current	Actual current encountered

Note: Points B and D are always for the *same* time.

cylinder—A solid having two parallel plane bases bounded by closed curves, and a surface formed by an infinite number of parallel lines called elements, connecting in the two curves. A cylinder is similar to a prism, but with a curved lateral surface, instead of a number of flat sides, connecting the bases. The axis of a cylinder is a straight line connecting the centers of the bases. A right cylinder is one having bases perpendicular to the axis. A circular cylinder is one having circular bases. The altitude of a cylinder is the perpendicular distance between the planes of its bases. The perimeter of a base is the length of the curve bounding it.

cylindrical projections (charts)—If a cylinder is placed around the earth, tangent along the equator, and the planes of the meridians are extended, they intersect the cylinder in a number of vertical lines. These lines, all being vertical, are parallel, or everywhere equidistant from each other, unlike the terrestrial meridians, which become closer as latitude increases. On a globe, the latitude circles are perpendicular to the meridians and become progressively smaller as latitude increases. On a cylinder they are perpendicular to the projected meridians, but because a cylinder is everywhere the same in diameter, the projected parallels of latitude are all the same length. If the cylinder is cut along a vertical line (a meridian) and spread out flat, the meridians appear as equally spaced vertical lines that do not converse, and the parallels as horizontal lines whose spacing progressively increases toward the poles.

D

Daily Memorandum—Provides navigators of ships in port with a printed copy of important safety information broadcast in the past twenty-four hours or since the previous working day. It is published by the Defense Mapping Agency Hydrographic Center each working day in two editions: the Atlantic edition (hydrolant) and the Pacific edition (hydropac). The Daily Memorandum is sent to fleet-operating bases, naval stations, customhouses, shipping-company offices, and so on, where it may be picked up by navigational personnel of vessels in the port.

danger angles—A predetermined angle, horizontal or vertical, used to locate a safe track past a hazard. If two landmarks are available, a horizontal angle is used; if one landmark, a vertical angle.

danger bearing—It is possible to keep a ship in safe water without fixes through the use of a danger bearings. If a ship must pass a hazard such as unmarked shoal water, draw a line from a landmark and well clear

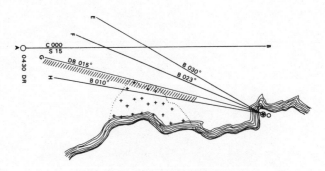

A danger bearing (XH). NMT means bearing
to H must not be more than '074°.

of the danger and label the line with its direction. This direction is the danger bearing. With the danger bearing as a line of demarcation, the mariner can tell whether he is outside or inside the danger area by checking the bearing to the land mark.

day beacons—In shallow waters, day beacons are often used instead of buoys, because they are less expensive to maintain. These are single piles or multiple-pile structures (dolphins) driven into the bottom on which are placed one or more sign boards, called "day marks," which convey information by color, shape, and numbers.

dead reckoning (DR)—The determination of position by advancing a previous position for courses steered and distances run. It is a reckoning relative to something stationary, or "dead," in the water, and hence applies to course and speeds through the water. Because of leeway due to wind, inaccurate allowances for compass error, imperfect steering, or error in measuring speed, the actual motion through the water is seldom determined with complete accuracy. Hence, a dead-reckoning position is an approximate one, which is corrected from time to time as opportunity allows. Dead reckoning is the only method by which a position can be determined at any time and therefore is considered fundamental to navigation, all other methods being used only to provide means for correcting the dead reckoning. If a navigator can accurately assess the disturbing elements, he can determine a better position than that established by dead reckoning alone; this is called an estimated position (EP). Because of the importance of dead reckoning, a log is kept of courses and speeds, changes, and compass errors. Navigators almost invariably keep their dead reckoning by plotting directly on the chart or a separate plotting sheet, drawing lines to represent the direction and distance of travel and indicating dead reckoning and estimated positions from time to time. This method is simple and direct. Large errors are often apparent as inconsistencies in an otherwise regular plot.

dead reckoning, current—In navigation it is customary to use the term "current" to include all factors introducing error in the dead reckoning. When a fix is obtained, the difference between it and the DR is assumed to be due to a current running from the DR position to the fix, and that the drift is equal to the distance in miles between these positions, divided by the number of hours since the previous fix.

dead-reckoning plot—A dead-reckoning plot originates at a fix or running fix. From the fix, the ship's course is drawn, and successive DR positions are marked at intervals along the course line. These positions are determined by the speed of the ship. The DR plot is a graphic

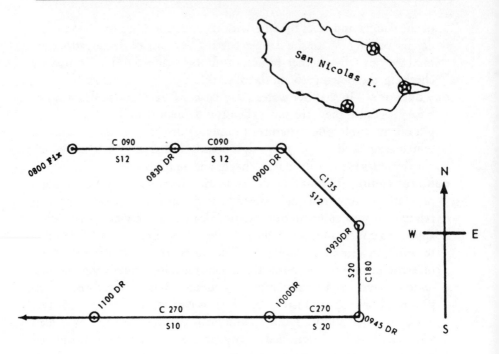

Dead-reckoning plot

history of the route the ship was thought to follow. It also may be referred to as the DR track or track line.

dead-reckoning terms:

HEADING (Hdg)—The horizontal direction in which a ship points or heads at any instant, expressed in angular units, clockwise from 000° through 360°, from a reference direction, usually north. The heading of a ship is also called ship's head (SH). Heading is a constantly changing value as a ship oscillates or yaws across the course owing to the effects of the sea and steering error.

COURSE (C)—As applied to marine navigation, the direction in which a vessel is to be steered, or is being steered; the direction of travel through the water. The course is measured from 000° clockwise from the reference direction to 360°. Course may be designated as true, magnetic, compass, or grid, as determined by the reference direction.

COURSE LINE—In marine navigation, the graphic representation of a ship's course, normally used in the construction of a dead-reckoning plot.

SPEED (S)—The rate of travel of a ship through the water; normally expressed in knots. (In some areas, where distances are stated in statute

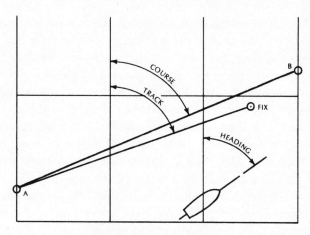

Heading and course

miles, such as on the Great Lakes, speed units will be miles per hour.)
It is used in conjunction with time to establish the distance run on each
of the consecutive segments of a DR plot.

FIX—A position established at a specific time by any of a number
of methods (*See later under* fix).

DR POSITION—A position determined by plotting only the course
and the distance along the course based on speed through the water,
without considering current.

ESTIMATED POSITION (EP)—In practical usage, the DR position
modified by the best additional information available.

ESTIMATED TIME OF DEPARTURE (ETD)—The estimate of the time of
departure from a specified location in accordance with a scheduled
move to a new location.

ESTIMATED TIME OF ARRIVAL (ETA)—The best estimate of the time
of arrival at a specified location in accordance with a scheduled movement.

dead water—The phenomenon that occurs when a ship of low propul-
sive power negotiates water that has a thin layer of fresher water over
a deeper layer of more saline water. As the ship moves, part of its
energy goes into generation of an internal wave, which causes a
noticeable drop in speed.

Decca (hyperbolic radio navigation system)—Decca is unique in that in
many areas it is privately owned and operated, supported by the sale
and lease of receiving equipment used on ships and aircraft. Decca uses
phase comparison for the determination of distance from one master
and three or four slave transmitters. The slaves are designated purple,

red, and green (orange if a fourth is used). Each of the stations transmits a continuous wave at a different frequency between 70 and 130 kHz. A receiver has three (or four) identical units, one for each frequency. Internal circuitry provides for comparison of the phase of the signal from each slave with that of the master. Decca charts showing hyperbolas printed in colors to agree with the colors of the slaves. Two slaves provide a fix; a third provides a check on the others and permits positioning in areas unfavorable to one of the other slaves. It is necessary to read only three dials, called decometers, to locate the intersection of the lines; no matching of signals or manipulation of controls is required. As with any phase-relationship system, the phases of the signals transmitted by master and slave are compared, rather than the travel times. Phase comparison gives a precise measure of the fractional part of a wavelength, or lane, but no indication of the total number of lanes existing. An auxiliary means of keeping track of the lanes is essential. The Mk 21 shipboard receiver has a digital lane-identification display for this purpose. Lane identification can also be accomplished from an accurate DR plot on the chart. The average reliable operational day and night range of Decca is about 250 miles (460 km). At this distance the average error in a line of position is approximately 150 yards (137 m) in daytime, and about 800 yards (730 m) at night. Decca coverage extends over much of Western Europe, the Persian Gulf, the Indian subcontinent, the Far East, Australian waters, and the Canadian maritime provinces.

Decca fix—In the Decca receiver, the zone letter, lane number, and fractional position within the lane to the nearest .01 are shown for each master/slave station pair on instruments called decometers. The face of the meter resembles a clock, with hands pointing to the lane number and lane subdivisions. A window in the lower part of the meter face shows the zone letter. Once the receiver has been set up for a particular Decca chain, the decometers provide continuous readings of the zone, lane, and lane position for each of the station pairs, until the vessel passes out of range of that chain.

declination—The *Nautical Almanac* tabulates declination for the sun, moon, and navigational planets for each hour of Greenwich mean time (GMT). The tabulated declination is prefixed by either N or S, indicating that the body is north or south of the celestial equator.

deep water—In wave forecasting, deep water means that the depth of the water is large compared with the wavelength of the longest wave generated. In general, waves are considered deep-water waves when the depth is greater than one-half wavelength.

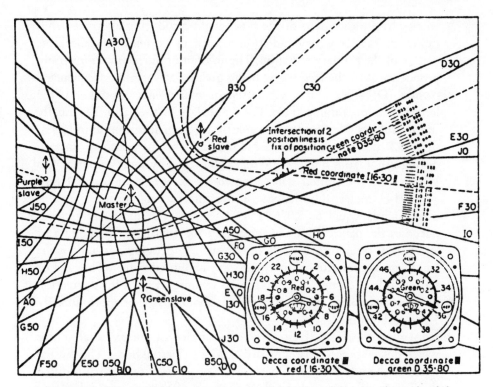

A plot of a Decca fix. Angle of a celestial body relative to the celestial equator; analogous to latitude.

deflection of the vertical (geodesy)—The angle at a point on the geoid between the vertical (direction of the plumb line) and the direction of the normal to the ellipsoid of reference. Deflection of the vertical is also called station error. This deflection is usually resolved into two components, one in the plane of the meridian and the other in the plane of the prime vertical (east–west direction).

depth finding—*See* echo sounder.

diffraction (radio waves)—When a radio wave encounters an obstacle, its energy is reflected or absorbed, causing a shadow beyond the obstacle. However, some energy does enter the shadow area by diffraction. Huygens's principle states that every point on the surface of a wave front is a source of radiation, transmitting energy in all directions ahead of the wave. No noticeable effect of this principle is observed until the wave front encounters an obstacle that intercepts a portion of the wave. From the edge of the obstacle, energy is radiated into the shadow area, and also outside of the area. The latter interacts with energy from other parts of the wave front, producing alternate bands in which the secondary radiation reinforces or tends to cancel the energy of the primary radiation. The amount of diffraction is inversely proportional to the frequency, being greatest at very low frequencies.

distance (D)—The spatial separation of two points, expressed as the length of a line joining them. On the surface of the earth it is usually stated in miles. Navigators customarily use the nautical mile (mi., M), of 1,852 meters exactly. It is often called the international mile to distinguish it from slightly different values used by some countries. On July 1, 1959, the United States adopted the exact relationship of 1 yard = 0.9144 meter. The length of the international nautical mile is consequently equal to 6,076.11549 U.S. feet. For most navigational purposes the nautical mile is considered the length of one minute of latitude, or of any great circle of the earth. A geographical mile is the length of one minute of the equator, or about 6,087 feet. The land or statute mile (mi., m), of 5,280 feet, is commonly used for navigation in rivers and lakes. The nautical mile is about 38/33, or approximately 1.15, statute miles.

diurnal circle—A small circle on the surface of the celestial sphere which describes the apparent daily path of a celestial body. The diurnal circle of the sun at the summer solstice projected to the earth is called the Tropic of Cancer; located 23.5° north of the equator and named for the sign of the zodiac containing the sun at that time, it marks the northern limits of the tropics. The diurnal circle of the sun at the winter solstice projected to the earth is called the Tropic of Capricorn; located 23.5° south of the equator, and named for the sign of the zodiac containing the sun at that time, it marks the southern limit of the tropics. When the sun is over the Tropic of Capricorn, the region north of 66.5° north latitude has continual darkness, and the region south of 66.5° south latitude has continual daylight. This is the basis for the establishment of the Arctic and Antarctic circles.

dividers—An instrument consisting of two hinged legs with pointed ends which can be separated at any distance from zero to some maximum imposed by its physical limitations. The setting is retained either by friction at the hinge, as in the usual navigational dividers, or by a screw acting against a spring. The principal use of dividers in navigation is to measure or transfer distances on a chart.

Doppler shift—The measurement of radio signals transmitted by a navigation satellite (NAVSAT) is based on the Doppler shift phenomenon, the apparent change in frequency of the radio waves received when the distance between the source of radiation (in this case the satellite) and the receiving station is increasing or decreasing because of the motion of either or both. The amount of shift is proportional to the velocity of approach or recession. The amount of this shift depends on the location of the receiving station with respect to the path of the satellite. Accordingly, if the satellite position (orbit) is known, it is possible by measurement of the Doppler shift to calculate the location of the receiver. Great accuracy is possible because of the quantities measured, frequency and time, can be determined to one part in a billion.

drift—The lateral movement of a craft over the bottom in contrast to its fore-and-aft movement. It is most often caused by current and, to a lesser degree, by wind. Drift caused by wind is called leeway. Also, the velocity of a current as opposed to its set, or direction.

dynamic water pressure (speed measurement)—When an object is moving through a fluid such as water or air, its forward side is exposed to a dynamic pressure that is proportional to the speed at which the object is moving. It can be used for determining speed. One of the most widely used means of measuring dynamic pressure is a Pitot tube, which is a tube open on its forward end.

E

earth coordinates—The earth is an oblate spheroid, or a sphere slightly flattened at the poles. The equatorial diameter is 6,888 miles; the polar diameter, 6,865 miles. The difference of 23 miles is sufficient to require attention in the making of charts and in many of the calculations involved in navigation over long distances.

Any plane surface passing through the center of a sphere intersects the surface of the sphere in a great circle; any plane passing through the poles and the center will intersect the surface of the sphere in a great circle called a meridian. The equator is an example of a great circle that does not include poles. Measurements made along the equator from the Greenwich, England meridian determine the longitude (Lo) of the meridian passing through the point to which the measurement is made. Longitude is measured in degrees, minutes ('), and seconds (") of arc up to 180°W and 180°E.

A plane passing through the sphere parallel to the equator will not pass through the center of the sphere. It forms a small circle at its intersection with the surface. As the plane approaches either of the poles, the radius of the small circle decreases. These small circles are parallels of latitude. There are 180° of arc along a meridian from pole to pole. Latitude (L) is the arc measured along a meridian from the equator to the parallel in question; values range from 0° to 90°N and 0° to 90°S. Latitude and longitude are coordinates that serve to locate any point on the earth's surface.

The distance measured along the equator between two meridians one degree apart is 60.12 nautical miles. One minute of longitude along the equator is then 1.002 nautical miles. Since meridians converge and meet at the poles, one minute of arc between them will be less than the equatorial value at any latitude other than the equator.

One minute of latitude measured along a meridian is 0.995 nautical miles near the equator, and 1.005 nautical miles at the poles. For practical purposes, one minute of latitude is one nautical mile at any latitude.

echo sounder—An instrument producing an underwater sound singal and measuring the elapsed time of its echo from the bottom. It is a form of sonar, although this term is usually applied only to equipment that directs the signal horizontally to measure distances. An echo sounder operating within the range of audible sound (20 to 20,000 cycles per second) is called a sonic depth finder; one using sound waves of a higher frequency, an ultrasonic depth finder. Echo sounders of American manufacture are calibrated for a speed of sound of 4,800 feet per second, although the actual speed varies with temperature, pressure, and salinity. A diaphragm (transducer) in contact with the water is vibrated by an electric circuit. The transducer is also used to receive the echo, which is amplified and fed to the depth indicator. Some echo-sounding instruments show the depth graphically. Others indicate it by meters, digital displays, or flashing lights.

Eckman current meter—A mechanical device for measuring ocean-current velocity. A sensitive impeller is turned by current action and the number of turns recorded on a dial. Speed is calculated from the number of impeller revolutions.

Eckman spiral—A representation of the theory that a wind blowing steadily over an ocean of unlimited depth and extent and of uniform viscosity would cause the surface layer to drift at an angle of 45° to the right of the wind direction in the Northern Hemisphere. Water at successive depths would drift more to the right until at some depth it would move opposite the wind. The depth at which this reversal occurs is around 100 meters. The net water movement is 90° to the right of the direction of the wind in the Northern Hemisphere.

ecliptic—The apparent path of the sun among the stars over a period of one year; a great circle on the surface of the celestial sphere lying in a plane that intersects the plane of the extended equator (equinoctial) at approximately 23.5°.

electromagnetic frequency spectrum—Radiation in electronics is in the form of electromagnetic waves called radio waves. Electromagnetic fields occur at all frequencies. The electromagnetic frequency spectrum extends from a single reversal (cycle) of polarity per second (1 Hertz) through the radio frequency spectrum, infrared frequencies, visible light frequencies, ultraviolet-ray, X-ray, and gamma-ray spectrums to approximately 10^{15}MHz (ten quadrillion Hertz).

Band	Abbreviation	Range of frequency	Range of wavelength
Audio frequency	AF	20 to 20,000 Hz	15,000,000 to 15,000 m
Radio frequency	RF	10 kHz to 300,000 MHz	30,000 m to 0.1 cm
Very low frequency	VLF	10 to 30 kHz	30,000 to 10,000 m
Low frequency	LF	30 to 300 kHz	10,000 to 1,000 m
Medium frequency	MF	300 to 3,000 kHz	1,000 to 100 m
High frequency	HF	3 to 30 MHz	100 to 10 m
Very high frequency	VHF	30 to 300 MHz	10 to 1 m
Ultra high frequency	UHF	300 to 3,000 MHz	100 to 10 cm
Super high frequency	SHF	3,000 to 30,000 MHz	10 to 1 cm
Extremely high frequency	EHF	30,000 to 300,000 MHz	1 to 0.1 cm
Heat and infrared*		10^6 to 3.9×10^8 MHz	0.03 to 7.6×10^{-5} cm
Visible spectrum*		3.9×10^8 to 7.9×10^8 MHz	7.6×10^{-5} to 3.8×10^{-5} cm
Ultraviolet*		7.9×10^8 to 2.3×10^{10} MHz	3.8×10^{-5} to 1.3×10^{-6} cm
X-rays*		2.0×10^9 to 3.0×10^{13} MHz	1.5×10^{-5} to 1.0×10^{-9} cm
Gamma rays*		2.3×10^{12} to 3.0×10^{14} MHz	1.3×10^{-8} to 1.0×10^{-10} cm
Cosmic rays*		$> 4.8 \times 10^{15}$ MHz	$< 6.2 \times 10^{-12}$ cm

*Values approximate.

Electromagnetic Spectrum

electromagnetic induction—A varying electric field is created by a varying magnetic field. The varying electric field in turn sets up a displacement current, which gives rise to a magnetic field. The varying magnetic field creates an electric field, and so on. The process whereby they mutually induce one another is called electromagnetic induction. The combination is called the electromagnetic field; this effect occurs at all frequencies. Once the initial field is created, it becomes independent of further electrical input. When the current stops, the field can continue to survive and propagate on into space.

electromagnetic log (EM log)—Consists essentially of a rod meter, sea valve, indicator-transmitter, and remote-control unit. The rod meter is a strut of streamlined cross-section. A sensing device near its tip develops a voltage proportional to the speed of the water past it. The indicator-transmitter houses all the moving parts of the equipment. It indicates the vessel's speed and it registers the distance the vessel has traveled through the water. The principle of the electromagnetic log is that any conductor will produce a voltage when it is moved across a magnetic field or when a magnetic field is moved with respect to the conductor.

electromagnetic wave—An electromagnetic wave is produced by a rapidly expanding and collapsing magnetic field, which in turn is produced by alternately energizing and de-energizing an electronic circuit designed for the generation of such waves. In electronics, such a generating circuit is referred to as an oscillator. An amplifer of some type is generally used to boost the power of the oscillator output, and an antenna is utilized to form the outgoing wave. An electromagnetic wave always resembles a sine wave; it can be characterized by its wavelength, frequency, and amplitude, as seen in the diagram below. In this figure, one complete electromagnetic wave or cycle is shown and terms used to describe it follow. A cycle is one complete sequence of values, from zero to positive, positive to zero, zero to negative and back to zero as the wave passes a point in space. The wavelength (λ) is the length of a cycle in meters or centimeters. The amplitude is the wave strength at any particular point along the wave. The frequency (f) is the number of cycles during one second. The phase of a wave is the amount by which a cycle has progressed from a specified origin. For most purposes it is stated in degrees, with a complete phase being 360°.

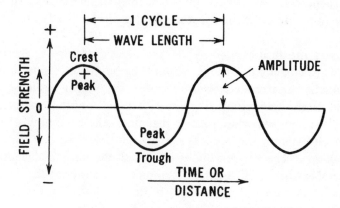

Electromagnetic wave terminology

epeiric seas—Shallow inland seas with restricted communications with the open ocean and having depths less than 250 meters (137 fathoms). Hudson Bay is an example.

equator—The terrestrial great circle whose plane is perpendicular to the polar axis. It is midway between the poles.

equatorial calms (doldrums)—Throughout the year a belt of low pressure surrounds the earth in the equatorial zone as a result of the overheating of the globe in this region. Late-afternoon showers are usual from the strong convection and resulting adiabatic cooling at this time of highest diurnal temperature. Most of the air motion is vertical, having in general a slight westward drift. The hot, sticky atmosphere, light winds, and slick seas were named doldrums in the days of sailing ships. During the northern winter the doldrums straddle the equator except in the vicinity of the eastern Indian Ocean. Here the equatorial low is displaced southward, by the warming of Australia in the southern summer. During the northern summer, a considerable northern displacement of the low-pressure belt occurs owing to the heating of the large continental areas. At this time of the year, the low-pressure belt becomes centered over Central America; in eastern longitudes an even more pronounced displacement, to southern Asia, takes place. The mean annual position of the doldrums generally lies north of the equator, owing to displacement during the northern summer.

equinoctial (nautical astronomy)—A great circle on the surface of the celestial sphere, always 90 degrees from the celestial poles. Sometimes called the celestial equator, the equinoctial lies in a plane that is the plane of the equator extended to intersect the celestial sphere and that is perpendicular to the axis of the earth (and of the celestial sphere). The equinoctial, like the equator, supplies a reference for north–south measurement.

equinoxes (nautical astronomy)—Two great circles on a spherical surface share two points of intersection. The points of intersection of the equinoctial and the ecliptic are called the vernal equinox (March equinox) and the autumnal equinox. The sun normally arrives at the vernal equinox on March 21; at that time (the beginning of spring), the declination of the sun is 0 and the sun passes from south to north declination. The sun normally arrives at the autumnal equinox on September 23; at that time (the beginning of autumn) the declination is also 0 and the sun passes from north to south declination.

Equivalent Temperature (Celsius and Fahrenheit)—

°C	°F	°C	°F	°C	°F	°C	°F	°C	°F
−10	14.0	0	32.0	10	50.0	20	68.0	30	86.0
−9	15.8	1	33.8	11	51.8	21	69.8	31	87.8
−8	17.6	2	35.6	12	53.6	22	71.6	32	89.6
−7	19.4	3	37.4	13	55.4	23	73.4	33	91.4
−6	21.2	4	39.2	14	57.2	24	75.2	34	93.2
−5	23.0	5	41.0	15	59.0	25	77.0	35	95.0
−4	24.8	6	42.8	16	60.8	26	78.8	36	96.8
−3	26.6	7	44.6	17	62.6	27	80.6	37	98.6
−2	28.4	8	46.4	18	64.4	28	82.4	38	100.4
−1	30.2	9	48.2	19	66.2	29	84.2	39	102.2

estimated position (EP)—A correction of the DR position, obtained by incorporating the effect of current. Although current, technically, is the horizontal movement of water, the term is used in navigation to include wind effect, steering error, and all other factors that tend to take a ship off its planned course. Estimated position is the most probable position when a fix or running fix is unobtainable. An EP may be either the DR position adjusted for current, or the nearest point to the DR on a bearing line.

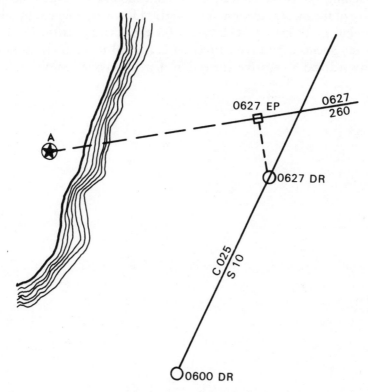

Estimated position, EP

estimated position (celestial navigation)—If an appreciable time has elapsed since the last fix of the ship's position at sea, the error in the DR plot may build to the point where the ship's actual position is a good distance away from her DR position. Under these circumstances, if a celestial LOP (line-of-position) can be obtained and plotted, an estimated position (EP) can be determined based on the LOP. If the LOP is accurate, the ship must have been located somewhere on it at the moment of observation. An estimate of the ship's likely location on the line can be made by dropping a perpendicular to the single LOP from the ship's DR position. After the EP has been plotted, the ship's DR track can be projected from it until such time as a second LOP from any source is obtained. If this subsequent LOP lies at an angle to the original celestial LOP, the earlier LOP may be advanced to form a running fix.

Etovos effect—The east–west component of the movement of the ship, including the effect of marine currents, modified by the centrifugal force of the earth's rotation. It is a vertical force experienced by a body moving in an east–west direction on the rotating earth. In gravity measurements a positive correction is applied if the body is moving eastward and a negative correction if it is moving westward.

F

fathom—The common unit of depth, equal to 6 feet (1.83 meters). It is also sometimes used in expressing horizontal distances, in which case 120 fathoms makes one cable, or very nearly one-tenth of a nautical mile.

fathometer—*See* Echo Sounder.

fix—A position determined without reference to any former position. It may be visual, sonic, celestial, electronic, radio, hyperbolic, loran, radar, etc., depending upon the means of establishing it. A pinpoint is a very accurate fix, usually established by passing directly over or near an aid to navigation or a landmark of small area. A line of position, however obtained, represents a series of possible positions, but not a single position. However, if two simultaneous, nonparallel lines of position are available, the only position that satisfies the requirements of being on both lines at the same time is the intersection of the two lines. This point is one form of fix. The angle between lines of position is important; ideal is 90°. If the angle is small, a slight error in measurement or plotting results in a large error in the position. Although two nonparallel lines of position completely define a position, an element of doubt always exists as to the accuracy of the lines, and additional lines of position can serve as a check on those already obtained.

FIX, RUNNING (R fix)—A fix obtained by means of lines of position taken at different times and adjusted to a common time. In piloting, common practice is to advance earlier lines to the time of the most recent observation. The time between observations should be no longer than necessary, for the uncertainty of direction and distance made good increases with time. On page 107 is a diagram of a running fix. The bearing (100°) taken on buoy A at 1014 has been advanced to the time

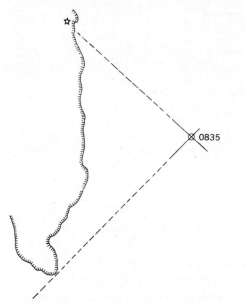

A fix by two bearing lines.

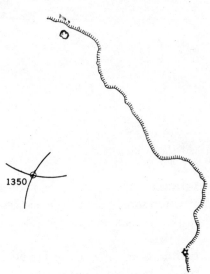

A fix by two distances.

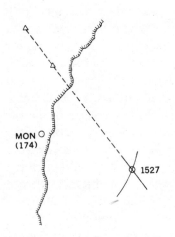

A fix by a range and distance.

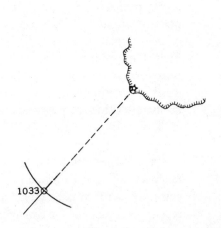

A fix by distance and bearing of single object.

Fixes

(1058) of the bearing (300°) on buoy B; the intersection of the two bearing lines is a running fix (R fix).

FIX BY HORIZONTAL ANGLES—A fix by the measurements of the two angles between three shoreside objects. The bearings of the objects are not measured; the angles are measured simultaneously, usually by sextant held horizontally.

FIX BY SOUNDINGS—A procedure characterized by the use of bottom contour lines as lines of position. First the time of crossing consecutive bottom contour lines and their depth are recorded. Second, the DR positions at the times the soundings were taken are noted. Third, on a sheet of tracing paper a line is drawn in the direction of travel. Fourth, the paper is placed over the DR position corresponding to the first recorded depth, and the contour line for that depth is traced. Fifth, the sheet is moved to successive DR positions, and the corresponding contour lines are traced. After three or more contours are plotted, their intersection is the fix.

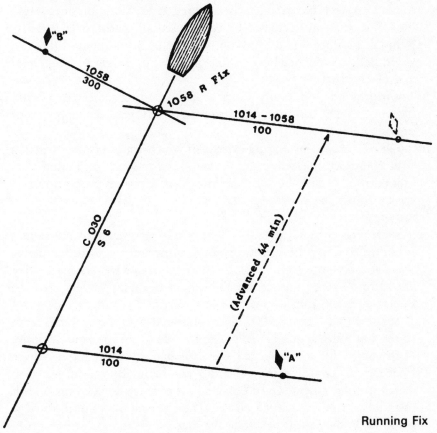

Running Fix

FIX BY BOW AND BEAM BEARINGS—A special case of the running fix. When the bearing of a landmark is 45° from the ship's heading, it is said to be broad on the bow. When the bearing increases to 90°, it is on the beam. By noting the time a landmark is broad on the bow and the time it is on the beam, one can compute the distance from the landmark; the distance when it is abeam is equal to the distance run between bow and beam bearings.

fog signals—Sounding-producing mechanisms operated in time of reduced visibility from a charted lighthouse, lightship, or buoy. The simpler fog signals are bells, gongs, or whistles on buoys. Such signals are operated by the motion of the sea and will not work in a calm. The only buoy that will signal its location under such conditions is the horn buoy, whose sounds are produced by batteries. At lighthouses, and lightships, signals are produced mechanically. Diaphones produce sound by compressed air. Diaphram horns produce sound by a disk vibrated by compressed air, steam, or electricity. Reed horns produce sound by a steel reed vibrated by compressed air. Sirens produce sound by a disk or a rotor actuated by compressed air, steam, or electricity. Whistles produce sound by compressed air or steam directed through a slot. Bells are sounded by a hammer actuated by a weight, compressed gas, or electricity.

following wind—Generally same as tail wind; specifically, a wind blowing in the direction of ocean-wave advance; the opposite of opposing wind.

force log—A speed-measuring system in which water pressure forces a strut against a calibrated spring. A flexible hydraulic hose transmits the motion to a speed indicator. The force on the strut is proportional to the square of the vessel's speed.

frequency:

HIGH (HF, 3 to 30 mHz)—The ground-wave range of HF signals is limited to a few miles, but elevation of the antenna increases direct-wave and sky-wave transmission distances. Usable frequencies by day are 10 to 30 mHz; during the night, 8 to 10 mHz. Widely used for ship-to-ship and ship-to-shore communications.

MEDIUM (MF, 300 to 3,000 kHz)—Ground-wave range varies from about 400 miles at the lower portion of the band to about 15 miles at the upper for a transmitted signal of one kilowatt. At the lower frequencies, sky waves are usable day and night. By careful selection of frequencies, ranges can be obtained for as much as 8,000 miles with one kilowatt of transmitted power. The frequency is critical, for if it is too high, the signals penetrate the ionosphere and are lost in space.

If too low, signals are weak. The standard broadcast band for commercial stations (535 to 1,605 kHz) and the frequencies for loran are in the MF band.

ULTRA HIGH (UHF 300 to 3,000 mHz)—Sky waves are not used in the UHF band, because the ionosphere does not reflect the waves. Ground waves reach about 15 percent beyond the visible horizon, owing to refraction. Reception of UHF signals is virtually free from fading and interference from atmospheric noise.

VERY HIGH (VHF, 30 to 300 mHz)—Communication limited primarily to direct wave, or direct wave plus a ground-reflected wave. Elevating the antenna results in increased range even though some interference between direct and ground-reflected waves is present. Diffraction (see entry) is much less than with lower frequencies, but is evident when signals cross sharp mountain peaks or ridges. Under suitable conditions, reflections from the ionosphere are sufficiently strong to be useful, but generally not. There is relatively little interference from atmospheric noise. The VHF band is much used for communication with aircraft and for radio aids to air navigation.

VERY LOW (VLF, 10 to 30 kHz)—As frequency is decreased to the LF band, the ionosphere becomes less useful as a reflector, diffraction decreases, ground losses increase, and range for a given power falls off rapidly. This is partly offset by more-efficient transmitting antennas, which can be made of a size practical for use aboard ship. The band is useful for radio direction finding and ground-wave transmission over medium distances.

G

Gee—A British hyperbolic navigation system resembling loran. In both systems the difference of the distances from two transmitters is determined by measurement of the time between receptions of synchronized, pulse-modulated signals. Gee operates in the 20–85 MHz range and is therefore limited to line-of-sight distances. Transmitting stations are arranged in groups of four, each group being considered a chain. One of the four is a master, controlling synchronization. Pulses are two to ten microseconds in length and the master transmits 500 per second. Two of the slaves transmit 250 pulses per second, synchronized with alternate pulses from the master. The third slave transmits 500/3 per second, synchronized with each third pulse from the master. As in other hyperbolic systems, maximum accuracy of position occurs along the line between transmitters (baseline).

geocentric latitude—The angle at the center of the ellipsoid (used to represent the earth) between the plane of its equator and a straight line (or radius vector) to a point on the surface of the ellipsoid. This differs from geodetic latitude because the earth is a spheroid rather than a sphere, and the meridians are ellipses. The difference between geocentric and geodetic latitudes has a maximum of about 11.6 at latitude 45°. Because of the oblate shape of the ellipsoid, the length of a degree of geodetic latitude is not everywhere the same, increasing from about 59.7 nautical miles at the equator to about 60.3 nautical miles at the poles.

geodesic line—A line of shortest distance between any two points on any mathematically defined surface.

geodetic datum—A datum is defined as any numerical or geometrical quantity or set of such quantities which may serve as a reference or base for other quantities. In geodesy, two types of datums are used; a horizontal datum, which is the basis for surveys in which the curvature of the earth is considered; and a vertical datum, to which elevations are referred. In other words, the coordinates for points in specific geodetic surveys and trinagulation networks are computed from certain initial quantities (datums).

geodetic latitude—The angle that the perpendicular to the ellipsoid at a station makes with the plane of the geodetic equator. A geodetic latitude differs from astronomic latitude by the amount of the meridional (N–S) component of the local deflection of the vertical.

geodetic leveling—In barometric leveling, one determines differences in height by measuring the differences in atmospheric pressure at various elevations. Air pressure is measured by mercurial or aneroid barometer, or the boiling point of water. Although the degree of accuracy possible with this method is not great, it obtains relative heights rapidly for points that are far apart. It is widely used in reconnaissance and exploratory surveys where more-exact measurements will be made later.

Differential leveling is the most accurate method. With the theodolite or transit locked in position, readings are made on two calibrated staffs held in an upright position ahead of and behind the instrument. The difference between readings is the difference in elevation between the points. The optical instrument (theodolite) used for leveling has a bubble tube to adjust it parallel to the geoid.

Trigonometric leveling involves measuring a vertical angle from a known distance with a theodolite and computing the elevation of the point. With this method, vertical measurement can be made at the same time horizontal angles are measured for triangulation. It is, therefore, a somewhat more economical method but less accurate than differential leveling. It is often the only practical method in mountainous areas.

geodetic longitude—The angle between the plane of the geodetic meridian at a station and the plane of the geodetic meridian at Greenwich. A geodetic longitude differs from astronomic longitude by the amount of the prime vertical (E–W) component of the local deflection of the vertical divided by the cosine of the latitude.

geographic position (GP)—As an observer looks at a star or other celestial body, its light rays pass through a single point on the earth's surface. This point is called the geographic position (GP) of the body; it is moving constantly westward, but its precise position on the earth's surface can be determined for any instant of time from information tabulated in an almanac. Knowing the exact location of the GP of a body, the navigator can develop a line of position by means of a sextant observation, very much as an LOP is obtained from observation of any landmark of known position on the earth's surface. To develop celestial lines of position, the navigator must obtain an accurate measurement of the altitude of a celestial body above the horizon.

geoid—The figure of the earth considered as if a mean-sea-level surface extended through the continents. The actual geoid is an equipotential surface to which, at every point, the plumb line (direction in which gravity acts) is perpendicular. It is the geoid that is obtained from observed deflections of the vertical and is the surface of reference for astronomical observations and for geodetic leveling.

geomagnetic electrokinetograph (GEK)—Shipboard current-measuring device used in depths greater than 100 fathoms. Dependent upon the principle that an electrolyte moving through the earth's magnetic field will generate an electric current. By means of two electrodes towed astern, beyond the magnetic influence of the vessel, one component of a current perpendicular to the course is measured. By measurement of two components, preferably measured on courses 90° apart, total current can be determined. Used primarily by oceanographers to study ocean currents.

geomagnetic equator—Great circle on the earth's surface that is everywhere equidistant from the geomagnetic poles; that is, the equator in the system of geomagnetic coordinates.

geomagnetic pole—Point where axis of a centered dipole that most nearly duplicates the earth's magnetic field would intersect surface of the earth. The earth's geomagnetic poles are located approximately 78.5°N, 69.0°W and 78.5°S, 111.0°E.

gimbaling error—That error due to the tilting of the compass. Directions are measured in the horizontal plane. If the compass is tilted, the projection of its outer rim onto the horizontal is an ellipse, and graduations are not equally spaced with respect to a circle. For normal angles of tilt this error is small and can be neglected. For accurate results, readings should be made when the card is horizontal. This error applies to the reading of the compass or its repeaters rather than to the compass itself. If the compass and its repeaters are installed so that the outer gimbals are in the longitudinal axis of the vessel, this error is minimized.

gnomonic projection (charts)—If a plane is tangent to the earth and points are projected geometrically from the center of the earth, the result is a gnomonic projection. Probably the oldest of the projections, believed to have been developed by Thales of Miletus (640–546 B.C.), who was chief of the Seven Wise Men of ancient Greece; founder of Greek geometry, astronomy, and philosophy; a navigator and cartographer. For the oblique case the meridians appear as straight lines converging toward the nearest pole. The parallels, except the equator, appear as curves. As in all azimuthal projections, bearings from the point of tangency are correctly represented. The distance scale, however, changes rapidly. The projection is neither conformal nor equal-area. Distortion is so great that shapes as well as distances are very poorly represented, except near the point of tangency. Gnomonic charts published by the U.S. Navy Hydrographic Office bear instructions for determining directions and distance on the charts. The principal navigational use of such charts is for plotting the great–circle track between points, for planning purposes. Points along the track are then transferred by latitude and longitude to the navigational charts, usually Mercator projection. The great circle is then approximated by following straight (rhumb) lines from one point to the next.

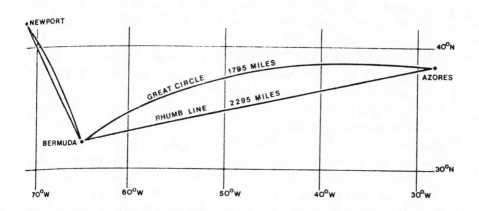

great-circle course—Is the shortest distance between two points on a sphere but cannot be exactly followed by a vessel, because direction on the circumference of a circle is constantly changing; selected chords of the circle are therefore plotted as rhumb-line straight courses to follow. Great circles and rhumb lines differ little for distances up to 600 miles, and on approximately north–south courses. The significantly shorter distance of a great circle is on east–west courses at distances of more than 600 miles. A great-circle course is obtained from a gnomonic, or "great-circle," chart and transported to a Mercator chart by (1) drawing a straight line on the gnomonic chart from departure to destination; (2) at convenient points along the line, writing down latitude and longitude; (3) transferring to a Mercator chart the latitudes and longitudes of the selected points on the gnomonic chart and connecting them. These (rhumb) lines are chords of the great circle courses to sail.

great diurnal range—The average difference in height between all mean higher high waters and all mean lower low waters measured over a nineteen-year period.

Greenwich hour angle (GHA)—Celestial equivalent of longitude, with the important difference that measurement from the Greenwich celestial meridian is westward through 360°, and not east and west of the meridian, as with longitude. Because direction west is understood, GHA does not have a suffix.

Greenwich interval—An interval referring to the transit of the moon over the meridian of Greenwich, as distinguished from local interval, which refers to the moon's transit over the local meridian.

Greenwich mean time (GMT)—Mean solar time measured with reference to the meridian of Greenwich. The mean sun transits the lower branch of the meridian of Greenwich at GMT 00-00-00 and again at 24-00-00 (which is 00-00-00 of the following day); the mean sun transits upper branch at 12-00-00. GMT is of great importance to the navigator, as it is the time used in almanacs for tabulating coordinates of all celestial bodies. The choice of the meridian of Greenwich as the reference meridian for time is logical, as it is also the reference meridian used in reckoning longitude.

grids—No system has been devised for showing without distortion the surface of the earth on a flat surface. Moreover, the appearance of any portion of the surface varies with the chart projection used and with the location of the chart's point or line of contact with the globe. For some purposes it is desirable to be able to identify a location by rectangular coordinates, using numbers or letters, or a combination of numbers and letters, without the necessity of indicating units or assigning a name (north, south, east, or west), thus reducing the possibility of a mistake. This is accomplished by means of a grid. In its usual form this consists of two series of lines that are perpendicular on the chart, Grid navigation uses a similar network to provide a uniform directional reference, particularly in polar regions. Difference in direction between magnetic north at any point and grid north at that same point is called grid variation or grivation.

grid direction—Because of the rapid convergence of the meridians in polar regions, true direction of an oblique line near the pole may vary considerably over relatively few miles. The meridians are radical lines meeting at the poles, instead of being parallel, as they appear on the Mercator chart. Near the pole, the convenience of using parallel meridians is attained by means of a polar grid. On the chart a number of lines are printed parallel to a selected reference meridian, usually that of Greenwich. Any straight line drawn on the chart then makes the same angle with all grid lines; this angle is called grid direction. North along the Greenwich meridian is usually taken as grid north in both Northern and Southern hemispheres.

ground waves (and sky waves)—Electromagnetic energy transmitted from an antenna radiates outward in all directions. A portion of this energy proceeds parallel to the earth's surface while the remainder travels upward until it strikes one or more layers of ionized gases (the ionosphere) and is reflected back to the earth. That portion of the radiated energy which follows along the surface of the earth is called the ground wave; the other, sky waves. Low-frequency ground waves penetrate the earth's surface, and the lower part of the wave is slightly impeded, but the upper portion of the wave is not. This causes the wave to curve along the earth's surface. It is this effect that makes possible the transmission of ground waves over great distances. Combined with the curvature of the wave is an energy loss by absorption into the earth. This effect necessitates high power to achieve long-distance transmission of the ground wave. The variation in surfaces of land areas complicates the prediction of ground-wave transmission. Conductivity of ocean surface, on the other hand, is quite constant, and propagation over ocean areas can be predicted quite accurately. Only low-frequency radio waves curve sufficiently to follow the earth's surface over great distances.

gyro compass—Essentially, one or more north-seeking gyroscopes with a suitable compass rose, housing, etc. Since a gyro compass is not affected by a magnetic field, it is not subject to magnetic-compass errors, nor is it useless near the earth's magnetic poles. If an error is present, it is the same on all headings, and no table of corrections is needed. An undesirable characteristic is that the directive force of the gyro compass decreases with latitude, being maximum at the equator and zero at the poles.

gyro compass repeater—A gyro compass is customarily located below deck, and its indications are transmitted electrically to various positions throughout the vessel. At each position is a repeater consisting of a compass rose. Although the repeater may be mounted in any position, including vertically on a bulkhead, it is generally placed in gimbals in a bowl similar to the mounting of a compass. This is true particularly of repeaters used for taking bearings. A repeater used primarily to indicate heading is called a ship's course indicator.

gyroscope—A conventional gyroscope consists of a massive, wheel–like rotor balanced in gimbals, which permit rotation in any direction about three mutually perpendicular axes. The three axes are called the spin axis, the torque axis, and the precession axis. The rapidly spinning rotor is balanced at its center of gravity and is in a state of neutral equilibrium. If the gimbal bearings were completely frictionless, the spin axis would retain its direction in space despite any motion of the system as a whole, as by the rotation of the earth. This property is called gyroscopic inertia. When a force is applied to change the direction of the spin axis, the reaction to the force is not in line with the force but perpendicular to it. This is called gyroscopic precession.

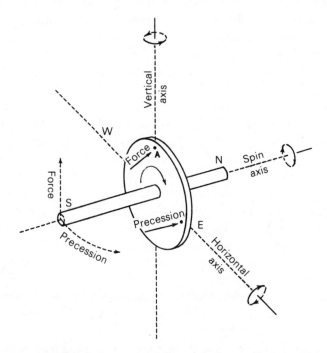

Axes of a gyroscope, and the direction of precession

gyroscope, rate—A simplified schematic of a rate gyroscope is shown below. Precession about the output axis is restrained by a spring. If a force tries to turn the gyro around its input axis, it will precess the gyro through angle θ until the precession is balanced by the spring.

As long as the rate of input torque remains constant, the gyro will maintain position. When the rate of input torque decreases, the gyro will return to its normal position.

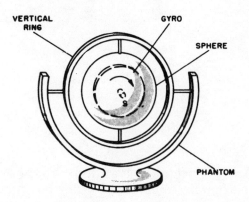

Schematic of a rate gyro

gyroscopic inertia—By Newton's first law (inertia), a mass will continue to move at constant speed and in the same direction unless it is acted upon by an outside force. Inertia also tends to keep the rotating wheel in the same plane and resists any force that tries to change its plane of rotation. If a gyroscope could be constructed free of mechanical error, with no friction on the axis of the rotating wheel or its gimbals, and operated in a vacuum with no air friction on the rotating wheel, the result would be a perpetual-motion machine. The direction of the spin axis would remain parallel to its original position when placed in motion, and the gyroscope would rotate forever.

gyroscopic laws—Of the four natural laws upon which gyro-compass operation depends, the first two are inherent: gyroscopic inertia (rigidity in space), and precession. The third and fourth are external: the ship's motion, and the earth's gravity.

H

hand lead—A lead-weighted length of rope heaved overboard by inducing a pendulum-like motion and letting go at such a time as to allow the lead to sink ahead of the boat. The leadsman calls out depths by referring to markings on the rope. In the end of the lead itself, a hollow permits "arming"; putting tallow or grease into the indentation in order to pick up samples of the bottom.

heading (Hdg., SH)—The direction in which a vessel is pointed, expressed as an angle, usually from 000° at north, clockwise through 360°. Heading should not be confused with course. Heading is a constantly changing value as a vessel oscillates or yaws back and forth across the course or as the direction of motion is temporarily changed, as in avoiding an obstacle. Course is a predetermined track and usually remains constant for a considerable time.

Hoey position plotter—A celluloid protractor with an attached drafting arm. The protractor has imprinted horizontal and vertical lines permitting alignment with parallels or meridians. After alignment, using the protractor and drafting arm, one may transfer lines that represent bearings or courses anywhere on the chart.

horizon—Celestial coordinates with which a navigator is directly concerned are based upon one of several horizons as the primary great circle. The line where the earth and the sky appear to meet is called the visible or apparent horizon. On land this is usually an irregular line unless terrain is level. At sea, the visible horizon appears very regular and often very sharp. However, its position relative to the celestial sphere depends primarily upon (1) refractive index of the air and (2) height of an observer's eye above the surface.

A plane perpendicular to the true vertical is a horizontal plane, and its intersection with the celestial sphere is a horizon. It is a celestial horizon if the plane passes through the center of the earth, a geoidal horizon if it is tangent to the earth, and a sensible horizon if it passes through the eye of the observer (see A below). Since the radius of the earth is negligible with respect to that of celestial sphere, these horizons become superimposed there, and most measurements are referred to the celestial horizon. If the eye of an observer is at the surface of the earth, his visible horizon coincides with the plane of the geoidal horizon; but when elevated above the surface, as at A, his eye becomes the vertex of a cone that, neglecting refraction, is tangent to the earth at small circle BB, and that intersects the celestial sphere in B'B', the geometrical horizon. For any elevation above the surface, the celestial horizon is usually above the geometrical and visible horizons, the difference increasing as elevation increases. It is thus possible to observe a body that is above the visible horizon but below the celestial horizon, that is, when the body's altitude is negative and its zenith distance is greater than 90°.

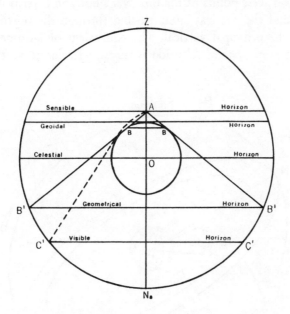

The horizons used in navigation

horizon coordinate system—In order to obtain a line of position by observation of a celestial body, the horizon system is required. It differs from the celestial coordinate system in that it is based on the position of the observer, rather than on the projected terrestrial equator and poles. The reference plane of the horizon system (corresponding to the plane of the equator in the terrestrial and celestial systems) is the observer's celestial horizon, defined as "a plane passing through the center of the earth, perpendicular to a line passing through the observer's position and the earth's center." The line extended outward from the observer to the celestial sphere defines a point on the sphere directly over the observer, called his zenith. The extension of the line through the center of the earth to the opposite side of the celestial sphere defines a second point directly beneath the observer, called his nadir. The observer's zenith and nadir correspond to the terrestrial and celestial poles, while the zenith–nadir line corresponds to the axis of the terrestrial and celestial spheres. The equivalent of a meridian in the terrestrial system and an hour circle in the celestial system is called a vertical circle in the horizon system; a great circle on the celestial sphere passing through the observer's zenith and nadir, perpendicular to the plane of the celestial horizon. The vertical circle passing through the east and west points of the observer's horizon is termed the prime vertical, and the vertical circle passing through the north and south points is the principal vertical. The equivalent of latitude is altitude in the horizon system. Altitude is measured relative to the celestial

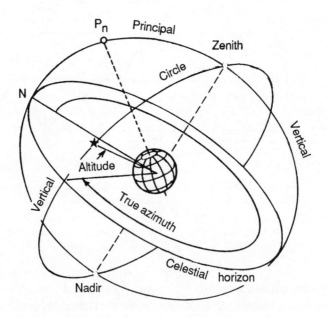

Observed altitude and true azimuth of a star
in the horizon coordinate system

horizon and termed observed altitude (Ho). The other horizon used as a reference for altitude measurements is the observer's visible or sea horizon, the line along which sea and sky appear to meet. The equivalent of longitude in the horizon system is true azimuth (Zn).

horizontal angle (piloting)—A fix may be obtained by means of the difference in bearing of several objects. Horizontal sextant angles are usually the most accurate source of such bearings. Customarily, two angles are measured between three objects. These angles are then plotted from a single point on a sheet of transparent material, or set on a mechanical device called a three-arm protractor. The three lines, or arms, are then moved around on a chart by trial and error until all three pass through the objects used for observation. The observer must be at the common intersection of the three lines. This method provides accurate results unless the three objects lie on or near a circle that passes through the observer. It has fallen into disuse because of the convenience and reliability of other methods.

hour angle—The angular distance of a body westward from a designated hour circle or celestial meridian, measured through 360°. In practice, one of three hour angles is measured: (1) Greenwich hour angle (GHA): the angular distance of a celestial body west from the Greenwich celestial meridian, tabulated in almanacs for the sun, moon, planets, and Aries. (2) Local hour angle (LHA): angular distance of a celestial body west from the celestial meridian of the observer, derived by applying observer's longitude (add east, subtract west) to GHA. (3) Meridian angle: a special case of local hour angle, equivalent to LHA except that it is measured east or west of the celestial meridian of the observer from 0° to 180°. Meridian angle is a factor in working most sight-reduction tables where, to conserve space, the value of LHA is presented to 180° rather than a full 360°. (4) Sidereal hour angle (SHA): the angular distance of a star west from the hour circle of Aries (♈). The SHAs of major stars are listed in almanacs. The GHA of a star is obtained by adding the SHA of the star and the GHA of Aries.

hour circle—A great circle through the celestial poles and a point or a body on the celestial sphere. It is similar to a celestial meridian but moves with the celestial sphere as it rotates about the earth, while a celestial meridian remains fixed with respect to the earth. The location of a body along its hour circle is defined by the body's angular distance from the celestial equator. This distance, called declination, is measured north or south of the celestial equator in degrees, from 0° through 90°, similar to latitude on the earth. A point on the celestial sphere may be identified as the intersection of its parallel of declination and its hour

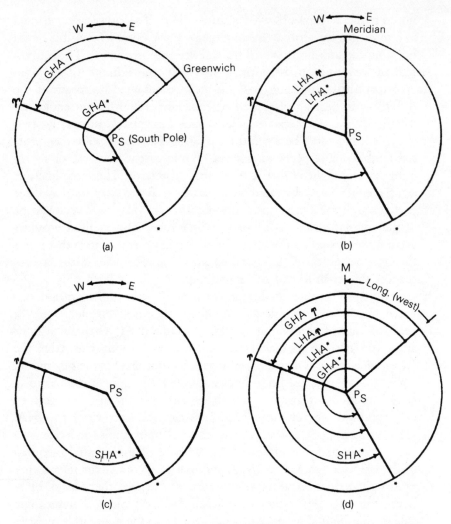

Hour angles (shown for a star): (a) Greenwich hour angles. (b) Local hour angles. (c) Sidereal hour angle (used only for a star). (d) Combined hour angles.

circle. Two basic methods of locating the hour circle are in use: (1) Its angular distance west of a reference hour circle through a point on the celestial sphere called the vernal equinox, or first point of Aries (♈), is called its sidereal hour angle (SHA). (2) Its angle eastward from the vernal equinox is called its right ascension and is usually expressed in time units, where 15° is equal to one hour.

I

impeller log—A speed-measuring system, which may be hull mounted or towed. The impeller (propeller) rotates as it moves through the water, its revolutions are proportional to the distance traveled, and its speed of rotation is proportional to the vessel's speed. These logs usually employ a magnetic pulse generator so that no physical contact, other than a bearing, is required between the rotor and the body of the instrument.

inertial navigation—The process of measuring and recording a craft's velocity and attitude changes (accelerations) since it left a known starting point. Inertial navigation is self-contained (independent of external aids to navigation) and passive, because no energy is emitted to obtain information from an external source. Inertial navigation is often referred to as a dead-reckoning method because position is obtained by measuring displacement from a starting point. As in other forms of dead reckoning, any error, small though it may be, will with time contribute to a position error. Accordingly, the position is periodically corrected using navigational information from external sources. The basic sensors used in inertial navigation are gyroscopes and accelerometers. The function of the accelerometers is to sense the accelerations of the craft with respect to the earth so that a computer can determine the craft's velocity, attitude, and position. The function of the gyroscopes is to maintain the accelerometers in correct orientation. Gimbals provide physical support for the gyroscopes and accelerometers and provide three axes of rotation with respect to the craft. The gimbals, gyroscopes, and accelerometers form a so-called stable platform, a reference system that stays vertical and points north.

inertial-navigation errors—Even if it were possible to make perfect sensors, inertial navigators would still have error, owing to uncertainties in knowledge of the physical environment. A particularly serious error in marine inertial-navigation systems is due to lack of knowledge of the gravitational environment, such as tilts of the actual (plumb bob) vertical relative to vertical on a reference ellipsoid, which is an approximation of the real earth.

Inherent errors of an inertial navigator are the 84.4-minute (Schuler) oscillation and the 24-hour oscillation. The 84.4-minute oscillation results from initial tilt or velocity errors. It can also be caused by any transient disturbance in the system. The 24-hour oscillation is a property of a properly functioning practical inertial navigator and is caused by initial errors in position, heading, or gyros. An initial error in either latitude or heading causes both quantities to oscillate about their true value in a twenty-four hour cycle. A gyro error causes latitude or heading to oscillate and may cause an ever-increasing (ramping) longitude error.

International Date Line—The International Date Line follows the 180th meridian with some offsets so that it does not bisect inhabited territory. The adjustment to the date is usually made at some convenient time shortly before or after the vessel crosses the date line. If a vessel has been steaming east, its clocks have been steadily advanced, and this is compensated for by reducing the date one day. Conversely, a vessel steaming west has been setting back its clocks, so that the date is advanced one day. This date change is made by every vessel crossing the date line, regardless of the length of the voyage. The change of date accounts for the two zone descriptions (ZD) associated with the 15° band of longitude centered on the 180th meridian. That part of the zone in west longitude has a ZD of (+12), and that part of the zone in east longitude has a ZD of (−12). The ZD is the same throughout the zone, but the date is one day later in the half that is in east longitude than it is in the half in west longitude.

Intertropical Convergence Zone (ITCZ)—An almost continuous trough or belt of low pressure at the earth's surface extends around the earth in the equatorial region. This is where northeast trade winds (of the Northern Hemisphere) and southeast trades (of the Southern Hemisphere) come together or converge. Seasonally, the ITCZ migrates from hemisphere to hemisphere. As the ITCZ migrates north and south in the course of a year, it passes the latitudes between its extreme positions twice, lagging behind the sun by about two months. As a result, many parts of the tropics have two rainy seasons and two dry seasons, the peaks of the rainy seasons occurring in December and April on the equator, in November and May at latitude 5°N, and in June and

October in latitudes 10°N. At latitudes 15°N and 15°S, the two rainy seasons merge into a single broad peak during the summer months. The total annual meandering of the ITCZ in the western Pacific sometimes amounts to as much as 44° latitude. The ITCZ reaches its northernmost latitude in August and its southernmost latitude in February. ITCZ is characterized by strong ascending air currents, cloudiness, frequent showers, and thunderstorms.

ionization—The earth's atmosphere is subjected to bombardment by intense ultraviolet rays from the sun. Electrons are excited by powerful ultraviolet electromagnetic forces, which reverse polarity approximately 10^{17} times per second. This oscillation causes electrons to separate from the positive ions with which they were combined. These freed electrons would eventually find their way to other, electron-deficient atoms, but this is prevented by continuing ultraviolet rays while they are in direct sunlight. The region of the upper atmosphere, generally above 30 miles (55km), where free ions and electrons exist in sufficient density to have an appreciable effect on radio-wave travel, is called the ionosphere; the ionization effect reaches it maximum when the sun is at its highest. Electrons and ions are not uniformly distributed in the ionosphere but rather tend to form layers. These change, disappear, combine, and separate. Four such ionized layers are involved in the phenomenon of radio-wave propagation. Each layer has the most intense ionization at the center. The greater the intensity of ionization in any layer, the greater is the bending back towards the earth of radio waves; lower frequencies are more easily reflected than higher frequencies, which have a tendency to penetrate the ionosphere and escape into space.

ionospheric layers—There are four ionospheric layers of importance in the study of radio-wave propagation: (1) The D layer is the closest to the earth's surface, about 60 to 90 kilometers high. It is less dense than the other layers and appears to be formed only during the daylight hours. (2) The E layer is located about 110 kilometers above the earth's surface. Its density is greatest beneath the sun and persists throughout the night with decreased intensity. (3) The F_1 layer occurs only in daylight regions of the upper atmosphere, usually between 175 and 200 kilometers above the earth's surface. (4) The F_2 layer is found at altitudes between 250 and 400 kilometers. Its strength is greatest by day, but because of very low density of the atmosphere at this height, the freed electrons in this layer persist several hours after sunset. There is a tendency for the F_1 and F_2 layers to merge thereafter to form the so-called F layer, which is ordinarily the only layer of importance to radio-wave propagation after dark. All layers of the ionosphere are somewhat variable, with main patterns seeming to be diurnal, seasonal, and by sunspot cycle. Layers may either be conducive to sky-wave transmission of a radio wave or may hinder or even entirely prevent such transmission, depending on frequency of wave, angle of incidence, and height and density of the various layers at the time of transmission. In general, frequencies in the MF and HF bands are most suitable for ionospheric reflection during both day and night, whereas frequencies in the LF and VHF bands produce usable sky waves only at night.

isallobars The change in atmospheric pressure in the three hours prior to an observation at a weather station is called the pressure tendency. Pressure tendency is reported along with other weather elements. Lines drawn connecting places having equal pressure tendencies are called isallobars.

isobath—Contour lines connecting points of equal water depths on a chart.

isobathytherm—Line or surface showing the depths in oceans or lakes which have the same temperature. Isobathytherms are usually drawn to show cross-sections of the water mass.

isogenic line—In the study of terrestrial magnetism, a line drawn through all points on the earth's surface having the same magnetic declination (variation). The particular isogenic line drawn through all points having zero declination is called the agonic line.

isomagnetic charts—Isomagnetic charts showing lines of equality of magnetic elements are published by the U.S. Navy Hydrographic Office in collaboration with the U.S. Coast and Geodetic Survey. There are three charts, consisting of one in the Mercator projection, covering most of the world, and one on a polar projection (azimuthal equidistant or stereographic) for each of the two polar areas. All charts included in the series are published at intervals of ten years, for each year ending in 5. Charts showing variation are also published for the years ending in 0.

K

katabatic wind—Varying conditions of topography produce a large variety of local winds throughout the world. Winds tend to follow valleys and to be deflected from high banks and shores. In mountain areas, wind flows in response to temperature distribution and gravity. An anabatic wind is one that blows up an incline, usually as a result of surface heating. A katabatic wind is one that blows down an incline. There are two types, foehn and fall wind. A dry wind with a downward component, warm for the season, is called a foehn. A cold wind blowing down an incline is called a fall wind.

Kelvin deflector—The relative magnetic directive force on various headings is determined by means of an instrument called a deflector. Measurement is made when the compass card has been rotated, or "deflected," 90° under certain standard conditions. The units are arbitrary "deflector units," which are used only for comparison with readings on other headings. The Kelvin deflector was developed by Sir William Thomson (Lord Kelvin). It consists of two permanent magnets hinged like a pair of dividers, with opposite poles at the hinge. The magnets are mounted vertically over the center of the compass with the hinged end on top. The separation of the lower ends can be varied by means of a screw. The amount of separation needed to change the compass 90° is indicated by a scale and vernier drums and is the reading used to determine the directive force.

Kepler's laws—The laws governing the motions of the planets in their orbits were discovered by Johannes Kepler and are known as Kepler's laws: (1) The orbits of the planets are ellipses, with the sun at one focus. (2) The straight line joining the sun and a planet (the radius vector) sweeps over equal areas in equal intervals of time. (3) The squares of the sidereal periods of any two planets are proportional to the cubes of their mean distances from the sun.

knoll—An elevation rising less than 1,000 meters from the sea floor and of limited extent across the summit.

knot (Kn)—A speed of one nautical mile per hour.

L

Lambert conformal conic projection—A projection in which meridians are represented by straight lines that meet in a common point beyond the limits of the map, and the parallels are concentric circles whose center is at the point of intersection of the meridians. Meridians and parallels intersect in right angles, and angles on the earth are correctly represented on the projection. This projection may have one standard parallel along which the scale is held exact; or there may be two such standard parallels, both maintaining exact scale.

Lambert conformal projection—The useful latitude range of a simple conic projection can be increased by using a secant cone intersecting the earth at two standard parallels. The area between the two standard parallels is compressed, and that beyond is expanded. Such a projection is called a secant conic or conic projection with two standard parallels. If, in such a projection, the spacing of the parallels is altered so that the distortion is the same along them as along the meridians, the projection becomes conformal. This is knowns as the Lambert conformal projection. It is the most widely used conic projection for navigation, though its use is more common among aviators than among mariners.

latitude—Angular distance from the equator measured northward or southward along a meridian from 0° at the equator to 90° at the poles. It is designated north (N) or south (S) to indicate the direction of measurement. The difference of latitude (l) between two places is the length of the arc of any meridian between their parallels. It is the numerical difference of the latitudes if the places are on the same side of the equator, and the sum if they are on opposite sides. It may be designated north (N) or south (S) when appropriate. The middle, or mid-, latitude (Lm) between two places on the same side of the equator is half the sum of their latitudes. Mid-latitude is labeled N or S to indicate whether it is north or south of the equator.

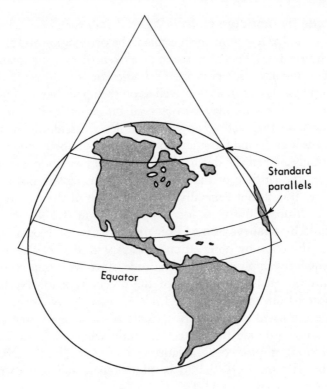

Lambert projection

Latitude

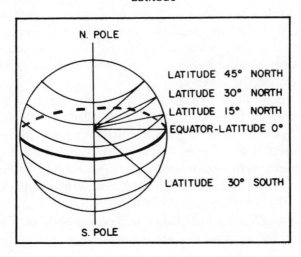

latitude by meridian sight—When the altitude of a celestial body is measured as it transits the meridian, the observation and the subsequent solution for a line of position is spoken of as a meridian sight. This sight includes observations of bodies on the lower branch of the meridian (lower transit) as well as on the upper branch (upper transit); circumpolar stars may be observed on either branch of the celestial meridian. In practice, however, bodies are seldom observed on the lower branch, and the sun is normally the only body observed. In polar latitudes, when the declination of the sun corresponds in name (N or S) to the latitude of the observer, the sun may be observed when in lower transit, but generally meridian sights of the sun are made when it is in upper transit at local apparent noon (LAN).

latitude by observation of Polaris—Polaris, the North Star, provides true direction by observation (always within 2° of true north) and is frequently employed to find latitude, since with minor corrections its altitude equals the latitude of the observer in the Northern Hemisphere. Both the *Nautical* and *Air Almanacs* provide simple tables for solution based on the LHA of Aries at the time of observation. Both almanacs provide the correct azimuth: when 000°, the LOP (line of position) is plotted as a latitude line through the DR longitude; otherwise the LOP should be plotted perpendicular to the azimuth passing through the DR.

leeway—The offsetting effect of wind; named for the direction in which it tends to move a boat off course; starboard leeway offsets to the right, port leeway to the left. Wind abeam creates maximum leeway; wind from forward or aft, none. In general, the deeper the keel the less leeway. Because leeway is hard to quantify, it is generally assumed to be an unknown contributor to the total offset plotted as current. However, when leeway can be estimated, as from a comparison of the wake angle with the heading, it may be applied as a compass correction to the course. Starboard leeway is an easterly correction; port leeway calls for a westerly conversion.

light—The term "light" covers a wide variety of aids to navigation, from short-range lights on a single pile in inland waters to multimillion candlepower seacoast lights on structures a hundred feet or more tall. These lights are assigned characteristic colors and (off-on) phases for identification. In some instances the shape and color of the supporting structure is of assistance in identification. When a light is required offshore, a lightship may be established.

light bobbing—When a light is first seen on the horizon, it will disappear if the observer tries to sight it from a point several feet, or one deck, lower and reappear when he returns to his original position. This is called bobbing a light, and can be helpful in estimating its distance. When a light can be bobbed, it is at the limit of its visibility for the observer's height of eye. By determining geographic range for the height of the light and for the observer's height of eye, and combining these two value, one may obtain an approximation of the distance. This distance, combined with a bearing, will give an approximate position.

lighthouse—Lighthouses, called "lights" in the light lists, are found along most of the world's coastlines and many interior waterways. Their principal purpose is to support a light at a considerable height above the water. The same structure may also house a fog signal and radio-beacon equipment and contain quarters for the keepers. However, in the majority of instances, the fog signal, the radio-beacon equipment, and the operating personnel are housed in separate buildings grouped around the tower. Such a group of buildings constitutes a light station.

lighthouse classes—The terms "primary seacoast" light, "secondary" light, and "river" or "harbor" lights (also called minor lights) indicate in a general way the wide variety of lighted aids to navigation that are "fixed," as distinguished from "floating" (as a buoy). The specific definition of each class is not of importance to a navigator. Lighthouses and major light structures are painted to make them readily distinguishable from the background, to distinguish one structure from others in the same vicinity, and for positive identification by a navigator making landfall. Solid colors, bands of colors, and various patterns are used for these purposes. Minor lights, such as river or harbor lights, that are part of a lateral system will normally have a numbered day mark of appropriate shape and color.

light lists—Lists for the United States and its possessions, including the Intracoastal Waterway, the Mississippi and its navigable tributaries, and the Great Lakes, including both the U.S. and Canadian shores, are published annually by the U.S. Coast Guard. Similar publications, called lists of lights, covering foreign coasts, are published by the Defense Mapping Agency Hydrographic Center (DMAHC) as publications nos. 111A, 111B, and 112 through 116. These light lists give detailed information regarding navigational lights, light structures, radio beacons, and fog signals. In addition, the light lists for the United States, published by the Coast Guard, give data on lighted and unlighted buoys and day beacons. Corrections to both sets of light lists are published weekly in Notices to Mariners.

light sectors—Sectors of colored glass are placed in the lanterns of certain lighted aids to navigation to mark shoals or to warn mariners off the nearby land. Lights so equipped show one color from most directions and a different color or colors over definite arcs indicated in the light lists and on charts. A sector changes the color of light when viewed from certain directions, but not the characteristics. Sectors may be a few degrees in width, marking an isolated rock or shoal, or of such width as to extend from the direction of the deep water toward shore. In the majority of cases, water areas covered by red sectors should be avoided, the exact extent of the danger being determined from an examination of the chart. In some cases, instead of indicating danger, a narrow sector may mark the best water across a shoal. On either side of the line of demarcation between white and a colored sector, there is always a small sector (about 2°) of uncertain color, as the edges of a sector cannot be cut off sharply. Bearings given on the lines of demarcation on the chart are true bearings of the light as seen from the ship. When a light is cut off by adjoining land or structures, the obscured sector is shown on the chart and described in the light list. The bearings on which the light is cut off are stated as for colored sectors, from ship toward the light. The exact bearings of cutoff may vary with the distance of the observer and his height of eye.

lightships—Serve the same purpose as lighthouses, being equipped with lights, fog signals, and radio beacons. Lightships mark the entrances to important harbors or estuaries and dangerous shoals lying in much-frequented waters and also serve as leading marks for transoceanic and coastwise traffic. Lightships in United States waters are painted red with the name of the station in white on both sides. Superstructures are white; masts, lantern galleries, ventilators, and stacks are buff. Relief (temporary replacement) lightships are the same color as the station ships, with the word RELIEF in white letters on the sides. The masthead lights, fog signals, and radio-beacon signals of lightships all have distinguishing characteristics, so that each lightship may be differentiated from others and also from nearby lighthouses. A lightship under way or off its station will fly the International code flag "LO." It will not show or sound any of the signals of a lightship but will display the lights prescribed by the international or inland rules for a vessel of her class. While on station, a lightship shows only the masthead light and a less brilliant light on the forestay. As lightships ride to a single anchor, the light on the forestay indicates the direction from which the combined wind and current are coming and the direction in which the ship is heading. By day, whenever it appears that an approaching vessel does not recognize the lightship or requests identification, the lightship will display the call letters of the station in flags of the International code.

light visibility—Light visibility is categorized by three ranges: geographic, nominal, and luminous. The geographic visibility range of a light is the number of nautical miles a light may be seen by an observer at a height fifteen feet above sea level, under conditions of perfect visibility, and without regard to candlepower. The nominal range is the maximum distance at which a light may be seen in clear weather, which is meteorologically defined as a visibility of ten nautical miles. The luminous range is the maximum distance a light may be seen under existing conditions of visibility.

line of position (LOP)—A line on some point of which the ship is presumed to be located, the exact point being unknown. An LOP is obtained by observation of a range, a circle of position, or a bearing. (1) Range. Where two fixed objects are in line with the ship, the ship is on the line through the objects. (2) Circle of position. When the distance to a fixed object is found by range finder, stadimeter, radar, sextant angle, or synchronized signals, the ship lies somewhere on the circumference of a circle, with the object at the center and the known distance as the radius. (3) Bearing. A bearing is the compass direction of one point on the earth's surface to another. The observer sights across a pelorus, hand-bearing compass, bearing circle, or gyro repeater toward a fixed, known object and determines the direction of the line of sight to that object; this is its bearing.

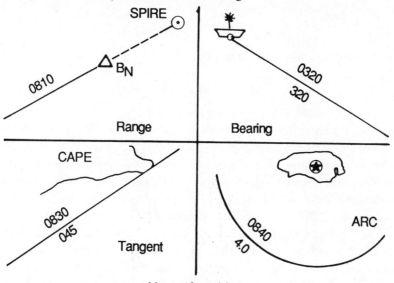

Lines of position

line of position labeling—A single line of position, whether a bearing, range, or distance, is labeled on the upper side of the line with the time of observation in four digits. A single line of position advanced to form a running fix is labeled with original time of observation and time to which it has been advanced. Direction is not normally labeled on an LOP but, if desired, can be added as a three-digit number directly beneath the time label (true direction is assumed; "M" is suffixed if magnetic). Simultaneous lines of position forming a fix need not be labeled, time of the fix being sufficient. Similarly, the second line of position in a running fix is not labeled; its time is that of the running fix.

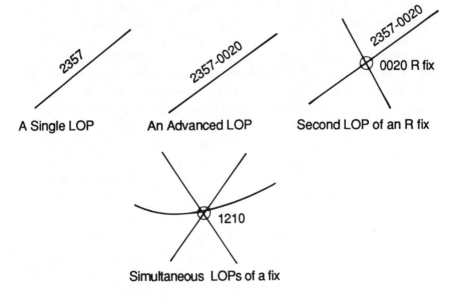

Labels for lines of position and fixes

local hour angle (LHA)—The angle between the celestial meridian of the observer and the hour circle of a body, measured westward along the arc of the equinoctial (equator) and expressed in degrees from 0 to 360. Also equal to the angle at the celestial pole between the local celestial meridian and the hour circle, measured westward. In west longitudes, LHA is found by subtracting the longitude of the observer from the GHA (Greenwich hour angle). In east longitudes, LHA is found by adding the longitude of the observer to the GHA.

local mean time (LMT)—Like zone time, LMT uses the mean sun as its celestial reference point. It differs from zone time in that the local meridian is used as the terrestrial reference rather than a zone meridian. Thus, the local mean time at each meridian differs from that of every other meridian, the difference being equal to the difference of longitude, expressed in time units (15° of longitude = one hour). At each zone meridian (center of a time zone), LMT and ZT (zone time) are identical. In navigation the principal use of LMT is to determine time of sunrise, sunset, and twilight.

log—Three types of logs are in general use on ships, some of which determine distance traveled as well as speed: the Pitot-static, the impeller, and the electromagnetic (EM) log. All use a rod meter projecting through the bottom of the ship. The rod contains the sensing device used to determine speed. The signal received from the sensing device is transmitted to display units throughout the ship.

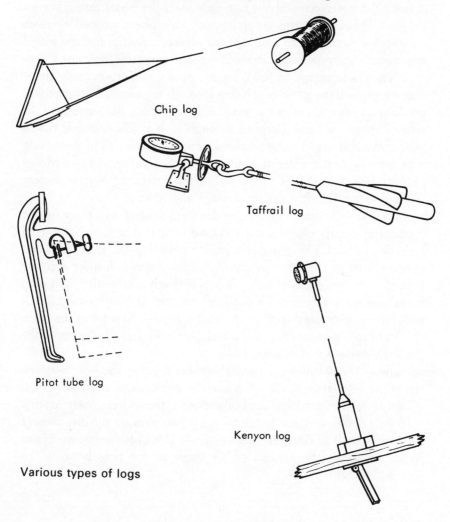

Chip log

Taffrail log

Pitot tube log

Kenyon log

Various types of logs

The rod meter of a Pitot-static log detects both dynamic and static pressure. As a ship moves through the water, the forward side of the rod meter is exposed to dynamic pressure, which is proportional to the speed of the ship. Dynamic pressure is the pressure on a surface resulting from a fluid in motion; it includes static pressure as well. A pitot tube is a devise by which the difference between dynamic and static pressures may be measured; the difference of the two pressures will vary with the speed of the ship. The device consists of two tubes, one inside the other. One tube opens forward and is subject to dynamic pressure; the other opens athwartships and is exposed to static pressure. Two are in general use: the pitometer log and Bendix underwater log.

The impeller log uses a propeller to produce an electrical impulse by which the speed and distance traveled are indicated. Typically, a rod meter head is projected about two feet from the vessel through a sea valve. The head contains an eight-pole, two-phase, propeller-driven frequency generator. The output of the generator is amplified and passed to a master transmitter-indicator and repeated at remote indicators.

The electromagnetic (EM) log is a device that produces a voltage that varies with the speed of the ship through the water. Saltwater will produce an electric current when it moves across a magnetic field, or when a magnetic field is moved through it. It is this principle that is used in the EM log. A magnetic field, produced by a coil in the sensing unit, is set up in the water in which the ship is floating, and two Monel buttons, one on each side of the rod meter, detect the electric current induced when the ship moves through the water.

log, chip—An old, simple measuring device consisting of a piece of line containing equally spaced knots and a wood float. The log was lowered over the stern of a ship under way. By counting the knots paid out over a period of time the navigator computed speed. A more accurate type of chip log consits of a chunk of wood and a stopwatch. The chip is thrown into the water forward of the stem and to leeward. As it passes the stem of the ship the stopwatch is started. As it passes the stern, the stopwatch is stopped. From the elapsed time and the length of the ship, the navigator computes speed.

longitude—The arc along a parallel or the angle at the pole between the prime (Greenwich) meridian and the meridian of any other point on the earth, measured eastward or westward from Greenwich through 180°. It is designated east (E) or west (W) to indicate the direction of measurement. The difference of longitude (DLo) between two places is the arc along the parallel or the angle at the pole between the meridians of the places.

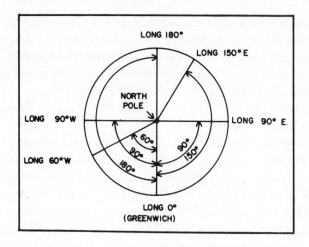

Longitude

N–S: Polar axis　　　　　　　　x: Point on meridian of long. 40°W
W–E: Plane of the equator　　　　y: Point on meridian of long. 10°E

longitude by prime vertical observation—A body is on the prime vertical (PV) when its position is directly east (90°) or west (270°) of the observer. At this instant a line of position from an observation of the body is a line of longitude. The opportunity for this observation occurs only when the observer's latitude and the declination of the body have the same name (N or S) and the latitude is greater than the declination. The observation can be made on any body but is usually employed only with the sun, which offers two daily opportunities. An observation made when the body is within 5° of the PV is sufficient for practical navigational purposes.

lorac—A hyperbolic navigation system using phase comparison of frequencies to measure distances from transmitters. Each chain consists of a central station and two side stations. Some installations also have an additional station, called the reference station. The continuous wave signals from the central station and one of the side stations are received at the second side station and also at the vessel. At each, the two signals are combined to obtain a signal in the audio frequency range. This audible signal (the beat frequency signal) is used to vary (modulate) the carrier wave of the transmitter at that station. This modulated signal is compared with another signal produced at the vessel, which is obtained from signals received at the ship from the central station and the first side station. The phase difference of these two signals varies with the position of the vessel and depends on the distances from the central station and the first side station. The readings appear automatically and continuously on dials. Charts showing the lines of position are needed. The name "lorac" is derived from "long-range accuracy." It is intended for use for distances up to 100 to 150 miles by day and 75 to 100 miles by night; accordingly, the baselines are about 35 miles long.

loran—A hyperbolic system of navigation by which distance from two fixed points onshore is determined by measurement of the time interval between reception of pulse-modulated, synchronized signals from transmitters at the two points. The name "Loran" is derived from "long-range navigation." Since it operates in the 1,750 to 1,950 kc frequency range, both ground waves and sky waves can be used to provide coverage over an extensive area with relatively few stations. Since ships do not need to transmit to use it (see Lorac), they can use loran without breacking radio silence. Usually, stations of a pair are located from 200 to 400 miles apart, although they may be as close as 100 miles or as far as 700 miles. The range at which signals are received varies considerably with the kind of signals (ground wave or sky wave), route of the signal (over land or water), time of day, atmospheric noise level, geographic region, ionospheric conditions, and directional properties of the receiving antenna. Pulse signals from each pair of stations are transmitted continually. Identification is by means of frequency and pulse repetitions rate (PRR). Frequency is identified by channel number, as follows:

Channel No.	Frequency
1	1950
2	1850
3	1900

The same frequency can be used for signals from a number of different station pairs by varying the rate at which the signals are transmitted. Three basic pulse repetition rates are used, as follows:

Special (S)	20 pulses per second
Low (L)	25 pulses per second
High (H)	33 1/3 pulses per second

The interval between the start of consecutive pulses is 50,000 μs (microseconds) for the special rate, 40,000 μs for the low rate, and 30,000 μs for the high rate. The special rate is for future use.

loran-A—System operates on medium frequency (MF) channels between 1850 and 1950 kHz. Both ground-wave and sky-wave reception are used, giving different ranges day and night, and different accuracies of fixes. Daytime use of ground waves extends out to about 500 miles (925 km) with fixes accurate to 1.5 miles (2.8 km) over 80 percent of the coverage area (accuracy is greatest along the baseline between the two transmitting stations). The use of sky waves extends the daytime range out to as much as 1,200 miles (2,222 km) and as much as 1,400 miles (2,600 km) at night; the accuracy of sky-wave fixes is roughly 5 to 7 miles (9 to 13 km). Loran-A stations are located at separations of 250 to 600 miles (460 to 1,100 km). At one time, there were 83 loran-A stations in operation giving coverage of both the North Atlantic and North Pacific oceans, the Gulf of Mexico, and the North Atlantic and North Sea, with some extensions into adjacent waters and land areas.

loran-A charts—Nautical charts overprinted with loran information that may be used for converting loran-A readings into LOPs and fixes. Loran-A charts have been made for those areas where loran-A signals are available. Loran-A charts show hyperbolic lines of position usually for each 20-microsecond time difference on large-scale charts and for each 100-microsecond time difference on small-scale charts. The lines emanating from different station pairs are identified by color as well as by rate and time difference. Charted hyperbolic lines are for ground-wave time differences; if sky waves are matched, then the time difference obtained must be corrected to comparable ground-wave time differences. Corrections are found at the intersections of meridians and parallels and are printed the same color as the rate to which they apply.

loran-C—A pulsed, hyperbolic, long-range electronic navigation system, operating on a single frequency centered on 100 kHz. Loran-C is similar to loran-A in that it is a pulsed, hyperbolic system of radio navigation available to ships and aircraft by day or night, in all weather conditions, over land and sea. In loran-A a single pulse is transmitted in each repetition interval. In loran-C a multiphase transmission is used. Each station radiates a group of eight pulses spaced 1,000 microseconds apart. Additionally, the master station transmits a ninth pulse, principally for identification. Multiple pulses are used so that more energy arrives at the receiver. Loran-C can supply position information to a higher degree of accuracy and at greater distances than loran-A. In both loran-A and loran-C, a time-difference reading is accomplished by comparing the arrival time of pulses from two transmitters. In addition, loran-C employs a cycle-matching technique for greater precision. A rough measurement is made of the difference in arrival time of the pulsed signals; this is refined by a comparison of the phase of the signal within the pulse. The phase comparison is accomplished automatically within the receiver and does not involve a separate operation by the navigator. Because of the use of a lower frequency, 100 kHz, rather than 1,850 or 1,950 kHz, and an increased baseline, 1,000 miles (1,850 km) or more, loran–C is able to provide position information out to 1,200 miles (2,225 km) by means of ground waves, and out to more than 3,000 miles (5,550 km) with sky waves.

loran-C chains—Composed of a master transmitting station, two or more secondary (slave) transmitting stations, and, if necessary, system area monitor stations. The transmitting stations are located so that the signals from the master and at least two secondary stations can be

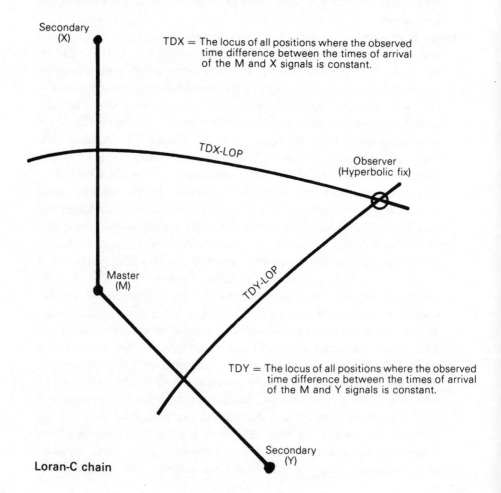

Secondary (X)

TDX = The locus of all positions where the observed time difference between the times of arrival of the M and X signals is constant.

TDX-LOP

Observer (Hyperbolic fix)

Master (M)

TDY-LOP

TDY = The locus of all positions where the observed time difference between the times of arrival of the M and Y signals is constant.

Secondary (Y)

Loran-C chain

received throughout the desired coverage or service area. For convenience, the master station is designated by the letter "M," and the secondary stations are designated "W," "X," "Y," or "Z." Thus, a particular master-secondary pair and the time difference (TD) it produces can be referred to by the letter designations of both stations or by just that of the secondary.

loran-C fix—Lines of position obtained by loran-C are plotted to form a fix in exactly the same manner as LOPs are determined by the use of loran-A. The DMAHC (Defense Mapping Agency Hydrographic Center) publishes nautical charts overprinted with loran-C hyperbolic patterns, which are similar in appearance to loran-A charts. A series of loran-C tables is also published by DMAHC as part of the publication no. 221 series of Loran tables, with a separate table for each Loran-C master/slave pair. They are designed for plotting short segments of the applicable loran-C hyperbolic grid on an unmarked navigational chart or plotting sheet.

loran-C plotting—In determining a vessel's position from loran-C, a loran-C chart of the area is examined for the time delays labeled on the various lines of position. Read one loran-C time difference from the receiver and find the pair of lines that lie on either side of this value; interpolate by eye for the exact LOP. The same procedure is followed for the second time difference as indicated by the receiver; the position is at the intersection of these lines.

loran-C signal format—The stations of a Loran-C chain transmit groups of pulses at a specified group repetition interval (GRI). A GRI is selected so that it contains time for transmission of the pulse group from each station (10,000 microseconds for the master and 8,000 microseconds for each secondary) plus time between each pulse group so that signals from two or more stations cannot overlap anywhere in the coverage area. Each station transmits one pulse group per GRI. The master pulse group consists of eight pulses spaced 1,000 microseconds apart, and a ninth pulse 2,000 microseconds after the eighth. Secondary pulse groups contain eight pulses spaced 1,000 microseconds apart. The master's ninth pulse is used for identification of the master, and to warn users that there is an error in the transmission of a particular station, by turning the ninth pulse on and off (blinking) in a specified code as shown on the next page. The secondary station of the unusable pair also blinks by turning its first two pulses on and off. Most modern receivers automatically detect blink and trigger warning indicators.

loran-D—Operates in the low-frequency band, in the range of 90 to 110 kHz. Its signal characteristics are very similar to those of loran-C.

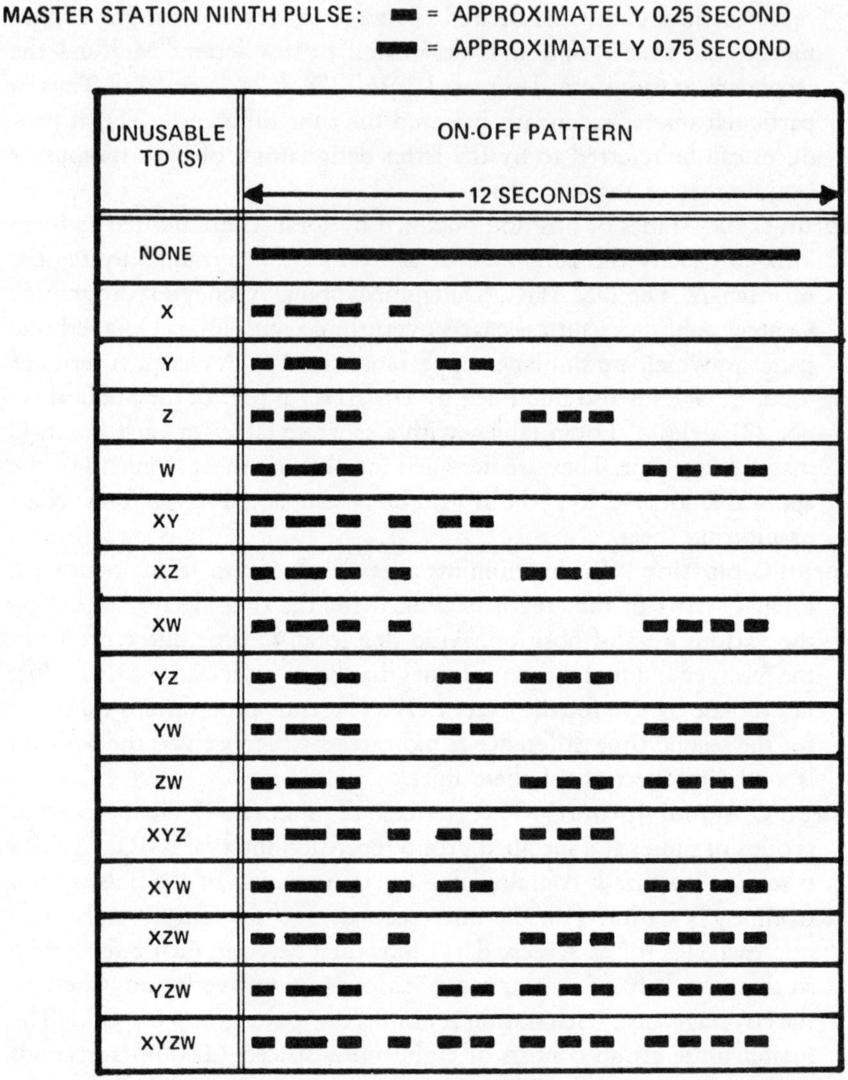

MASTER STATION NINTH PULSE: ■■ = APPROXIMATELY 0.25 SECOND
                               ■■■ = APPROXIMATELY 0.75 SECOND

UNUSABLE TD (S)	ON-OFF PATTERN (12 SECONDS)
NONE	
X	
Y	
Z	
W	
XY	
XZ	
XW	
YZ	
YW	
ZW	
XYZ	
XYW	
XZW	
YZW	
XYZW	

SECONDARY STATION FIRST TWO PULSES:

TURNED ON (BLINKED) FOR APPROXIMATELY 0.25 SECONDS EVERY 4.0 SECONDS. ALL SECONDARIES USE SAME CODE, AUTOMATICALLY RECOGNIZED BY MOST MODERN LORAN—C RECEIVERS.

Loran-C blink code

Three or four transmitting stations operate together on a time-shared basis to provide ground-wave signals of high accuracy over a range of about 500 miles. Under good conditions it will establish position to one-tenth of a mile at a range of 250 miles from the transmitters. Its signals are equally dependable over land or water. Primarily, loran-D differs from loran-C in its signal, which uses repeated groups of sixteen pulses, spaced 500 microseconds apart. The system is resistant to electronic jamming, and stations can be set up within twenty-four hours.

M

magnetic azimuth (of a celestial body)—The body most frequently used for this purpose is the sun. A time of day should be selected when the sun's altitude is below about 30°, because it is difficult to measure its azimuth (true bearing) accurately at high altitudes. Azimuths can be looked up in Defense Mapping Agency Hydrographic Center (DMAHC) publication no. 229 or special tables of azimuths of the sun, such as publication no. 260. Having determined the azimuth, one applies the variation for the locality to obtain magnetic azimuth. To put the ship on a desired magnetic heading, find the magnetic azimuth for the appropriate time; then find the angle between the desired magnetic heading and the magnetic azimuth. Rotate the azimuth circle on the compass so that the line of sight through the vanes forms the same angle with the lubber's line. Adjust course right or left until the sun appears in the vanes.

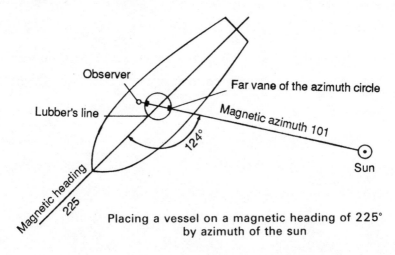

Placing a vessel on a magnetic heading of 225°
by azimuth of the sun

144

magnetic charts—The Defense Mapping Agency Hydrographic Center (DMAHC) publishes a series of magnetic charts of the earth as a whole (Mercator projection) and for the north and south polar areas (azimuthal equidistant projection). Separate charts are prepared for variation and vertical inclination (dip) and for intensity of field, horizontal, vertical, and total; they are revised when required by changes in the earth's magnetic field. Of greatest interest to the navigator is DMAHC chart 42, "Magnetic Variation Chart of the World."

magnetic compass error—Directions relative to the northerly direction along a geographic meridian are true. If a compass card is oriented so that a line from its center to 000° points to true north, any direction measured by the card is a true direction and has no error. If the card is rotated so that it points in any other direction, the amount of rotation is the compass error. The error is named east or west to indicate the side of true north on which compass north now lies. If a magnetic compass is influenced by no magnetic field other than that of the earth, and there is no instrumental error, its magnets are aligned with the magnetic meridian at the compass, and 000° of the compass card coincides with magnetic north. All directions indicated by the card are magnetic. The angle between geographic and magnetic meridians is called variation; if a compass is aligned with the magnetic meridian, compass error and variation are the same.

magnetic deviation—The angle between the magnetic meridian and the axis of a compass card, expressed in degrees east or west to indicate the direction in which the northern end of the compass card is offset from magnetic north. Deviation is caused by disturbing magnetic influences in the immediate vicinity of the compass.

magnetic dip (I)—The angle between the horizontal at any point and a magnetic line of force through that point. The magnetic latitude of a place is equal to the magnetic dip of the place.

magnetic direction—The direction that a magnetic compass or chart indicates.

magnetic diurnal variation—Oscillations of the earth's magnetic field which have a period of about one day and depend on local time and geographic latitude.

magnetic equator—The imaginary line on the earth's surface where magnetic inclination (dip) is zero degrees; that is, the magnetic field is horizontal.

magnetic latitude—At any point on the earth's surface the angle of the magnetic dip at that point.

magnetic meridians—At the surface of the earth, lines of force become magnetic meridians. These are irregular lines caused by the nonuniform distribution of the magnetic material in the earth.

magnetic secular change—The earth's magnetic field is not constant in either intensity or direction; its changes are daily, yearly, or secular (occuring over long periods of time). The secular change in direction is a real factor in navigation. Although it has been under observation for more than 300 years, the length of its period has not been established. The change generally consists of a reasonably steady increase or decrease in the variation, which is the difference between the magnetic meridian and the true meridian at a given place. This change may continue for many years in the same direction, sometimes reaching a large value; then it remains nearly stationary for a few years, and then reverses.

magnetic variation—Magnetic meridians indicate the direction of the earth's magnetic field, but only in a very few places do magnetic and true meridians coincide. The difference at any location between the directions of the magnetic and true meridians is the variation, sometimes called magnetic declination. It is called easterly (E) if the compass needle, aligned with the magnetic meridian, points eastward or to the right of true north, and westerly (W) if it points to the left. The magnetic variation and its annual change are shown on charts, so that directions indicated by the magnetic compass can be corrected to true directions. Since variation is caused by the earth's magnetic field, its value changes with the geographic location of the ship but is the same for all headings of the ship.

magnetism—As a result of the earth's magnetic materials, it may be treated as a large magnet. The magnetic poles are located approximately 74N, 101W; and 68S, 144E. To avoid confusion when speaking of the action of poles, colors have been assigned. The earth's north magnetic pole is designated "blue," and the south magnetic pole is designated "red." The magnetic lines of force that connect the magnetic poles are called magnetic meridians. Because of the irregular distribution of magnetic material in the earth, the meridians are irregular, and the planes of the magnetic meridians do not necessarily pass through the center of the earth. Midway between the magnetic poles a circle called the magnetic equator crosses the magnetic meridians. The earth's magnetism undergoes diurnal, annual, and secular changes. Diurnal changes are daily changes that are caused by the movement of the magnetic poles in an orbit having a diameter of about fifty miles. Annual changes represent the yearly permanent change in the earth's magnetic field. The direction and intensity of the earth's magnetic field may be resolved into horizontal and vertical components. At the magnetic equator the horizontal component is of maximum strength, and at the magnetic poles the vertical component is of maximum strength. A magnetic compass reacts to the horizontal components of the earth's magnetic field, and therefore its sensitivity reaches a maximum at the magnetic equator and decreases with increases in magnetic latitude.

mariner's compass—In a mariner's compass several strong magnets are attached to the compass card so that card and magnet rotate as a unit on a central jewel bearing. If local disturbances are disregarded, the magnets will line up with the earth's magnetic field, with one end pointing to the north magnetic pole. The compass-card graduations will then show angular direction around the entire horizon, measured clockwise from magnetic north. The housing of a marine compass, which will be rigidly attached to the boat, has a vertical mark called the lubber's line. When the compass is installed, it must be set so that a line through the central pivot and the lubber's line will be parallel to the keel of the boat. The zero of the compass card will always point to magnetic north, while the lubber's line will rotate with the boat as it changes direction. The intersection of the lubber's line with the graduations on the compass card will give the direction in which the boat is heading.

marine VHF-FM—At the power permitted a station in this band, the practical range of a marine VHF station is limited to the line of sight distance between the antennas of transmitter and receiver. The reflected sky wave is too weak to be useful or to interfere with a distant station using the same frequency. Effective range may be ten to thirty miles between a boat and a land station and, owing to lower antenna height, only five to fifteen miles between boats. Channels of particular interest to operators of small boats are listed on the next page.

mechanical protractors—A ruler connected by gears to a compass rose which automatically causes the compass rose to indicate whatever course or bearing the ruler is placed on.

Mercator projection—A conformal projection in which the meridians and parallels are portrayed as parallel lines at right angles to one another. The scale is chosen to be true along the equator. This projection can be equivalently described as the development of a rhumb line on the earth, since it is a straight line on the projection. The distinguishing feature of the Mercator projection among cylindrical projections is that both the meridians, and parallels expand at the same ratio with increased latitude. The expansion is equal to the secant of the

Designated noncommercial VHF-FM channels available for small-boat radio communication

Channel	Frequency Coast	MHz Ship	Points of Communication	Conditions of Use
16	156.800	156.800	Coast to ship	Distress, safety, and calling
65	156.275	156.275	" " "	Port operation
66	156.325	156.325	" " "	" "
12	156.600	156.600	" " "	" " , Coast Guard
73	156.675	156.675	" " "	" "
14	156.700	156.700	" " "	" "
74	156.725	156.725	" " "	" "
20	161.600	157.000	" " "	" "
15	156.750	None	" " "	Weather, state of sea, time signal, notices to mariners, hazards
17	156.850	156.850	" " "	State control
68	156.425	156.425	Coast to ship Intership	For small noncommercial boats having limited number of channels
09	156.450	156.450	Coast to ship	Commercial and noncommercial
69	156.475	156.475	" " "	For marinas, yacht clubs, service to noncommercial vessels
71	156.575	156.575	" " "	Same as channel 69
78	156.925	156.925	" " "	Same as channels 69 and 71
70	None	156.525	Intership	For recreational boats during maneuvers, cruises, rendezvous
72	None	156.625	"	Same as for channel 70
26	161.900	157.300	Coast to ship	Public correspondence
27	161.950	157.350	" " "	" "
28	162.000	157.400	" " "	" "

latitude, with a small correction for the ellipticity of the earth. Since the secant of 90° is infinity, the projection cannot include the poles. Expansion is the same in all directions and angles are correctly shown (the projection is said to be conformal). Rhumb lines appear as straight lines, the direction of which can be measured directly on the chart. Distances can also be measured directly, to practical accuracy but not by a single span over the entire chart, unless the spread of latitudes is small. Great circles, except meridians and the equator, appear as curved lines concave to the equator. Small areas appear in their correct shape but of increased size unless they are near the equator. Plotting of positions by latitude and longitude is done by means of rectangular coordinates, as on any cylindrical projection.

The Mercator is commonly pictured as being developed from a cylinder tangent to the earth's equator. For the transverse Mercator the cylinder has been turned through 90° and is tangent along a selected meridian. For the polar regions it has the same desirable properties that the original Mercator possesses near the equator. As with the original Mercator projection, there has to be expansion of the parallels as one moves away from the line of tangency in order to maintain the relative shapes of areas. Now, however, the areas of distortion are those distant from the pole. The transverse Mercator has been used for some charts of the polar regions where its properties and methods of use are practically identical with those of the Lambert. Its chief disadvantage is the curvature of the meridians, making them less suitable for measurements with a protractor. Within the limits of a single chart, however, this is usually negligible. The cylinder of the mercator can be turned through angles other than 90°; in this case it is often known as the oblique Mercator, and sometimes as the transverse Mercator.

meridian—A great circle through the geographical poles of the earth; therefore, all meridians meet at the poles, and their planes intersect each other in a line, the polar axis. The term "meridian" is usually applied to the upper branch only, that half from pole to pole on the observer's side of the earth. The other half is called the lower branch.

meridian angle (t)—The angle between the celestial meridian of the observer and the hour circle of a body measured eastward or westward along the arc of the equinoctial; expressed in degrees from 0 to 180. Meridian angle always carries a suffix "E" or "W" to indicate the direction of measurement. When LHA (local hour angle) is less than 180°, t equals LHA and is labeled west. When LHA is greater than 180°, t equals 360-LHA and is labeled east.

meteorological optical range (International Visibility Code)—

Code	Weather	Visual Range	
0	Dense fog	Less than 50	yards
1	Thick fog	50 to 100	"
2	Moderate fog	200 to 500	"
3	Light fog	500 to 1,000	"
4	Thin fog	.5 to 1	mile
5	Haze	1 to 2	miles
6	Light haze	2 to 5.5	"
7	Clear	5.5 to 11	"
8	Very clear	11.0 to 27.0	"
9	Exceptionally clear	Over 27.0	"

mid-latitudes—For some navigational calculations, the mid-latitude (Lm) is needed. This is the latitude at which the arc of the parallel between the meridians of the start and finish of a voyage would be equal to the departure (difference in longitude expressed in nautical miles). As this is difficult to calculate, the average or mean latitude is normally used. When both points are on the same side of the equator, this is the arithmetical mean of the two latitudes.

moon—The earth's only natural satellite, it is at an average distance of 385,000 km (239,000 miles) from the earth. Its orbit is elliptical; a moderate degree of eccentricity results in a distance of approximately 356,000 km (221,000 miles) at perigee, and 407,000 km (253,000 miles) at apogee. As with the sun, this change in distance causes a variation in apparent diameter of the moon between 29.4 and 33.4 minutes of arc. The diameter of the moon is roughly 3,480 km (2,160 miles). Its period of revolution about the earth and its axial rotation are the same, 27 1/3 days; thus it always presents essentially the same face to the earth.

moon phases—The moon passes through its cycle of phases during a 29.5-day (synodic) period. The synodic period of a celestial body is its average period of revolution, with respect to the sun, as seen from the earth. It differs from the 360° sidereal period because of the motion of the earth and the body in their orbits. When the moon is between the sun and the earth, its sunlit half faces away from the earth, and the body cannot be seen; this is the new moon. As it revolves in its orbit, (counterclockwise), an observer on the earth first sees a part of the sunlit half as a thin crescent, which will then wax, or grow, slowly through the first quarter, when it appears as a semicircle. After passing through the first quarter, it enters the gibbous phase, until it becomes full, and the entire sunlit half can be seen. From full it is said to wane, becoming gibbous to the last quarter, and then crescent until the cycle is completed.

most probable position (MPP)—Since information sufficient to establish an exact position is seldom available, the navigator is frequently faced with the problem of establishing the most probable position of the vessel. If three reliable bearing lines cross at a point, there is usually little doubt as to the position, and little or not judgment is needed. But when conflicting information or information of questionable reliability is received, a decision is required to establish the MPP.

N

nautical direction—On the next page is a diagram of directions referred to a vessel.

nautical mile—Distance unit used in marine navigation equal to one minute of arc of a great circle on a sphere; roughly 6,080 feet.

nautical slide rule—Circular plastic slide rule used for the rapid solution of problems involving time, distance, and speed. (See page 153.) Given any two of these factors, the third may be obtained. The time scale shows hours in red, and minutes and seconds in black; seconds are shown separately to 120. The yards scale is based on the assumption that 1 nautical mile equals 2,000 yards; this is an assumption frequently used in marine navigation, the slight error (1.25 percent) is ignored for the convenience gained. Therefore, if the distance scale is set at 3 miles, it will also read 6,000 yards.

NAVAREA warnings—Contain information that may affect the safety of navigation on the high seas and are broadcast in accordance with international obligations. The Defense Mapping Agency Hydrographical Center is responsible for disseminating navigational information for ocean areas (Atlantic and Pacific) designated as NAVAREA IV and XII of Worldwide Navigational Warning Systems. Warnings for NAVAREA IV and XII may be superseded by a numbered paragraph in the Notice to Mariners. Printed copies are published each working day in the appropriate edition of the Daily Memorandum. The text of effective warnings for NAVAREA IV and XII is printed in the weekly Notice to Mariners.(*See also* Daily Memorandum.)

navigational accuracy—Normally expressed in terms of the error between the point desired and the point achieved during navigation. The error is expressed as a distance unlikely to be exceeded in some percentage of cases. Therefore, this distance does not indicate the separation

151

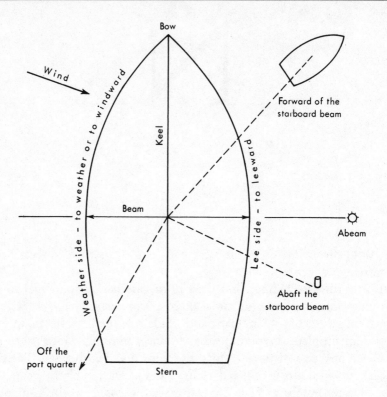

Visual bearings are given in points referring to bow, beam, or quarter. Portside bearings follow the same scheme.

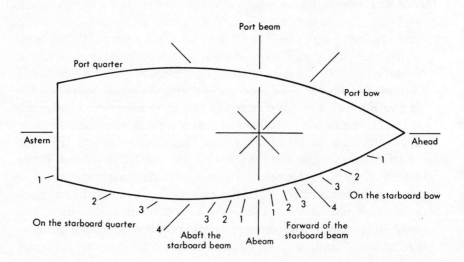

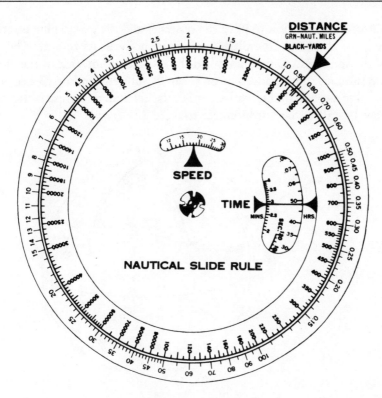

Nautical slide rule

between the fixed position and the observer's actual position, except by chance. In a navigational system, predictability is the measure of the accuracy with which the system can define the position in terms of geographic coordinates; repeatability is the measure of the accuracy with which the system permits the user to return to a position as defined in terms of the coordinates peculiar to that system.

navigational triangle—A triangle formed by arcs of great circles on a sphere is called a spherical triangle. A spherical triangle on the celestial sphere is called a celestial triangle. The spherical triangle of particular significance to navigators is called the navigational triangle. It is formed by arcs of a celestial meridian, an hour circle, and a vertical circle. Its vertices are the elevated pole, the zenith, and a point on the celestial sphere. The terrestrial counterpart is also called a navigational triangle, being formed by arcs of two meridians and the great circle connecting two places on the earth, one on each meridian. The vertices are the two places and one pole. In great-circle sailing these places are the points of departure and destination. In celestial navigation they are the assumed position (AP) of the observer and the geographic position (GP) of the body (the place having the body in its zenith). The GP of the sun is also sometimes called the subsolar point, that of the moon the sublunar point, and that of a star its substellar point. When used to solve a celestial observation, either the celestial or terrestrial triangle may be called the astronomical triangle (*see entry*).

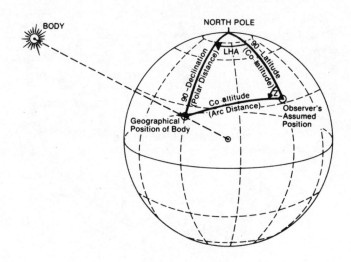

Navigational triangle

The coaltitude is the side of the navigational triangle joining the assumed position (AP) of the observer and the geographic position (GP) of the body. Since the maximum possible altitude of any celestial body is 90°, the coaltitude is always 90° minus the altitude of the body.

The polar distance is the side of the navigational triangle joining the elevated pole and geographic position (GP) of the body. For a body in the same hemisphere, the length of polar distance is 90° minus the declination (latitude) of geographic position (GP); for a body in the opposite hemisphere, its length is 90° plus the declination of the GP.

NAVSTAR global positioning system (GPS)—A navigational system of satellites orbiting 20,183 km (10,898 miles) above the earth. It provides extremely accurate position (three-dimensional), velocity, and time information.

node—That part of a standing wave where vertical motion is least and horizontal greatest. Nodes are associated with resonant wave reflections in a harbor or bay.

node cycle—Time required for regression of the moon's nodes (the two points where the plane of the moon's orbit intersects the ecliptic) to complete a circuit; a period of approximately 18.6 years. It is accompanied by a corresponding cycle of changing inclination of the moon's orbit relative to the plane of the earth's equator with resulting inequalities in the rise and fall of the tide and speed of the tidal current.

Notice to Mariners—Published weekly by the Defense Mapping Agency Hydrographic Center (DMAHC) and prepared jointly with the National Ocean Survey and the U.S. Coast Guard. Published to advise mariners of important matters affecting navigational safety, including new hydrographic discoveries, changes in channels and aids to navigation, etc. The information is published later in charts, sailing directions, light lists, and other publications produced by DMAHC, the National Ocean Survey, and the U.S. Coast Guard.

null—*See* radio direction finding.

ocean-current systems—A number of well-defined, permanent current systems exist in the open oceans. The chief cause of these currents is winds, such as the various trade winds, that blow almost continuously in the same direction, over large areas of the globe. The direction, steadiness, and force of a prevailing wind determine to a large extent the set, drift, depth, and permanence of the current it generates. However, currents with a generally northerly or southerly set are affected by Coriolis, force caused by the rotation of the earth. In the Northern Hemisphere, deflection is clockwise; in the Southern Hemisphere, counterclockwise. Coriolis is responsible for the circular pattern of the currents in the North and South Atlantic, the North and South Pacific, and the Indian Ocean. Because of seasonal variations in the wind systems, and because of other seasonal changes, the characteristics of most ocean currents change at certain times of the year. Currents are often described as warm or cold. The terms are relative and are based on the latitude in which they originate and on the effect they have on climate. For example, the Northeast Drift current, off the northern coast of Norway, is a "warm" current, although it may be lower in temperature than the cold Labrador current off New England.

ocean-floor landmarks—Charted "landmarks" on the ocean floor can often assist the navigator in determining position. Such marks include submarine canyons, trenches, troughs, escarpments, ridges, seamounts, and guyots. These terms describe submarine topographical features that are similar to counterparts on dry land. An escarpment is a long, steep face of rock, a submarine cliff. A seamount is an elevation of relatively small horizontal extent rising steeply toward, but not reaching, the surface. A guyot is a flat-topped seamount, rather similar to the mesas found in the southwestern United States. Canyons are found off most continental slopes; they are relatively steep-sided, and their axes descend steadily. A canyon, when crossed approximately at right angles, is easily recognized on a depth sounder or recorder. It will serve to establish a line of position. Trenches, troughs, ridges, and escarpments can also yield a line of position.

Omega—A hyperbolic navigational system, similar to loran-A. A long-range, pulsed, phase-difference, very-low-frequency (VLF) system, operating on a frequency of 10 to 14 kHz. It is a worldwide all-weather system, of use to ships, aircraft, and submerged submarines. Its accuracy is about one mile during the day and two miles during the night. As with loran, shore transmitting stations are used. Theoretically, six such stations are required for worldwide coverage; however, two additional stations are required to provide for station repair. In contrast to other hyperbolic navigational systems, any two stations produce a line of position. Special charts are provided by the U.S. Naval Oceangraphic Office for Omega plotting. Long baselines of as much as 6,000 miles are used, so the system is accurate to about 6,000 miles. For greatest accuracy, the navigator should select station pairs yielding lines of position that will cross at angles of 60° to 90°.

omega, differential—The 1 to 2 miles accuracy of the Omega system is adequate for the high seas, but it is not precise enough for coastal areas. Accuracy can be improved to approximately 0.5 nautical mile (0.9 km) by the technique known as differential Omega. This technique is based on the principle that propagation corrections will be the same for all receivers within a local area of perhaps 100 to 200 miles (185 to 370 km) radius. A monitor station develops corrections on a continuous basis; these are then transmitted to ships with Omega receivers. When these are applied, positions can be fixed to within 0.25 miles (0.5 km) at a distance of 50 miles (93 km) from the monitoring station, degrading to about 0.5 mile (0.9 km) at 200 miles (370 km). At times of sudden ionospheric disturbances (SIDs) and polar-cap disturbances (PCDs), its accuracy is retained while that of the basic system is seriously degraded; at such times the improvement by the differential technique may be as great as 10:1.

omega position tables—Omega charting coordinate tables (also called Omega lattice tables) are Omega lines of position in tabular form. If a navigator lacks an Omega chart he may simply put Omega lines directly onto a convenient chart or blank plotting sheet. These tables are published by DMAHC as publication no. 224.

omni—An omni receiver will fix a vessel's line of position to within two compass degrees. Its drawback is its short range; unlike ordinary radio beams, which can be bounced off the atmosphere, omni beams go in a direct line and thus become ineffective beyond the horizon. The key element in an omni system is the complex, very-high-frequency (VHF) beam sent out by each transmitting station. The beam is actually a composite of two VHF radio waves. When transmitted together, these two waves combine into a signal whose nature varies depending upon the direction in which it travels. Thus the portion of the signals that are sent out to the north differs from the signals aimed east or west. An omni receiver detects these differences and displays them as bearings between the station and the boat.

optical bearing beacon—Beacon composed of two lanterns and colors with their flashing characteristics arranged to provide an observer the true bearing from the beacon without use of a compass. One lantern consists of a rotating lens, which emits a pencil beam every 60°. The six beams rotate in a clockwise direction at a rate of one revolution per minute, and the light is seen to flash once every ten seconds. Five of the six beams are either red or green, the sixth white. The white beam is considered the key beam. The other lantern is omnidirectional and is a xenon flash tube. Xenon light is very crisp and distinct and slightly bluish. When the white flash of the rotating beacon passes through true north, the xenon flashes. To obtain true bearing from the beacon, measure the seconds from the xenon flash to the white beam of the rotating beacon. The time in seconds multiplied by six, equals the true bearing from the beacon. An accuracy of 0.5 second will provide a bearing accurate to 3°.

orthographic projection—If terrestrial points are projected geometrically from infinity (projecting lines parallel) to a tangent plane, an orthographic projection results. This projection is neither conformal nor equal-area. Its principal use is in navigational astronomy, where it is useful for illustrating or graphically solving the navigational triangle and for illustrating celestial coordinates. If the plane is tangent at a point on the equator, the usual case, the parallels (including the equator) appear as straight lines and the meridians as elipses, except that the meridian through the point of tangency appears as a straight line and the one 90° away as a circle.

orthophoto charts—The National Ocean Survey publishes some charts using a combination of aerial photographs and conventional chart symbols; these are called orthophoto charts. Usually of harbor areas, such charts assist a navigator by providing greater land details for

An orthographic map of the Western Hemisphere

fixing his position. The orthophoto format also aids in the production of charts by eliminating the hand drafting of intricate details such as roads, buildings, and other man-made objects.

over-bottom speed—The actual geographical speed of a craft. A boat doing a through-water speed of six knots against a two-knot current will be accomplishing a four-knot over-bottom speed.

P

parallax—The difference in the altitude of a celestial body when viewed from the surface of the earth and from its center is called a parallax. Parallax is greatest when the body is near the horizon and least when the body is near the observer's zenith; the maximum value, occurring when a body is on the horizon, is called horizontal parallax (HP). In the figure below, the angle called the observed altitude (Ho) at the center of the earth between the celestial horizon and the line of sight to the body is greater than a similar angle called the altitude apparent (Ha) at the surface because of the radius of the earth. Moreover, the closer the body to the earth, the greater the difference in the two angles. Consequently, the parallax of the moon is most pronounced, followed by the parallax of the sun and finally that of the planets and stars. A star is so distant that parallax is negligible, while the effect for the moon is so great that the

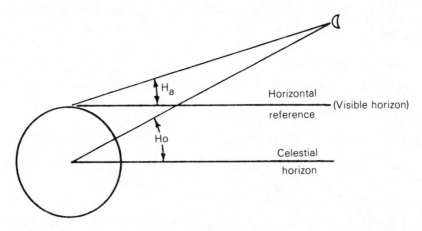

The effect of parallax

160

values of horizontal parallax are tabulated for each hour in the daily pages of the *Nautical Almanac.* The parallax correction for the sun is included in the altitude correction tables in the almanac and is the basis for the additional corrections for Mars and Venus.

parallel of latitude—A circle on the earth, parallel to the plane of the equator. It connects all points of equal latitude. The equator is a great circle connecting points of 0° latitude. The poles, single points at latitude 90°, are the other limiting case. All other parallels are small circles.

parallel ruler—Instrument for transferring a line parallel to itself. In its most common form, it consists of two parallel bars or rulers connected in such a manner that when one is held in place on a flat surface, the other can be moved away parallel to it. The principal use of parallel rulers in navigation is to transfer a charted line to a compass rose, and vice versa.

parhelion—A form of halo consisting of an image of the sun at the same altitude and some arc distance away from it, usually 22°, but occasionally 46°. A similar phenomenon at an angular distance of 120° (sometimes 90° to 140°) is called a paranthelion. One at an angular distance of 180° (a rare occurrence) is called an anthelion. A parhelion is popularly called a mock sun. Similar phenomena in relation to the moon are called paraselene.

parsec—From the words "parallax" and "second"; is the distance at which a body, viewed from the earth and from the sun, will differ in position by one second of arc. This amounts to about 19.1 trillion (1.91 × 10^{13}) miles (3.07 × 10^{13} km), or 3.24 light-years. Since this value is less than the distance from earth to Rigil Kentaurus, the navigational star nearest to our solar system, at a distance of about 4.3 light-years, any star viewed from the sun and from the earth will differ in direction by less than one second of arc. This small angle is known as the star's heliocentric parallax.

pelorus—Since a clear view in all directions may be unobtainable from the compass, peloruses, or dumb compasses, may be mounted at convenient points, such as the wings of a bridge. A pelorus consists of a flat ring mounted in gimbals on a vertical stand. The inner edge of the ring is graduated in degrees, from 0° at the ship's head clockwise through 360°. This ring snugly encloses a compass card. The card, flush with the ring and the top of the bowl, is rotatable, so that any degree of its graduation may be set to the lubber's line. Upon the card is mounted a pair of sighting vanes similar to those of a bearing circle (*see entry*). They may be revolved independently and held in position by a clamp screw. On some models an electric light inside the stand illuminates the card from underneath.

phase—The phase of a wave is the amount the cycle has progressed from a specified origin. For most purposes it is stated in circular measure, a complete cycle being considered 360°. The origin is not important, principal interest being the phase relative to that of some other wave. Thus, two waves having crests one-fourth cycle apart are said to be 90° out of phase. If the crest of one wave occurs at the trough of another, the two are 180° out of phase.

phonetic alphabet—Internationally agreed upon alphabet, recommended for clarity in spelling out words or numerals by all persons using voice radio.

Alphabet:	A	Alpha	J	Juliet	R	Romeo
	B	Bravo	K	Kilo	S	Sierra
	C	Charlie	L	Lima	T	Tango
	D	Delta	M	Mike	U	Uniform
	E	Echo	N	November	V	Victor
	F	Foxtrot	O	Oscar	W	Whisky
	G	Golf	P	Papa	X	X ray
	H	Hotel	Q	Quebec	Y	Yankee
					Z	Zulu
Numerals:	1	Wun	5	Fi-yev	8	Ait
	2	Too	6	Six	9	Niner
	3	Tree	7	Seven	0	Zay-roe
	4	Foe-were				

pilot charts—Published by the U.S. Navy Hydrographic office for the North Atlantic Ocean and the North Pacific Ocean. Pilot charts are also published in atlas form for the northern North Atlantic Ocean; the South Atlantic Ocean and Central American waters; and the South Pacific and Indian oceans.

pinger—A battery-powered device that transmits sound waves. When the pinger is lowered into the water, the direct and bottom-reflected sound can be monitored with a listening device. The difference between arrival time of the direct and reflected waves is used to compute the distance of the pinger from the ocean bottom.

plan position indicator (PPI)—The maplike presentation on a radar scope. On the PPI, the range of a target is measured from the center of the scope by a series of concentric rings, or by one adjustable ring (variable range marker). Bearing is indicated by the direction of an echo from the center of the scope. To facilitate measurement of direction, a movable, radial guideline or cursor is provided, and a compass rose is placed around the outside of the scope. In the "heading upward" presentation, relative bearings are indicated, the top of the scope representing the direction of ship's head. In the "north upward" presentation, gyro north is always at the top, regardless of the heading. True bearings are indicated if there is no gyro error. On this presentation, a radial line customarily shows the heading of the vessel.

plotters—Most plotters consist of some form of protractor and a straightedge. Typical is the Weems Mark II, a protractor of 180° mounted on a straightedge, intended primarily for measuring courses or bearings relative to a meridian. An auxiliary scale is included, which permits measuring from a parallel. The Mark II plotter was designed primarily for aircraft use.

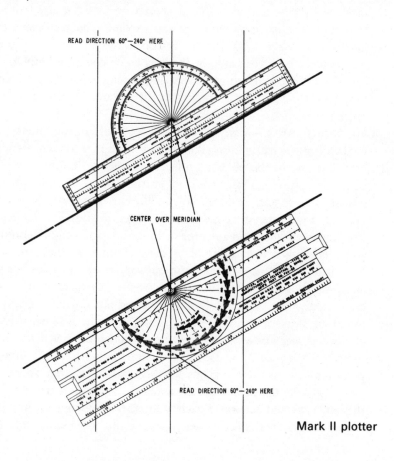

Mark II plotter

plotting sheets—Designed for use by the navigator at sea when no large-scale charts are available, they are blank Mercator charts showing only meridians and parallels with a compass rose in the middle. Plotting sheets are particularly useful in plotting celestial fixes. The fix is then transferred to the chart. There are two types available: those printed for a given band of latitude; and universal plotting sheets (UPS), which can be used at any latitude. The Defense Mapping Agency Hydrographic Center (DMAHC) publishes several series at different scales. One may use the same plotting sheets for either north or south latitudes by inverting the sheet. DMAHC chart nos. 900–910 are plotting sheets covering 8° of latitude with a longitude scale of 1° = 4 inches. Chart nos. 920–933 are smaller in overall size and cover varying amounts of latitude, from 8° near the equator to 3° at 65° latitude.

Universal plotting sheets (UPS) have a compass rose, unnumbered parallels of latitude, and a single meridian in the center of the sheet. They are unusual in that they may be used for any latitude and longitude, exclusive of the polar areas where a Mercator chart is not practical. On the UPS the navigator draws in meridians properly spaced for the mid–latitude of the area to be covered. Universal plotting sheets are published by DMA Aerospace Center with the designation VP-OS. They are 13 inches by 14 inches and have a scale of 20 miles per inch.

polar coordinates—Many of the concepts of measurement that are used in normal navigation take on new meanings, or lose their meanings entirely, in the polar regions. In temperate latitudes, one speaks of north, south, east, and west; of latitude and longitude; of time; of sunrise and sunset; and of day and night. Each of these terms is associated with specific concepts. In temperate latitudes, the lengths of a degree of latitude and a degree of longitude are roughly comparable, and meridians are thought of as parallel lines, as they appear on a Mercator chart. But meridians run outward from the poles like spokes, and longitude becomes a direction. At the North Pole all directions are south; at the South Pole all directions are north. A bearing to a mountain peak can no longer be considered a rhumb line. It is a great circle and, because of the rapid convergence of meridians, must be plotted as such. Time as used in temperate zones has little meaning in polar regions. As the meridians converge, so do the time zones. A mile from the pole, the time zones are a quarter of a mile apart. At the pole, the sun rises and sets once each year, the moon once a month. The visible stars circle the sky endlessly, essentially at the same altitudes, and only half the celestial sphere is visible. The planets rise and set once each sidereal period (from 225 days, for Venus, to 29.5 years, for Saturn). A day of twenty-four hours at the pole is not marked by the usual periods of daylight and darkness, and "morning" and "afternoon" have no significance. In fact, the day is not marked by any observable phenomenon except that the sun makes one complete circle around the sky, maintaining essentially the same altitude (equal to its declination) and always bearing south (or north).

polar distance—The angular distance of a celestial body from the elevated pole measured along the body's hour circle. When declination and elevated poles are of the same name (both north or both south), polar distance is the complement of declination and may be referred to as codec. When elevated pole and declination are of different names (one north and one south), polar distance equals 90° plus declination.

polarization—Radio waves have both electric and magnetic fields. The two are conceived as having an orientation to their vibrations. The direction of the electric field is called the polarization of the combined fields. Thus, if the electric component is vertical, the wave is said to be "vertically polarized," and if horizontal, "horizontally polarized." A wave traveling through space may be polarized in any direction; traveling along the surface of the earth it is always vertically polarized because the earth, a conductor, short-circuits the horizontal component. The magnetic and electric fields are always mutually perpendicular.

polyconic projection—The latitude limitations of the secant conic projection (*see* Conic) can be eliminated by the use of a series of cones, a polyconic projection. In this projection a parallel is the base of a tangent cone. Parallels appear as nonconcentric circles and meridians as curved lines converging toward the poles and concave to the central meridian. The polyconic projection is widely used in atlases, particularly for areas of large range in latitude and longitude. Since it is not conformal, this projection is not customarily used in navigation, except in hydrographic surveying.

precession of the equinoxes—The axis of the earth is undergoing a precessional motion similar to that of a top spinning with its axis tilted. In about 25,800 years the axis completes a cycle and returns to the position from which it started. Since the celestial equator is 90° from the celestial poles, it too is moving. The result is a slow westward movement of the equinoxes and solstices, which has already carried them about 30°, or one constellation, along the ecliptic from the positions they occupied when named, more than 2,000 years ago. Since sidereal hour angle is measured from the vernal equinox and declination from the celestial equator, the coordinates of celestial bodies would be changing even if the bodies themselves were stationary. This westward motion of the equinoxes along the ecliptic is called precession of the equinoxes. The total amount, called general precession, is about 50″27 (seconds of arc) per year (in 1975). Because of precession, the celestial poles are describing circles in the sky. The north celestial pole is moving closer to Polaris, which it will pass at a distance of approximately 28′ (minutes of arc) in about the year 2120. Other stars in their turn will become the pole star. Similarly, the south celestial pole will someday be marked by stars of the False Southern Cross. The precession of the earth's axis is the result of gravitational forces exerted principally by the sun and moon on the earth's equatorial bulge. The spinning earth responds to those forces in the manner of a gyroscope. Regression of the nodes of the moon's orbit introduces another irregularity known as nutation, in the precessional motion.

prime meridian—That meridian used as the origin for measurement of longitude. The prime meridian used universally is that through the original position of the British Royal Observatory at Greenwich, near London, England.

prime vertical—The vertical circle passing through the east and west points of the horizon. The prime vertical arc above the horizon terminates at the points of intersection of the equinoctial (plane of the equator) and the celestial horizon.

protractor, three-arm—A circular metal or celluloid disk graduated in degrees with a fixed arm, at 000°, and two movable arms, attached to the center. After a sextant observation of two horizontal angles, defined by three objects with the observer at the vertex, the three-arm protractor is set to the two angles and oriented through the objects on the chart; the center of the protractor is the position of the observer.

psychrometer—Two thermometers mounted side by side in a wooden case. One is the "dry bulb." The other, the "wet bulb," has a small container of water connected to its surface by a wick. The evaporation of water around the wet bulb lowers the temperature. By comparing the two thermometer readings and consulting a table contained in *The American Practical Navigator* (Bowditch), one determines the relative humidity, which is useful in weather predicting.

quadrant, storm—The 90° sector of a storm centered on a designated cardinal point of the compass. An eight-point compass rose is used when one is referring to quadrants. As an example, the north quadrant refers to the sector of a storm from 315° through 360° to 045°.

quadrantal error—If a body mounted in gimbals is not balanced, a disturbing force will cause it to swing. A swinging body tends to rotate so that its long axis of weight is in the plane of the swing. A rolling vessel introduces the forces needed to start a gyro compass swinging. The effect reaches a maximum on intercardinal headings, midway between the two horizontal axes of the compass, and is called quadrantal error. It is corrected by the addition of weights to balance the compass so that the weight is the same in all directions from the center. Without a long axis of weight, there is no tendency to rotate during a swing.

R

racon (radar)—Racons transmit a pulse or pulses, but only when triggered by receipt of a pulse from a ship's radar. They not only give a stronger return than a reflector; they can be coded for positive identification and range measurement. The reply pulse consists of a number of pulses transmitted at selected intervals; these appear on the ship's plan position indicator (PPI) scope as segments of concentric arcs. The number of segments and their distance apart form the identification code.

radar (Radio Detection And Ranging)—Electronic equipment designed to determine distance by measuring the time required for a radio signal to travel from a transmitter to a "target" and return, either as a reflected "echo" (primary radar) or a retransmitted signal from a transponder triggered by the original signal (secondary radar). Since primary radar uses a directional antenna, the direction of the target is also determined. Returning echoes are displayed by a cathode-ray tube on a plan position indicator (PPI), which gives an aerial-map appearance to the presentation, with the ship centered. The range of a target is proportional to the distance of its echo signal (blip) from the radar scope's center and is measured by a series of concentric circles. Bearing is indicated by the direction of a blip from the scope center. When the presentation is calibrated so that the top of the scope represents the ship's heading, the bearings are relative. When a movable compass rose is positioned concentric with the outer rim of the scope, true or magnetic bearings are obtained. Radar's effective distance depends on the height of the scanner antenna and the height of the target.

radar chart comparison unit (CCU)—By means of this device an image of a chart is superimposed over the plan position indicator (PPI), or an image of the PPI is superimposed over the chart. Either method permits direct comparison of radar image and chart, if the two are of the same scale. Although distortion of the PPI presentation is not the same as that of the chart, an experienced person can usually effect a reliable match, providing reasonably accurate determination of position.

radar echoes—Indirect or false blips are caused by reflection of the main lobe of the radar beam off ships' structures. When such reflection does occur, the echo will return from a legitimate radar contact to the antenna by the same, indirect path. Consequently, the echo will appear on the PPI at the bearing of the reflecting surface. The indirect echo will appear on the PPI at the same range as the direct echo, assuming that the additional distance by the indirect path is negligible. Characteristics by which indirect echoes may be recognized are: (1) They usually occur in shadow (blind) sectors. (2) They have constant bearings. (3) They appear at the same ranges as the corresponding echoes. (4) When plotted, their movements are usually abnormal. (5) Their shapes may indicate that they are not direct echoes.

Second-trace echoes are echoes received from a contact at an actual range greater than the radar range setting. If an echo from a distant target is received after the following pulse has been transmitted, the echo will appear on the radarscope at the correct bearing but not at the true range. Second-trace echoes are unusual except under abnormal atmospheric conditions or conditions of super-refraction. Second-trace echoes may be recognized by changes in their position on the radarscope when changing the pulse repetition rate (PRR); hazy, streaked, or distorted shapes; erratic movement on plotting.

Side-lobe effects are readily recognized because they produce a series of echoes on each side of the main echo at the same range. Semicircles or even complete circles may be produced. Because of the low energy of the side lobes, these effects will normally occur only at the shorter ranges. The effects may be minimized or eliminated through the use of the gain and anticlutter controls. Slotted waveguide antennas have largely eliminated the problem.

radar fixes—The following are used in piloting to establish a radar fix: (1) Range and bearing of an object. (2) Two or more bearings. Because of bearing inaccuracy this is not a preferred method. (3) Two bearings and a range. If the range arc does not pass through the point of intersection of the bearings, the fix should be established at the point on the range arc equidistant from each bearing line. (4) Two or more range arcs. This provides the best fix.

radar reflectors—Because radar beams reflect poorly or not at all from wooden or fiberglass boats, many small-craft skippers use radar reflectors. Commonly about fifteen inches in diameter, the reflectors are made of thin, interlocking metal disks. Usually kept folded and stowed away, they can be assembled and hoisted aloft for cruising at night or in bad weather.

radio beacons—Marine radio beacons are important aids to electronic navigation and are described in DMAHC publication no. 117, "Radio Navigational Aids." The letters "RBn" denote their location on a nautical chart. They are particularly useful in piloting during periods of poor visibility. Transmitting in the medium-frequency range, and identified by Morse code, their transmissions may be directional, rotational, or circular. Directional radio beacons transmit beams along a fixed bearing. Rotational radio beacons revolve a beam of radio waves in a manner similar to the revolving light of certain lighthouses. Circular radio beacons, the most common type, send out waves in all directions for reception by radio direction finder. Radio bearings may be taken on any received radio signal within frequency range of the receiver. At many locations radio beacons are provided for this purpose. Their locations and identifying signals are shown on the chart by appropriate symbol and the abbreviation "Ra Bn," and are tabulated in Hydrographic Office publication no. 117, "Radio Navigational Aids." Where bearings are taken in other stations, one should be careful to determine the location of the transmitting antenna from which the signal is coming. This may not always be the same as a receiving antenna associated with the same station, and the signal may possibly be rebroadcast from another station.

radio bearing (reciprocal bearing)—Unless a radio direction finder has a sensing antenna, there is a possible 180° ambiguity in the reading. If such an error is discovered, the reciprocal of the incorrect reading should be taken and the correction for the new direction applied. If there is doubt as to which of the two possible directions is the correct one, wait long enough for the bearing to change appreciably and take another reading. The transmitter should draw aft between reading. If the reciprocal is used, the station will appear to have drawn forward.

radio-bearing errors—A radio wave crossing a coastline at an oblique angle undergoes a change of direction because of the difference in conducting and reflecting properties of land and water. It is avoided by not using, or regarding as doubtful, bearings of beams that cross a shoreline within 150° to 20° of parallel.

When radio waves arrive at a receiver, they are influenced somewhat by the environment. An erroneous radio-direction-finder bearing results from currents induced in the direction finder antenna by reradiation from the vessel's superstructure and distortion due to the dimensions and contours of the vessel's hull. This quadrantal error is a function of the relative bearing, normally being maximum for bearings broad on the bow and broad on the quarter. Its value for various bearings can be determined, and a calibration table made.

The direction of travel of radio waves may undergo alteration near sunrise or sunset, when great changes are taking place in the atmosphere. This is sometimes called night effect. The error can be minimized by the averaging of several readings, but any radio bearings taken during this period should be considered doubtful.

radio direction finding (RDF)—The simplest and most widespread of radio-navigational systems found on most medium-size or larger recreational craft, fishing vessels of all sizes, and oceangoing ships. The extent of regular use varies with availability of more-sophisticated equipment but remains a basic radio navigational system. Modern RDF systems for marine navigation use shore-based nondirectional transmitters and direction-sensitive antennas on ship-based receivers. The radio bearing is taken aboard the vessel and plotted directly. Bearings are best taken from marine radio beacons, which are designed and constructed solely for this purpose, but they can also be taken on commercial broadcasting stations (standard AM band), aeronautical radio beacons, and some other stations. A bearing obtained from any of these sources can be used in the same manner as any other line of position. The exact location of the transmitting antenna must be known; nautical charts show all marine radio beacons and often show the position of aeronautical radio beacons and some commercial broadcasting stations (whose antennas are frequently not in the town or city whose name is used in the station identification). Typically, a radio direction finder makes use of the directional properties of a loop antenna. If such an antenna is parallel to the direction of travel of the radio waves, the signal received is of maximum strength. If the loop is perpendicular to the direction of travel, the signal is of minimum strength or entirely missing. When a dial is attached to such a loop antenna, the direction of the antenna and hence the direction of the transmitter can be determined. The pointer indicates the direction of the transmitter from the receiver when the loop is perpendicular to this direction, when the minimum signal is heard. The minimum, generally called the "null," rather than the maximum is used because a sharper reading is obtained. Since radio waves travel a great circle, a correction must be applied for plotting on a Mercator chart. A Lambert chart permits direct plotting of all radio bearings.

radio direction-finding equipment—May be either manual (RDF) or automatic (ADF). In the former case, the antenna is rotated by hand until a direction is obtained. The point of minimum signal (null), rather than the maximum, is used, as it is sharper and can be judged more precisely. There will be two positions of the antenna, 180° apart, which will give a null; a separate, "sense" antenna is used to resolve the ambiguity, unless the correct direction is readily apparent from other information such as the DR position. Automatic direction finders rotate the antenna mechanically or electronically. A visual display continuously indicates the bearing of the transmitter being received, corrected for ambiguity; the operator of an ADF set needs only to tune and confirm the identification of the station.

Radio bearings are plotted and labeled in the same manner as visual bearings. RDF bearings are, however, usually less accurate; a position found with one or more radio bearings must be identified as an RDF fix or as an estimated position (EP). A new DR track is not customarily plotted from an EP, but a course line should be drawn to determine whether or not there is any possibility of the ship's standing into danger. A series of estimated positions obtained from RDF bearings and supplemented by a line of soundings can often locate a vessel's position with acceptable accuracy.

radio frequency bands—The tremendous demand for communication channels has required allotment of bands of frequencies to specific uses. The most familiar band is the commercial broadcast, 550–1600 kHz. Besides entertainment, this band carries a considerable amount of weather information of interest to the mariner. A vessel with direction-finding equipment may use commercial broadcasting stations for position finding, although more exact positions can be established by the use of radio beacons, assigned frequencies in the 285–325 kHz band. A nationwide network of transmitters in the 200–400 kHz band broadcast continuously for airplane guidance. Signals from some of these stations near the coast can be useful for position finding by boats. In addition, the air-navigation transmitters broadcast weather reports at regular intervals, usually at fifteen and forty-five minutes after the hour. The lowest band of interest to small-boat skippers is for Consol and Consolan, 190–200 kHz. Two frequency bands have been assigned for the use of small-craft radiotelephones. Four frequencies have been designated for marine distress calls and direction finding for search and rescue:

500 kHz	The LF international distress and calling frequency used by ships carrying licensed radio operators.
2182 kHz	The MF international distress and calling frequency for ships not carrying a licensed radio operator. The distress signal on this frequency is MAYDAY.
8364 kHz	The HF international survival craft radio distress and direction-finding frequency for search and rescue.
156.8 MHz	The VHF international distress and calling frequency. The distress signal on this frequency is MAYDAY.

Radio frequency spectrum—*See* electromagnetic spectrum and frequency entries.

radio-navigation systems—According to the nature of the lines of position provided, radio-navigation systems are described as hyperbolic, ranging, azimuthal, or composite. Radio-navigation systems are described as short-range if their capability is limited to coastal regions, or to making a landfall; examples are radar and the radio direction finder (RDF). Systems are described as medium-range if limited to ranges permitting reliable positioning for about one day prior to making landfall; Decca is an example. The maximum range of a radio-navigation system depends upon frequency, transmitter power, and signal-to-noise ratio, which is often a more realistic indicator of range than power. Radio-navigation systems are also classified as to availability. Those systems that do not require the user to transmit and can be used simultaneously by an unlimited number are described as passive and nonsaturable.

radio-navigation systems (hyperbolic)—So called because of the hyperbolic lattices formed in their signal fields and the associated hyperbolic lines of position produced. Gee, loran and Decca are examples (*see separate entries*). Hyperbolic systems provide the greatest potential for coverage of large areas with the smallest number of transmitting sites, and the best compromise between accuracy and coverage. The accuracy of the fix provided by a hyperbolic radio-navigation system is dependent upon the accuracy of each line of position and their angle of intersection. Since the velocity of a radio wave is approximately one foot per nanosecond, for accuracies of tens or hundreds of feet, measurements must be made to tens or hundreds of nanoseconds. The receiver's ability to make these measurements accurately is dependent upon signal-to-noise ratio. The user's position relative to the transmitting stations governs the gradient or spacing between consecutive lines of position. Lines are most closely spaced, giving highest accuracy, along the baseline between stations. As the distance between lines increases, the accuracy decreases, being so low along the baseline extensions that the use of this part of the lattice is normally avoided.

radio-navigation systems (ranging mode)—*See* Rho-Theta navigation and Raydist.

radiotelephony—Citizens Band Class D radio, in the high-frequency 27 MHz band, is a limited system for personal, "walkie-talkie" conversations and does not satisfy the safety and operational requirements for coastal cruising.

The Marine Band, of 2000–3000 kHz (2–3 MHz), is the primary offshore safety and operating network, keystoned by the international calling and distress frequency of 2182 kHz. Ship-to-ship calls are initiated on 2182 kHz. Nonemergency traffic, after establishing initial contact, then shifts to a working frequency. The U.S. frequencies for nonemergency traffic are:

MHz Band	Frequency	Purpose
2–3 MHz	2003 kHz	Great Lakes
	2142 kHz	Pacific Coast daytime, south of lat. 42°N
	2638 kHz	All areas
	2670 kHz	Coast Guard, including ship-to-shore
	2738 kHz	All areas except Great Lakes and Gulf of Mexico
	2830 kHz	Gulf of Mexico

radio time signals—Broadcast worldwide by several U.S. Navy and Bureau of Standards radio stations, among which are stations NSS (Annapolis, Maryland), WWV (Fort Collins, Colorado), and WWVH (Maui, Hawaii). Although the signals are used on U.S. Navy ships primarily for checking the accuracy of chronometers and other shipboard timepieces, they can be used to set the comparing watch or stopwatch prior to celestial observations. The time transmitted by station WWV (Bureau of Standards) is based on the resonance of the cesium atom and is called coordinated universal time (UTC).

ramarks—Radar beacons can be of two different designs, ramarks and racons. Ramarks are continuously transmitting beacons that display on the PPI (plan position indicator) scope a bright radial line or narrow sector on the bearing of the mark. There are two general types of ramarks. One operates within the marine radar frequency band; the other transmits in the adjacent radar "beacon" band on a frequency of

9310 MHz. There are two methods of providing identification: by having the radial line on the PPI broken up into dots and dashes, or by transmitting the signal only during some of the revolutions of its antenna (time coding). Ramarks operating in the beacon band are simpler but require that the ship have either a separate receiver or a means of shifting the main radar from its normal working frequency to 9,310 MHz.

range lights—Two lights located some distance apart with one higher than the other, visible usually from one direction only, so positioned that a mariner can hold his ship on the axis of a channel by steering to keep the far ("rear") light directly above the near ("front") light. Entrance channels are frequently marked by range lights. The lights of ranges may be red, green, or white and may be fixed, flashing, or occulting, the principal requirement being that they stand out from their surroundings. The U.S. Coast Guard has standardized quick-flashing for the front light and equal-interval, six-second flashes for the rear light. Range-light structures are usually fitted with conspicuous marks for daytime use.

Raydist—A midrange navigation system, it employs radio distance measuring to produce either circular or hyperbolic lines of position. Raydist uses two transmitters on a baseline with a separation of as much as 100 miles. Operating frequencies are in the 1.6–5 MHz range, permitting effective transmission beyond line of sight. Depending upon power, ranges up to 200 miles may be reached. Transmissions differ by 400 cycles per second, which permits phase comparison for locations. An accuracy of one to three meters may be achieved. Raydist equipment, including the transmitters, is small, compact, light and fully automatic.

reciprocal bearing—*See* radio direction finding.

reference direction—A number of reference directions are used in navigation. If a direction is stated without a reference, its reference is true (geographic) north. When grid navigation is used in high latitudes, grid north is generally used as a reference direction. The reference direction for magnetic directions is magnetic north, and that for compass directions is compass north. For relative bearings it is the heading of the ship. For amplitudes the reference direction is east or west, 090° or 270° true.

reference station—Place where tide or tidal-current constants have been determined from observation. It is the place for which daily predictions are given in tide or tidal-current tables and from which predictions are made for other nearby locations.

reflection (radio waves)—When radio waves strike a surface, they are reflected in the same manner as light waves. The strength of the reflected wave depends upon the angle between the incident ray and the horizontal, type of polarization (*see entry*), and properties of the surface. Low-frequency waves penetrate the surface, and very low frequencies can be received below the surface of the sea. A change of phase also takes place when a wave is reflected. The amount varies with the conductivity of the surface and the polarization of the wave, reaching a maximum of 180° for a horizontally polarized wave reflected from seawater. When direct waves (those traveling from transmitter to receiver without reflection) and reflected waves arrive at a receiver, the total signal is the vector sum of the two. If the signals are in phase, they reinforce each other, producing a stronger signal. If there is a phase difference, the signals cancel each other, cancellation being complete if the phase difference is 180° and the two signals have the same amplitude. This interaction is called interference.

refraction—Light, or other radiant energy, is assumed to travel in a straight line at uniform speed, if the medium in which it is traveling has uniform properties. But if light enters a medium of different properties, particularly if the density is different, its speed changes somewhat. If the light is traveling in a direction perpendicular to the surfaces of the two media, all parts of each wave enter the new medium at the same time, so all parts change speed together. But if the light enters the denser medium at an oblique angle, the change of speed occurs progressively along the wave front as the different parts enter the denser medium. This results in a change in the direction of travel. This change in direction is called refraction. If the change in densities is sudden, as along the surface separating water and air, the change in direction is equally sudden. However, if a ray of light travels through a medium of gradually changing densities (indices of refraction), its path is curved. This is the situation in the earth's atmosphere, which decreases in density with height. This gradual change of direction is called atmospheric refraction.

A ray of light entering the atmosphere from outside, as from a star, undergoes atmospheric refraction, and the effect makes the celestial body appear higher in the sky. If a body is in the zenith, its light is not refracted. At an altitude of 20° it is about 2.'6; at 10°, 5.'3; at 5°, 9.'9; and at the horizon, 34.'5. A table of refraction is given on the inside cover of the *Nautical Almanac* in the column headed "Stars and Planets." As height above the surface of the earth increases, light from an outside source travels through less atmosphere, and refraction decreases. At shipboard heights the difference is negligible, but at aircraft heights it is a consideration.

relative bearing (RB)—A bearing relative to the heading, or to the vessel itself. It is sometimes measured right or left from 0° at the ship's head through 180°. To convert a relative bearing to a bearing (Bn) from north, express the relative bearing in terms of the 0°–360° system and add the heading: Bn = RB + SH. The pelorus can be used for taking relative bearings by setting the 000° graduation of its card to the lubber's line, then observing the object and reading the card.

Rho-Theta navigation—Range-direction navigation utilizes a combination of circular (ranging) systems for distance measurement, together with azimuthal or directional measuring systems. The Omnirange (VOR) system in general use for aviation throughout the United States provides bearing information. A large number of the stations are also equipped with distance-measuring equipment (DME) to provide a complete Rho-Theta system. The military version is known as TACAN. These systems are sufficiently accurate for general navigational purposes but are limited to a line-of-sight range. The principle of Omnirange navigation is based on phase comparisons of two radio signals. One is nondirectional, with a constant phase throughout 360° of azimuth. The other signal rotates and varies in phase with change in azimuth. Equipment on the aircraft translates the received signals and shows the pilot the bearing "TO" or "FROM" the ground station.

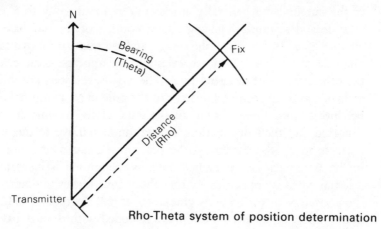

Rho-Theta system of position determination

rhumb line—For practical purposes, a rhumb line (also known as a loxodrome or loxodromic spiral) is a line that crosses every meridian of the earth at the same angle. In other words, a ship could maintain the same heading from starting point to destination (disregarding current, wind, and changing magnetic variation).

right ascension—The angle between the hour circle of the first point of Aries and the hour circle of a body, measured eastward along the arc of the equinoctial, and expressed in either degrees or in hours. Right ascension (in degrees) plus sidereal hour angle equals 360°.

RPM counters—The engine-revolution counters (tachometers) provide a means of determining speed and distance. One is provided for each shaft. By means of a master counter, the average revolutions made by all propellers can be obtained. If the number of revolutions made during any interval of time is divided by the number of revolutions known to drive the ship one mile, the distance traveled is obtained. The speed trials of a ship furnish data as to the revolutions required for a mile, as well as revolutions per minute (RPM) for various speeds. A table is made out for use on the bridge while the ship is under way which gives the RPM required for each knot. In making use of engine revolutions as speed indicators, the draft of the ship, the condition of its bottom, and the state of the sea are also considered.

Rude star finder—Designed to permit the determination of the approximate altitude and azimuth of any of the fifty-seven selected navigational stars tabulated in the *Nautical* and *Air* almanacs, it can also be set up to obtain the position of the navigational planets, any other stars, and even the sun or moon. The device can also be used to identify an unknown body, given its altitude and true azimuth. The accuracy of the star finder is generally considered to about $\pm$ 3° to 5° in both altitude and azimuth. The star finder consists of the star base, white circular plate with a pin in the center, and ten transparent overlays. On one side of the base the north celestial pole appears at the center; on the other, the south celestial pole. The fifty-seven stars are shown on each side at their positions relative to the pole in an azimuthal equidistant projection. The positions of the stars relative to one another are distorted, but their declinations and azimuths relative to the poles are correct; hence, the pattern of the stars on the star base is not as seen in the sky. Each star is named, and its magnitude is indicated. The celestial equator appears as a circle about four inches in diameter, and the periphery of each side is graduated in half degrees of LHA (local hour angle). There are ten templates included with the star base. Nine of these are printed with a blue altitude–azimuth grid; the tenth, printed in red, is for plotting bodies other than the fifty-seven selected stars.

S

sailing charts—The smallest-scale charts used for planning, for fixing position at sea, and dead reckoning while one is on a long voyage. The scale is generally 1:600,000 or smaller. The shoreline and topography are generalized, and only offshore soundings, the principal lights, buoys, and landmarks are shown.

Sailing Directions (Planning Guide)—Each of the eight Sailing Directions (Planning Guides) contains five chapters, covering (1) countries, (2) ocean-basin environment, (3) warning areas, (4) ocean routes, and (5) Navaid systems. The Planning Guides are relatively permanent because of the nature of the material they contain. The Sailing Directions (Enroute) are affected by relatively frequent changes, and so is the World Port Index. The Sailing Directions are designed to assist in planning a voyage of any extent, particularly if it involves an ocean passage. Each of the Sailing Directions covers one of eight areas based on division of the world's seaways into "ocean basins."

sailings—Dead reckoning involves the determination of position by means of course and distance from a known position. A closely related problem is that of finding the course and distance from one point to another. Although both of these problems are customarily solved by plotting directly on the chart, it occasionally becomes desirable to solve by computation, frequently by logarithms or traverse table. The various methods of solution are collectively called the sailings.

Great-circle sailing is used to take advantage of the shorter distance along the great circle between two points, rather than to follow the longer rhumb line, which appears the more direct route on a Mercator chart because of distortion. Since a great circle is continuously changing directions as one proceeds along it, no attempt is customarily made to follow it exactly. Rather, a number of points are

179

selected along the great circle, and rhumb lines are followed from point to point, taking advantage of the fact that over short distances, a great circle and a rhumb line almost coincide. Great-circle sailing by computation involves solution for an initial course, distance, latitude and longitude of the top of the circle (vertex), and latitude and longitude of the intersections of rhumb lines and the great circle. The computation involves successive solutions of the navigational spherical triangle, and many methods can be used.

Mercator sailing provides a mathematical solution of the plot as made on a Mercator chart. It is similar to plane, but uses meridianal differences and difference of longitude in place of difference of latitude and departure, respectively.

Middle- (or mid-) latitude sailing involves the use of a mid- or mean latitude (Lm) to convert departure (nautical miles traveled east or west) to difference of longitude (DLo) when the course is not due east or due west. The formulas for the conversion are: DLo = p sec Lm, and p = DLo cos Lm, where p is the departure. The mean latitude (Lm) is half the sum of the latitudes of two places on the same side of the equator. If a course crosses the equator, that part on each side is solved separately.

Plane sailing is a method of calculating course and distance, difference of latitude, and departure, when the earth is regarded as a plane surface. The method provides solution for the latitude of the point of arrival, but not for its longitude, one of the spherical sailings being needed for this. Because of the basic assumption that the earth is flat, this method is not used for distances of more than a few hundred miles.

Traverse sailing combines the plane-sailing solutions when there are two or more courses. A traverse is a series of courses or a track consisting of a number of course lines, as might result from a sailboat's beating into the wind. Traverse sailing is the finding of a single equivalent course. Solution is usually made by means of traverse tables by which the distance made good to north or south and to east or west on each course is tabulated and the change in latitude and longitude is found.

scalar and vector quantities—A scalar is a quantity that has magnitude only; a vector quantity has both magnitude and direction. If a vessel is said to have a tank of 5,000-gallon capacity, the number 5,000 is a scalar. In navigation, speed alone can be considered a scalar, while speed and direction are considered to constitute velocity, a vector quantity. Distance and direction also constitute a vector quantity. A scalar can be represented fully by a number. A vector quantity requires, in addition, an indication of direction. This is conveniently done graphically by means of a straight line, the length of which indicates the magnitude, and the direction of which indicates the direction of application of the magnitude. Such a line is called a vector. Since a straight line has two directions, reciprocals of each other, an arrowhead is placed along or at one end of a vector to indicate the direction represented, unless this is apparent or indicated in some other manner.

sextant—A precision optical instrument that uses two mirrors to measure angles, usually the vertical angle between a celestial body and the sea horizon. Its chief purpose is in calculating a position on the earth. The sextant can also be useful as a piloting instrument to measure the horizontal angle between two aids to navigation or a vertical angle, such as that between the top and base of a lighthouse, to compute distance off. In order to view both the body and the horizon simultaneously, the lower (horizon) mirror is vertically divided, half-clear, half-mirrored. The horizon appears through the clear glass and the body's image is reflected from the upper mirror onto the mirrored half. Once the body is observed through the horizon glass to be level with the horizon, its altitude is found by reading a calibrated scale and a micrometer drum. The optical principle of the sextant is illustrated below, with the solid line representing the path of a light ray from a celestial body being observed. The instrument is constructed in such a way that the angle BDC between the body and the horizon is always twice the angle between the index (upper) mirror and the horizon (lower) glass, angle BGC, which is marked on the sextant arc.

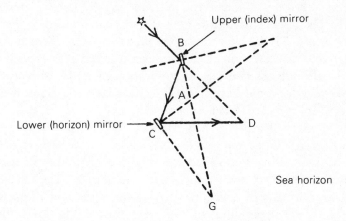

Upper (index) mirror

Lower (horizon) mirror

Sea horizon

Optical principle of the sextant

In use, the image of the body is reflected from the upper, or index, mirror, to the lower, or horizon, mirror, and then by tilting the index mirror, it is brought into coincidence with the horizon, seen through the clear portion of the horizon mirror.

sextant corrections:

AIR TEMPERATURE—The *Nautical Almanac* refraction table is based upon an air temperature of 50°F (10°C) at the surface of the earth. At other temperatures the refraction differs somewhat, becoming greater at lower temperatures and less at higher temperatures. The accompanying table provides the correction to be applied to the altitude. This correction can also be applied with reversed sign to the refraction from the almanac, and a single refraction applied to the altitude. A combined correction for nonstandard air temperature and nonstandard atmospheric pressure is given on page A4 of the *Nautical Almanac*. The correction for air temperature varies with the temperature of the air and the altitude of the celestial body, and applies to all celestial bodies, regardless of the method of observation. However, except for extreme temperatures or low altitudes, this correction is not usually applied unless results of unusual accuracy are desired.

APPARENT ALTITUDE—For purposes of routine navigation, corrections to the sextant altitude can be applied in any order using the Hs (raw sextant reading) as entering argument in the various correction tables. Where greater accuracy is desired, however, or at low altitudes where small changes in altitude can result in significant changes in the correction, the order of applying the corrections is important. To obtain maximum accuracy, the three corrections for nonadjustable instrument error (I), index error (IC), and dip (D) are first applied to the Hs. The Hs so corrected is termed the apparent altitude (Ha), and the value of Ha is used in entering the tables to obtain corrections. The R (refraction) correction is always negative, and it is applied to all celestial altitude observations. Its application to the Hs corrects the Hs to the value it would have if the light rays from the body were not refracted by the earth's atmosphere.

ARTIFICIAL HORIZON—When an artificial horizon is used, index correction (IC) is first applied. The result is then divided by two. Other corrections are then applied to the result, as applicable in the same manner as for observations using the visible horizon. The sun and full moon are normally observed by bringing the lower limb of one image tangent to the upper limb of the other image. The lower limb is observed if the image seen in the horizon mirror is above the image seen in the artificial horizon, unless an inverting telescope is used, when the opposite relationship holds. With a gibbous or crescent moon, judgment may be needed to establish the positions of the limbs. In some cases better results may be obtained by superimposing one image over the other, as with a planet or star. When this is done, the center of the body has been observed and no correction is applied for semidiameter (or irradiation, phase, or augmentation). There is no correction for dip (or sea-air temperature) when an artificial horizon is used.

ATMOSPHERIC PRESSURE—The *Nautical Almanac* refraction table is based upon an atmospheric pressure of 29.83 inches of mercury (10/10 millibars) at sea level. At other pressures the refraction differs, becoming greater as pressure increases and smaller as it decreases. Table 24 provides the corrections to be applied to the altitude for this condition. A combined correction for nonstandard air temperature and nonstandard atmospheric pressure is given on page A4 of the *Nautical Alamanac*. If the correction is to be applied to the refraction, reverse the sign. This correction varies with atmospheric presssure and altitude of the celestial body and is applicable to all celestial bodies, regardless of the method of observation. However, except for extreme pressures or low altitudes, this correction is not usually applied unless results of unusual accuracy are desired.

AUGMENTATION—If a celestial body is on the observer's horizon, its distance is approximately the same as from the center of the earth; but if the body is on the zenith, its distance is less by about the radius of the earth. Therefore, the semidiameter increases as the altitude becomes greater.

This increase is called augmentation. For the moon, the augmentation from horizon to zenith is about 0.3 at the mean distance of the moon. At perigee it is about $2''$ greater, and at apogee about $2''$ less. Augmentation of the sun from horizon to zenith is about 1/24 of one second of arc. For planets it is correspondingly small, varying with the positions of the planets and the earth in their orbits. At any altitude the augmentation is equal to the sine of the altitude times the value at the zenith. Augmentation increases the size of the semidiameter correction, whether positive or negative. It is included in the moon correction tables on the inside back cover and facing page of the *Nautical Almanac*.

BACK SIGHT—An altitude measured by facing away from the celestial body being observed may be used when an obstruction, such as another vessel, obscures the horizon under the body, when that horizon is indistinct, or when observations are made in both directions, either to determine dip or to avoid error due to suspected abnormal dip. Such an observation is possible only when the arc of the sextant is sufficiently long to permit measurement of the angle, which is the supplement of the altitude. For such an observation of the sun or moon, the lower limb is observed when the image is brought below the horizon, appearing as a normal upper-limb observation, and vice versa. To correct such an altitude, subtract it from 180° and reverse the sign of correction of the first two groups (under sextant corrections), normally only index corrections and dip.

DIP—Dip of the horizon is the angle by which the visible horizon differs from the horizontal at the eye of the observer (sensible horizon). Thus it applies only when the visible horizon is used as a reference, and not when an artificial horizon, either internal or external to the sextant, is used. It applies to all celestial bodies. If the eye of the observer were at the surface of the earth, visible and sensible horizons would coincide, and there would be no dip. This is never the situation aboard ship, however, and at any height above the surface, the visible horizon is normally below the sensible horizon. Normally, an altitude measured from the visible horizon is too great, and the correction is negative. It increases with greater height of the observer's eye. Because of this, it is sometimes called height-of-eye correction. If there were no atmospheric refraction, dip would be the angle between the horizontal at the eye of the observer, and a straight line from this point tangent to the surface of the earth. The amount by which refraction alters dip varies with changing atmospheric conditions.

INDEX (IC)—Due primarily to lack of parallelism of the horizon and index mirrors at zero reading. Until the adjustment is disturbed, the index correction remains constant for all angles and is applicable to all angles measured by the instrument. It may be either positive or negative. Normally, artificial-horizon sextants do not have index corrections.

IRRADIATION—When a bright surface is observed adjacent to a darker one, a physiological effect in the eye causes the brighter area to appear to be larger than is actually the case; conversely, the darker area appears smaller. This is called irradiation. Since the sun is considerably brighter than the sky background, the sun appears larger than it really is; and when the sky is considerably brighter than the water, the horizon appears slightly depressed. The effects on the horizon and lower limb of the sun are in the same direction and tend to cancel each other, while the effect on the upper limb of the sun is in the opposite direction to that on the horizon and tends to magnify the effect.

PARALLAX—Parallax is the difference in apparent position of a point as viewed from two different places. If one of the nearer stars were observed from the earth and from the sun, it would appear to change slightly with respect to the background of more-distant stars. This is called heliocentric parallax or stellar parallax. The nearest star has a parallax of less than 1″. Even if the value were greater, no correction to sextant altitudes would be needed, for the difference would be reflected in the tabulated position of the body. However, positions of celestial bodies are given relative to the center of the earth, while observations are made from its surface. The difference in apparent position from these two points is called geocentric parallax. The maximum value for a visible body occurs when the body in on the horizon. At this position the value is called horizontal parallax (HP). Since the earth is an oblate spheroid and not a sphere, the parallax varies slightly over different parts of the earth. The value at the equator, called equatorial horizontal parallax, is greatest, and the value at the poles, called polar horizontal parallax, is least. The difference is not enough to be of practical navigational significance. As the distance of the moon varies, so does the parallax, becoming greater as the moon approaches each side of the value at mean distance. For the sun, mean equatorial horizontal parallax, called solar parallax, is 8″80. Daily values of horizontal parallax for the sun, moon, and planets are given in the *American Ephemeris* and *Nautical Almanac* to a precision of 0″01. In the *Nautical Almanac,* mean values for the sun are included in the two sun correction tables, given on the inside front cover and facing page. Horizontal parallax of the moon is tabulated at intervals of one hour on the daily pages. This value is used to enter the lower part of the moon correction table, on the inside back cover and facing page.

PHASE—Because of phase, the actual centers of planets and the moon may differ somewhat from the apparent centers. Average values for this difference are included in the additional corrections for Venus and Mars given on the inside front covers of the *Nautical Almanac.* They should be applied only when these bodies are observed during twilight. At other times, the magnitude and even the sign of the correction might differ from those tabulated, because of a different relationship between the body and the horizon. The phase correction for navigational planets other than Venus and Mars is too small to be significant. A phase correction may apply to observations of the moon if the apparent center of the body is observed, as with an artificial-horizon sextant. However, no provision is made for a correction in this case; the need for it can be avoided by observing one of the limbs of the body.

REFRACTION—Light, or other radiant energy, is assumed to travel in a straight line at uniform speed, if the medium in which it is traveling has uniform properties. But if light from space enters a medium of different properties, such as air, it is bent, and the source appears higher in the sky (*see* refraction). The correction is always negative and is given in the *Nautical Almanac*.

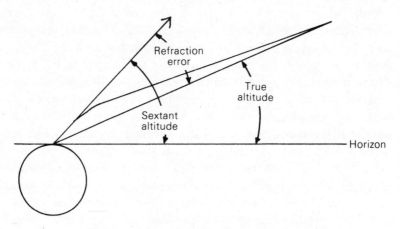

Atmospheric refraction causes bending of light rays

SEA–AIR TEMPERATURE DIFFERENCES—Under normal atmospheric conditions, temperature and pressure both decrease at standard rates with increase in height above the surface. Accordingly, the density of the atmosphere also decreases at a standard rate, which is uniform over the heights encountered aboard ship. The effect of refraction upon dip, as given in the tables, is based upon the standard rate. When there is a difference between sea and air temperature, the air is warmed or cooled by the water, upsetting the normal rate of decrease near the surface. The effect is greater as the temperature differences increase. If conditions are not too extreme, the dip is altered, but observations may seem normal. If the water is warmer than the air, the horizon is depressed and the dip is increased. Under these conditions the measured altitudes are too great. Therefore, as a correction to the altitude, the sea-air temperature difference correction is negative when the water is warmer than the air. When the air is warmer, the reverse is true, and the altitude correction is positive.

SEMIDIAMETER (SD)—Semidiameter of a celestial body is half the angle subtended at the observer's eye by the visible disk of the body.

Because the position of the lower or upper limb (edge) of the sun with respect to the visible horizon can be judged with greater precision than that of its center, it is customary to observe one of the limbs and apply a correction for semidiameter. The semidiameter of the sun varies from a little less than 15ʹ.8 early in July, when the earth is at its greatest distance from the sun, to nearly 16ʹ.3 early in January, when the earth is nearest the sun. In the *Nautical Almanac,* the semidiameter of the sun is given to the nearest 0ʹ.1 at the bottom of the GHA column. The altitude correction tables of the sun, given on the inside front cover and facing page, are divided into two parts, to be used during different periods of the year. The mean semidiameter of each period is included in the tables of both upper- and lower-limb corrections. The semidiameter each day is listed to the nearest 0ʹ.01 in the *American Ephemeris* and *Nautical Almanac.* In the *Air Almanac* the semidiameter to the nearest 0ʹ.1 is given near the lower-right-hand corner of each daily page.

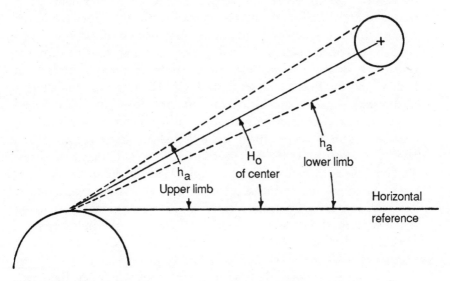

Effect of semidiameter on the altitude of a body

sextant index error (IE):

    BY SEA HORIZON—Index error should be determined each time the sextant is used. In the daytime, this is usually done by an observation of the horizon. With the index arm set at 0° and the sextant vertical, the horizon is observed. In nearly all instances the horizon will not appear as a continuous line in the direct and reflected views. The micrometer drum is adjusted until the reflected and direct images of the horizon coincide, forming a straight line. The amount of index error is read in minutes and tenths and used as the index correction (IC). If IE is positive, the micrometer drum reads more than 0.0' and the sign of the IC is negative; if the micrometer drum reads less than 0.0' the error is negative and the sign of the correction is positive.

INDEX ERROR BY A STAR—With the index set approximately at zero, direct the telescope at a low-lying star; superimpose the true and reflected stars and read the vernier or the micrometer drum. If the reading is exactly zero, there is no index error. Should the reading be "on" the arc, for example 2', then 2' would be subtracted. It would be written as IE+2', IC−2'. Should the reading, however, be 58' (2' "off" the arc), then 2' would be added to observed angles, and written as IC + 2', IE−2'.

INDEX ERROR BY SEA HORIZON—The index error may be found both by vertical and by horizontal angles in which the sun's diameter is measured both "on" (behind the zero mark) and "off" (forward of the zero mark) the arc. It is generally more convenient to observe horizontal diameters because it is awkward to observe the sun at high altitudes, and at low altitudes vertical diameters may be distorted by refraction. Hold the sextant horizontal; set the index to 32' (approximate diameter of the sun) "on" the arc. Bring the left limb (edge) of the reflected image into exact contact with the limb of the direct image. Read the angle and write it down. Bring the reflected sun across the actual sun until the opposite limbs are in contact (this will occur at about 32' "off" the arc). Note down this angle. Half the difference between the two angles is the index error. If the greater of these two angles is "on" the arc, then the index error is positive and is subtracted (−); if the greater of the two angles is "off" the arc, the index error is negative and is added (+).

sextant types:

CLAMPING SCREW—In the clamping-screw sextant, when the index bar is in approximately the required position on the arc, a thumbscrew attached to the back of the arc, called the clamping screw, is tightened. This holds the index bar firmly against the arc. The index bar may now be moved a short distance backwards and forwards along the arc by means of the tangent screw so that an exact reading may be made. The exact reading of the angle observed is read on a small arc, adjacent to the main arc, called a vernier. The vernier can be moved only to the limit of the tangent screw. This is inconvenient in practice because frequently, when altitudes are being observed, the screw gets to the end of its thread and it is necessary to unclamp, turn the screw back to the middle of its thread, and restart the observation.

ENDLESS TANGENT—This type is an improvement over the clamping screw, because by pressing (or keeping pressed between thumb and forefinger) a quick release at the foot of the index arm, one can move it readily along the arc. When this has been done, the tangent screw can be brought into play, and as this has an endless thread, the index arm can be moved slowly along from one end of the arc to the other without interruption. Even though the clamping screw has been eliminated by a quick release, the sextant still has to be read by a vernier.

MICROMETER DRUM—Known also as the micrometer tangent-screw sextant. The tangent screw moves the index along the arc, which shows the whole degrees of observed angle, while the micrometer shows minutes and tenths. This is the modern type of instrument in which the index arm is first of all fixed at a rough position in the same way as the endless tangent-screw sextant by a quick-release clamp. The tangent screw is worked by a micrometer screw fitted with a large

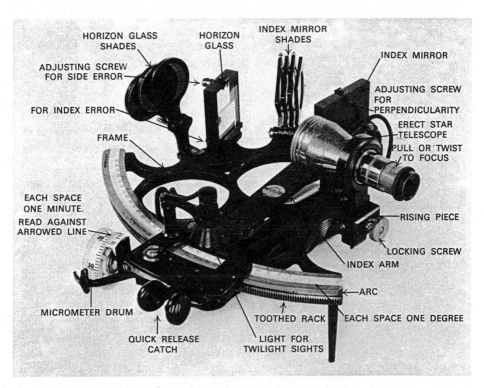

Parts of a micrometer sextant

micrometer head or drum (about an inch in diameter), on which minutes of arc are marked in black on a white ground, the graduations being easily discernible at arm's length in daylight. Whole degrees are read from the arc and the minutes from the micrometer head, thus dispensing entirely with the vernier and its tiny magnifying glass.

sextant usage:

SWINGING THE ARC—When the sun is to be observed, the sextant is initially set at 0°, and then it is held vertically in the right hand with the line of sight directed at the sea horizon below the sun. Suitable shade glasses are moved into position, depending on the brightness of the horizon and of the sun, and the index arm is moved by means of the quick release until the image appears in the horizon glass alongside the direct view of the horizon. Next, the micrometer drum is slowly rotated until the sun appears to be resting exactly on the horizon. To check the perpendicularity of the sextant, the instrument is then tilted slightly to either side around the axis of the telescope, causing the sun to appear to swing in an arc across the horizon. This is called swinging the arc. While one swings the arc several times, the image of the sun is adjusted so that at the bottom of the arc it is tangent to the horizon, and the altitude is read.

TAKING HORIZONTAL ANGLES—Three objects marked on a chart are required, and horizontal angles are measured between the middle one and that on either side of it. This gives a fix independent of the compass. To find the horizontal angle between two objects, hold the sextant horizontally (flat), mirrors upward, and bring the reflection of the right-hand object directly below the left-hand object seen through the plain part of the horizon glass. To pick up the reflection of the right-hand object, set the index bar at zero, and look directly toward the left-hand object. If it is necessary to reflect the left-hand object over the right-hand object, the sextant must be held upside down.

TAKING VERTICAL ANGLES—Set the index bar at zero. Look directly at the object and, by moving the tangent screw (or micrometer-drum), bring the reflection of the upper part of the object (seen in the silvered half of the horizon glass) down to the level of the lower part of the object (seen through the plain glass in the horizon mirror), generally the horizon. When observing the sextant angle of a lighthouse, it is the center of the glass lamp that must be reflected down to the sea (high-water mark should be strictly accurate) and not the top of the lighthouse. In practice, no allowance is made for height of tide or height of eye, as by ignoring these the observer is led to believe he is closer to the object than he really is, and therefore has an added

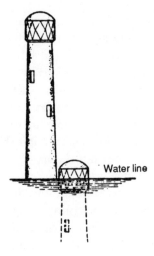

Water line

Taking the vertical angle

margin of safety. The height of the lighthouse and headlands, above the high water, are shown on the chart in the light lists.

THREE-POINT PROBLEM—Normally, three charted objects are selected for measuring horizontal sextant angles to determine the observer's position, one of the objects being common to each angular measurement. With simultaneous or nearly simultaneous measurements of the horizontal angles between each pair of objects, the observer establishes two circles of position. For each pair of objects there is only one circle that passes through the two objects and the observer's position. The solution of what is known as the three-point problem is affected by placing the hairlines of the arms of a plastic three-arm protractor over the three observed objects on the chart. With the arms so placed, the center of the protractor disk is over the observer's position on the chart at the time of the measurements. In plotting the three-point fix without a three-arm protractor, the procedure is to draw the circles of equal angle (*see entry*).

ship motion—In perfectly calm water a carefully steered ship moves along a straight course. A point that corresponds to the center of gravity of the ship also moves along this straight line at a constant velocity. In a wave system, however, this point deviates from this simple, straight-line motion in six ways: (1) heave, the up-and-down motion of this point as it travels along; (2) surge, the fore-and-aft motion of this point, as the ship speeds up and slows down when she encounters waves; (3) sway, the athwartship motion as the point departs from a straight-line path; (4) roll, the athwartship rotation about the point which occurs as the ship heels first to one side and then to the other; (5) pitch, the fore-and-aft rotation about the point which occurs as the bow and stern alternately rise and fall; and (6) yaw, the horizontal rotation about this point which occurs as the direction of the ship's keel is deflected from the direction of her course. The first three motions are translational motions; the last three are rotational motions. In other words, the first three motions are such that the center of gravity departs from a straight line, and the last three motions are such that the center of gravity does not depart from its position.

shoran—A form of secondary radar using two beacons located ashore and an indicator aboard a ship to measure the distance from each beacon. By this means two distances are continually available, permitting rapid determination of position. Special charts are not needed, but where they have been provided they show a number of circles centered upon each beacon. Approximate positions can be plotted by inspection. The name "shoran" was derived from "short-range navigation." Because of the high frequency used (230–310 mHz), shoran is limited in range by the curvature of the earth.

sidereal hour angle (SHA)—The angle between the hour circle of the first point of Aries and the hour circle of a body measured westward along the arc of the equinoctial, expressed in degrees from 0 to 360. "Sidereal" means "of or pertaining to the stars," and the SHA for fifty-seven navigational stars is tabulated in the *Nautical Almanac*. SHA, unlike the other hour angles, does not increase with time but remains relatively constant. The reason for this is that the hour circles between which the measurement is made are traveling at practically the same speed and thus have a relative speed of nearly zero.

sidereal time—Sidereal time uses the first point of Aries (vernal equinox) as its celestial reference point. Since the earth revolves around the sun, and since the direction of the earth's rotation and revolution are the same, it completes a rotation with respect to the stars in less time (about $3^m56\overset{s}{.}6$) than with respect to the sun, and during one revolution about the sun (one year) it makes one complete rotation more with respect to the stars than with the sun. This accounts for the daily shift of the stars nearly 1° westward each night. Hence, a sidereal day is shorter than a solar day, and its hours, minutes, and seconds are correspondingly shorter. The sun is at the first point of Aries at the time of the vernal equinox, about March 21. However, since the solar day begins when the sun is over the lower branch of the meridian, apparent solar and sidereal time differ by twelve hours at the vernal equinox. Each month thereafter, sidereal time gains about two hours on solar time. By the time of the summer solstice, about June 21, sidereal time is six hours behind solar time. By the time of the autumnal equinox, about September 23, the two times are together, and by the time of the winter solstice, about December 22, the sidereal time is six hours ahead of solar time.

sight reduction—The process of deriving from a celestial observation the information needed for establishing a line of position is called sight reduction. The observation itself consists of measuring the altitude of a celestial body and noting the time. The process of finding a line of position may be divided into six steps: (1) Correction of sextant altitude. (2) Determination of Greenwich hour angle (GHA) and declination. (3) Selection of assumed position (AP) and finding final local hour angle (LHA) or meridian angle (t) at that AP. (4) Computation of altitude and azimuth at the AP. (5) Comparison of computed and observed altitudes. (6) Plot of the line of position. The expression is often limited to the tables for computation of altitude and azimuth. A great variety of such tables exists. Although the dead reckoning (DR) or estimated position (EP) can be used, one can avoid unnecessary interpolation when using modern sight-reduction tables by selecting an AP that will result in two of three variables being whole numbers. In these tables, altitudes and azimuths are given for each whole degree of latitude and each whole degree of either meridian angle or local hour angle. Therefore, the whole degree of latitude nearest to the DR or EP at the time of the sight is selected as the assumed latitude (aL). The assumed longitude (aλ) is also selected so that no minutes of arc will remain after it is applied to GHA to make LHA.

"Sight Reduction Tables" (publication no. 229)—A set of tables entitled "Sight Reduction Tables for Marine Navigation," generally referred to as "Pub. 229" (and sometimes by their former number, H.O. 229). They are inspection tables of precomputed altitudes and azimuths. The publication is a joint U.S.–British project involving the U.S. Naval Oceanographic Office, the U.S. Naval Observatory, and the Royal Greenwich Observatory; volumes with identical tabular contents are published separately in England. The publication no. 229 tables are in six volumes, arranged by latitude. Each volume contains data for a 16° band of latitude, north or south, with an overlap of 1° between volumes. In each volume, the latitudes are separated into two "zones" as shown on the next page.

Publication no. 229 is designed to provide computed altitudes (Hc) correct to the nearest 0.1′ when all corrections are employed, and azimuth angle to 0.1° for all combinations of latitude, local hour angle

Vol. no.	First zone of latitude	Second zone of latitude
1	0° – 7°	8° – 15°
2	15° – 22°	23° – 30°
3	30° – 37°	38° – 45°
4	45° – 52°	53° – 60°
5	60° – 67°	68° – 75°
6	75° – 82°	83° – 90°

(measured westward from the observer's celestial meridian through 360°), and declination at a uniform interval of 1° in each of these arguments. It may be used for reduction from DR position to the same degree of precision, and directions for such reduction are given in each volume. However, it is primarily intended to be used with an assumed position (AP). The latitude of the AP is the integral degree nearest the vessel's DR or EP latitude; its longitude is selected to give a whole degree of local hour angle within 30' of the vessel's DR or EP longitude. These tables offer maximal precision and also permit the reduction of an observation of any navigational body, at any altitude, including negative ones; there are no limitations of latitude, hour angle, or declination.

solar time—The period of the earth's rotation relative to the sun is called the solar day. The solar year is based on the period of the earth's revolution about the sun, which requires approximately 365.5 days. Mean solar time is based on an imaginary sun, termed the mean sun, which has an hour circle moving westward along the celestial equator

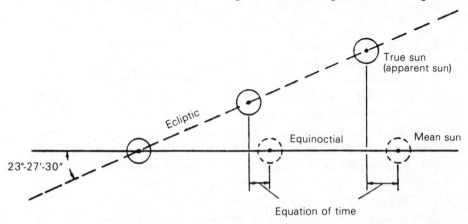

Relationship of mean to apparent solar time

at a constant rate. Mean solar time is nearly equal to the average apparent solar time; it is the time kept by the ship's chronometers and the great majority of timepieces. The difference between the apparent and the mean day is never as great as a minute, but it is cumulative, so that the difference between suns (equation of time) amounts to approximately a quarter hour at certain times of the year.

solstices—When the sun reaches its maximum northern declination (23.5 N), on or about June 22, the moment is spoken of as the summer solstice (the beginning of summer). When the sun reaches its maximum southern declination (23.5 S), on or about December 22, we speak of the time as the winter solstice (the beginning of winter).

sonar (SOund NAvigation Ranging)—Operates in the same manner as the echo sounder, except that it radiates its signal in a horizontal, rather than a vertical, direction. Excellent ranges on underwater objects may be obtained with sonar, and as the sonar transducer can be rotated horizontally, accurate bearings may also be obtained. Sonar can be of great assistance in piloting in thick weather, particularly in rocky areas. In Arctic regions, sonar is sometimes helpful in locating ice when steaming at low speed, as approximately nine-tenths of the ice is located below the water. Large bergs may sometimes be detected at a range of 6,000 yards (3 miles) or more, but the service range is usually less.

sounding (*see* echo sounding)—The most important use of sounding is to determine whether the depth is sufficient to provide a reasonable margin of safety for the vessel. Under favorable conditions, soundings can be a valuable aid in establishing the position of a vessel. If the echo sounder produces a continuous recording of the depth, called a bottom profile, this can be matched to the chart in the vicinity of the course line.

sound velocity—The rate at which sound moves through a medium, usually expressed in feet per second. The velocity of sound in sea water is a function of temperature, salinity, and the changes in pressure associated with changes in depth. An increase in any of these factors tends to increase the velocity. Sound propagates at 4,742 feet per second at 32°F, one atmosphere of pressure, and a salinity of 35 parts per million (PPM).

speed curves—Logs are commonly used on sailboats and on some powerboats whose owners like to have a direct speed indication at all times. The majority of powerboat operators, however, make use of the speed of the main engine, indicated by tachometer. The relationship between engine speed (rpm) and boat speed depends on many factors, including the shape of the hull, condition of the underwater surfaces, loading, fore-and-aft and lateral trim. Therefore, a graph known as a speed curve must be prepared relating engine speeds to boat speeds. Speed trials may be run on one of the measured-mile courses laid out by the Coast Guard or on any straight run of a mile or more between charted markers. A suitable engine speed is selected, and the boat is then put on her proper course with the first marker well ahead, to ensure a steady speed by the time the first marker comes abeam. Runs should be made in pairs, in opposite directions, to eliminate the effects of wind and current. Each pair should be made in quick succession to avoid changes in wind and current. The two speeds calculated from each pair of runs are averaged to obtain the speed in still water.

speed triangle—A diagram consisting of properly related straight lines called vectors. These indicate direction and rate of travel. The center of the diagram is labeled with the small letter "e," for the earth, the reference for movement. The course and speed of one's own ship is represented by the vector "er," while the course and speed of the other (target) ship is represented by the vector "em." The vector "rm" then represents the direction of relative movement (DRM) and the speed of relative movement (SRM). All course and speed vectors are drawn from "e." The directions of the vectors are also shown by arrows; the vector "rm" is always drawn in the direction from "r" toward "m."

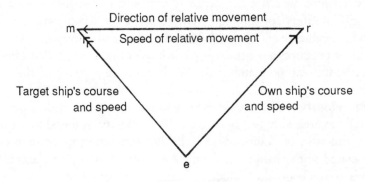

Speed or vector triangle

split fix—On occasion, the mariner must obtain what is called a split fix through observations of two pairs of charted objects, with no objects being in common. As with the three-point fix, the mariner obtains two circles of equal angle (*see entry*).

stable platform—(*See* inertial navigation.)

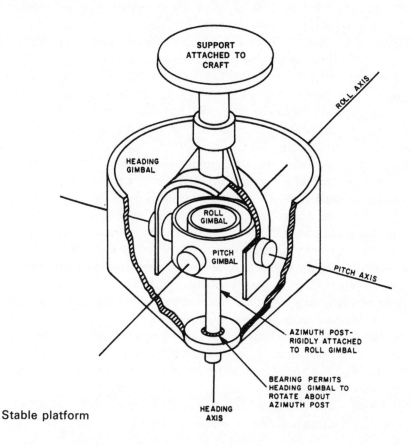

Stable platform

stadimeter (specialized sextant)—For determining ranges of 200 to 10,000 yards, the stadimeter is utilized. The principle employed is that in a right triangle, if one knows the length of one leg and the value of the opposite angle, the length of the other leg may be computed. On the index arm of the stadimeter the height of a shoreside object in feet is set; this moves the index mirror through a small arc and thus introduces one needed value. Through a sighting telescope, a direct image of the object appears on the left and a reflected image appears on the right. By moving a micrometer drum, one brings the top of the reflected image into coincidence with the bottom of the direct image. This movement of the micrometer drum measures the subtended arc (the second needed value) and automatically solves the triangle for the length of the adjacent leg (the distance to the object). From the drum, the range in yards is read directly.

star—The average navigator regularly uses not more than perhaps 20 to 30 stars. The *Nautical Almanac* gives full navigational information on 19 first-magnitude stars and 38 second-magnitude stars, in addition to Polaris. Abbreviated information is given for 115 more. Additional stars are listed in the *American Ephemeris* and *Nautical Almanac* and in various star catalogues. About 6,000 stars of the sixth magnitude or brighter (on the entire celestial sphere) are visible to the unaided eye on a clear, dark night. Stars are designated by one or more of the following: (1) Name. Most names now used were given by the ancient Arabs, and some by the Greeks and Romans. (2) Bayer's names. Most bright stars have been given a Greek letter followed by the possessive form of the name of the constellation, as α Cygni (Deneb, the brightest star in the constellation Cygnus, the Swan). Roman letters are used when there are not enough Greek letters. Usually the letters are assigned in order of brightness within the constellation, but in some cases the letters are assigned in another order where it seems logical to do so. (3) Flamsteed's number. A similar system, accommodating more stars, numbers them in each constellation, from west to east, in the order in which they cross the celestial meridian. (4) Catalogue number. Stars are sometimes designated by the name of a star catalogue and the number of the star as given in that catalogue. In these catalogues stars are listed in order from west to east, without regard to constellation, starting with the hour circle of the vernal equinox. This system is used primarily for dimmer stars having no other designation.

star charts—Star charts are based upon the celestial-equator system of coordinates, using declination and sidereal hour angle (or right ascension). The zenith of the observer is at the intersection of the parallel of declination equal to his latitude, and the hour circle coinciding with his celestial meridian. A star globe is similar to a celestial sphere, but with stars (and often constellations) shown instead of geographical positions. On a star globe the celestial sphere is shown as it would appear to an observer outside the sphere. Constellations appear reversed. Star charts may show a similar view, but more often they are based upon the view from inside the sphere, as seen from the earth. On these charts, north is at the top, as with maps, but east is to the left and west is to the right.

NAUTICAL ALMANAC—The *Nautical Almanac* has four star charts. The two principal ones are on the polar azimuthal equidistant projection, one centered on each celestial pole. Each chart extends from its pole to declination 10°. Below each polar chart is an auxiliary chart on the Mercator projection, from 30°N to 30°S. The horizon is

90° from the zenith. The charts can also be used to determine the location of a star relative to the surrounding stars.

star identifier—*See* Rude star finder.

  KOTLARIC'S—A booklet of eighteen pairs of star charts with a plastic template enclosed. It depicts the 57 selected (navigational) stars plus 125 other stars, for a total of 182 stars. All of the 173 stars listed in the *Nautical Almanac* are depicted. This star finder provides greater reliability in identification than Rude. Each pair of star charts shows the Western and Eastern hemispheres separately, using a stereographic projection on a plane tangent to the celestial equator. The stars are plotted with different symbols, according to their magnitude; selected stars in black, the others in green. Stars in constellations are connected by a broken yellow line; paths to find important alignments are plotted with solid yellow lines. Since the list of stars near the back of the *Nautical Almanac* is not compiled in alphabetical order, an alphabetical index of stars with rounded values of SHA and declination is included with the star finder to facilitate location in the list.

stereographic projection—If points on the surface of the earth are projected onto a tangent plane from a point on the side of the earth opposite the point of tangency, a stereographic projection results. The scale of a stereographic projection increases with distance from the point of tangency, but more slowly than in a gnomonic projection. An

A stereographic map of the Western Hemisphere

entire hemisphere can be shown on a stereographic projection without excessive distortion. As in other azimuthal projections, great circles through the point of tangency appear as straight lines. All other circles, including meridians and parallels, appear as circles or arcs of circles. The principal navigational use of the stereographic projection is for charts of the polar regions and devices for mechanical or graphical solutions of the navigational triangle.

sun—The sun, with a diameter of 864,400 miles, situated 93 million miles from earth, provides the basis of the earth's timekeeping and is the celestial body most frequently observed in navigation. The sun does not rise and set daily in the true east and west (except for two days in the year), because it does not follow the path of the celestial equator; rather, its path (the ecliptic) is S-shaped, reaching northward to a maximum declination of 23.5°N about June 21 and retreating to 23.5°S about December 22, crossing the equator at the approximate mid-dates of September 23 and March 21, the latter time being the vernal equinox, or first point of Aries. Because the sun is relatively close to the earth, its diameter is prominent, and a difference of altitude will be registered on a sextant depending upon whether the center, the lower limb (bottom edge) or, the upper limb (top edge) is measured from the horizon. Most observations are made of the lower limb, but at times the upper limb is more convenient. Correction tables are therefore given in all almanacs to find the semidiameter, or center, when a limb has been observed. Greenwich hour angle (GHA) and declination of the sun are tabulated in the almanacs. Observations of the sun are customarily taken at the approximate times it is on the prime vertical (90° east or 270° west of the observer) to establish longitude, and at or near the time of local apparent noon (LAN), which provides latitude since the sun is then either due north or south depending upon the observer's latitude. Observations at other times are taken to obtain bearings for a running fix, often by combination with the latitude or longitude observations.

super high frequency radio signal (SHF)—*See* radar.

T

taffrail (patent) log—Consists of a rotator and sinker attached to a registering device located on an after rail or taffrail. Towed sufficiently far astern to avoid the wake, the rotator turns by the action of the water against its spiral fins. Through the line, the register, which is calibrated to indicate miles and tenths of miles, is driven. The log tends to read slightly high in a head sea and slightly low in a following sea.

telescopic alidade—Similar to a bearing circle, only having a telescope in lieu of sight vanes. A reticule within the telescope, together with a prism, facilitates reading bearings while the telescope magnifies distant objects. When a ship is yawing, it is easy to lose sight of an object using the telescope alidade because the field of vision is very limited. To overcome this handicap, the telescope can be mounted on a compass card driven by the master gyro. It is possible then to set the alidade on a desired bearing and observe an object without having the telescope deviate from the bearing because of the motion of the ship. This is the self-synchronous alidade.

thermograph—A mechanical device consisting of a metallic element whose curvature varies with temperature. One end of the curved element is connected to a lever, which has a pen at its end. The pen rests on a cylinder, which rotates by means of an inner clockwork. A sheet of graph paper is wrapped around the drum and is divided into days and hours, horizontally, and temperature, vertically. Changes in temperature cause variations in curvature of the metal element, which deflects the pen arm upward or downward, and a line is traced that indicates the temperature at any time during the recording interval.

thermometers—Two thermometers are often mounted together in an instrument shelter, a box with louvered sides to protect the instruments from direct rays of the sun and other conditions that would render their readings inaccurate. One of the thermometers has its bulb covered with a wet fabric. The rate of evaporation of the water is dependent on the relative humidity of the air or on the relative amount of water vapor in the air. The evaporating water cools the bulb of the thermometer; the result is a lower temperature. When one knows the air temperature (reading of the dry-bulb thermometer) and the difference between this and the reading of the wet-bulb thermometer, one can easily determine the relative humidity and dew point (the temperature to which the air must be cooled for condensation to take place). Relative humidity and dew point are of interest to the mariner in connection with the formation of fog. This combination of wet and dry thermometers is known as a psychrometer.

three-point problem—*See* sextant usage.

tidal constants—Tidal relations that remain essentially the same for any particular locality.

tidal current—Horizontal flow of water resulting from the rise and fall of tides, its phases being directly related to, but seldom coincident with, a tidal movement. A tidal current moving upstream or toward shore is a flood current; the reverse movement is an ebb. Slack current is comparable to the stand of a tide, the motionless period before reverse of direction. Offshore, the current experienced may be a combination of tidal and ocean current. In a restricted area (such as a river or estuary) a tidal current flows in opposite directions and is termed a reversing or hydraulic current. A tidal current in unrestricted waters is rotary, flowing through all points of the compass during the tidal period. Countercurrents and eddies are found near straits and bights. Tide rips are formed by a rapid current moving over an irregular bottom.

tidal-current charts—Tidal-current charts for U. S. harbors are published by the U.S. Coast and Geodetic Survey. Each of the nine sets consists of twelve charts, which depict the direction and speed of the tidal current for each hour of the tide cycle, thus presenting a comprehensive view of the tidal-current movement in the respective waterways as a whole, and supplying a means for determining for any time the direction and speed of the current. The charts are intended for use in connection with the tidal-current tables for the same areas, except for New York harbor, where the tide tables are to be used.

tidal-current tables—Published annually by the U.S. Coast and Geodetic Survey, tabulate daily predictions of the times of slack water and times and speeds of maximum flood and ebb currents for a number of waterways. Also include other useful information, such as methods for obtaining the speed of a tidal current at any time and the duration of slack water. Information on the Gulf Stream is included in the tidal-current tables for the Atlantic coast of North America. Tidal-current tables are available in two separate volumes for the Atlantic coast of North America and the Pacific coast of North America and Asia.

tidal cycles—Tides go through a number of cycles. The shortest cycle (semidiurnal), completed in about twelve hours and twenty-five minutes, extends from any phase of a tide to the next recurrence of the same phase. During a lunar day (averaging twenty-four hours and fifty minutes) there are thus two highs and two lows at places having semidiurnal tides.

tidal reference planes—The expression "height of tide" is not to be confused with "depth of water." The latter refers to the vertical distance from the surface of the water to the bottom; the former refers to the vertical distance from the surface of the water to an arbitrarily chosen reference plane or datum, such plane being based on a selected low-water average. The charted depth is the vertical distance from this reference plane to the bottom. A second reference plane, based on a chosen high-water average, is used as a basis for the measurement of heights and clearances above the water. If the adopted low-water average is mean low water, and the high-water average is mean high water, then the difference between these two planes is called the mean range of the tide. These terms are always shown on the chart. It should be remembered that the water level is occasionally below the reference plane. That is, the depth of water can be less than the charted depth. This is indicated by a minus sign placed before the height of tide in the tide tables. When there is a negative tide, one subtracts the numerical value of the height of tide from the charted depth to find the depth of water. In many coastal areas, the actual height of tide at any time may be influenced by winds from a particular direction, especially if the winds are strong and persist for several days. The reference plane chosen differs with the locality and the country making the survey on which the chart is based. The principal planes used are:

Mean low water, the average of all low tides. The plane is used on NOS (National Ocean Survey) charts of the Atlantic coast, and on nearly all DMAHC (Defense Mapping Agency Hydrographic Center) charts. The Gulf Coast low-water datum is essentially the same plane.

Mean lower low water, the average of the lower of the two daily tides. This plane is used on charts of the Pacific coast of the United States, the Hawaiian islands, the Philippines, and Alaska.

Mean low-water springs, the average of the low waters at spring (full and new-moon) tides, or mean lower-low-water springs, the average of the lower of the two daily low tides at spring. It is not necessary to know the reference planes of various localities because the tide tables are always based on the same plane used for the largest-scale charts of the locality.

tide(s)—The oceans are affected by the gravitational attraction between the earth and the moon, and by the centrifugal forces resulting from their revolution around a common center (bary center), a point located within the earth about 810 miles (1,500 km) beneath the surface. The gravitational and centrifugal forces are in balance, and as a result the earth and the moon neither collide nor fly away from each other in space. Although the earth-moon system as a whole is in equilibrium, individual particles on the earth are not. The centrifugal force is the same everywhere, since all points on the earth's surface describe the same motion around the common center of mass; these forces are all parallel to each other and to a line joining the center of the earth and the moon. On the other hand, the gravitational force is not everywhere the same; particles nearer the moon feel a greater attractional force than those on the far side of the earth; these forces are not parallel, each being in the direction from that particle to the center of the moon. As the earth rotates each day on its axis, the line of direction toward the moon changes, and so each point has two highs and two lows.

Tides are the result of lunar and solar influences. When these two bodies are in line with the earth, as at new and full moon, the two influences act together, and the result is higher-than-average high tides and lower-than-normal low tides; these are called spring tides. When the directions of the sun and moon are 90° apart, as at first- and third-quarter (half) moons, the sun partially counteracts the moon's influence. At these times, the high tides are lower and low tides are higher than normal; these are neap tides. Since the moon revolves about the earth once each lunar month (roughly twenty-eight days), it transits any meridian on earth approximately every twenty-four hours and fifty minutes. This is the usual tidal period of two high waters and two low waters and is called a tidal day; the period for one high and one low is referred to as a tidal cycle. In actuality, the daily rotation of the earth on its axis has a frictional effect on the tides, so that high tides normally lag behind the time of the moon's transit across the meridian of any given location. Tides in the open oceans are only one to two feet high (with tides on the far side being about 5 percent less than those on the near side). Coastal tides are often much greater, in some places as much as 40 or 50 feet (12 to 15 m) more. This is the result of large landmasses restricting the flow of water, of ocean-bottom and shoreline variations, of the internal friction (viscosity) of the flowing water, and other factors. These interrelate to establish natural periods of oscillation for seas, gulfs, large bays, and estuaries, which enhance the basic tidal influences.

tide tables—Tide tables for various parts of the world are published in four volumes by the U.S. Coast and Geodetic Survey. Each volume is arranged as follows: Table 1 contains a complete list of the predicted times and heights of the tide for each day of the year at a number of designated reference stations. Table 2 gives differences and ratios, which can be applied to the tidal information for the reference stations to make predictions for a large number of subordinate stations. Table 3 provides information for use in finding the approximate height of the tide at any time between high water and low water. Table 4 is a sunrise–sunset table at five-day intervals for various latitudes from 76°N to 60°S. Table 5 provides an adjustment to convert the local mean time of table 4 to zone or standard times. Table 6 (two volumes only) gives the zone time of moonrise and moonset for each day of the year at certain selected places. Table 7 gives certain astronomical data. In the two volumes not having moonrise-moonset tables, this is table 6.

time—For the most part, the navigator uses mean solar time, reckoned according to the travel of the mean sun with respect to one of three reference meridians: the Greenwich, or prime, meridian; the central

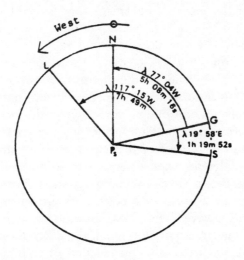

The difference in time between places is equal to the difference in their longitudes, converted to time units.

meridian of the time zone in which he is located; the meridian passing through his position. Time reckoned according to the position of the mean sun relative to the prime meridian is called Greenwich mean time (GMT). Time using the central meridians of the various time zones as reference is called zone time (ZT), and time using the observer's meridian as a reference is local mean time (LMT).

time, atomic (AT)—The principle of the atomic clock is that electromagnetic waves of a particular frequency are emitted when an atomic transition occurs. In 1967 the atomic second was defined by the Thirteenth General Conference on Weights and Measures as the duration of 9,192,631,770 periods of transition between two levels of the ground state of the cesium 133 atom. The atomic second became the unit of time in the International System of Units.

time, ephemeris (ET)—The uniform measure of time defined by the law of dynamics and determined in principle from the orbital motion of the planets, specifically the orbital motion of the earth as represented by Newcomb's *Tables of the Sun*. Ephemeris time is the time in which Newcomb's *Tables of the Sun* agree with observation. Ephemeris time is based on the ephemeris second, defined as $1/3155625.9747$ of the tropical year for 1900 January 0^d12^h ET. The ephemeris day is 86,400 ephemeris seconds. The ephemeris second is a fundamental invariable unit of time. The ephemeris time at any place is obtained by comparing observed positions of the sun, moon, and planets with gravitational predictions of their coordinates; observations of the moon are most effective for this purpose. Ephemeris time is used by astronomers for fundamental ephemerides (almanacs) of the sun, moon, and planets, but is not used by navigators.

time, local mean—Just as Greenwich mean time is mean solar time, measured with reference to the meridian of Greenwich, local mean time (LMT) is mean solar time measured with reference to a given (local) meridian. Local mean time was generally used after the introduction of time based on a mean sun, and every city kept time based on the mean sun's transit of that city's local meridian. As a result, a number of different times were used in a comparatively small geographic area. Before electronic communication, when travel was at the speed of a man, a horse, or a river, such disparities were of no real importance. However, when development made communication instantaneous and transportation rapid, the differences could no longer be tolerated; this led to the introduction of zone time (ZT).

time, sidereal—Time defined by the daily rotation of the earth with respect to the equinox or first point of Aries. Sidereal time is measured by the hour angle of the equinox, that is, the position of the equinox in its daily rotation. One rotation of the equinox (two consecutive upper-meridian transits) is a sidereal day; it is divided into twenty-four sidereal hours, reckoned from 0^h at upper transit, which is known as sidereal noon. The equinox is the intersection of the celestial equator and the ecliptic; the time measured by its daily rotation is apparent sidereal time. The position of the equinox is affected by the nutation (nodding) of the axis of rotation of the earth which introduces irregular inequalities into apparent sidereal time and the length of the sidereal day. The time measured by the daily motion of the mean equinox, which is affected only by secular (long-term) inequalities owing to the precession of the axis, is mean sidereal time. The average difference between apparent and mean sidereal time is only a little over a second, and its greatest daily change is a little more than a hundredth of a second.

time, zulu—In communications involving ships or activities in different time zones, it is common to use Z, or Greenwich mean time. This is popularly known as "zulu time," as Zulu is the International Phonetic Alphabet equivalent for the letter Z.

time and arc—One day represents one complete rotation of 360° of the earth with respect to a selected celestial point. Each day is divided into twenty-four hours of sixty minutes, each minute having sixty seconds. Any time interval, therefore, can be expressed as an angle (arc) of rotation, and vice versa. To convert one to the other:

Time	Arc
1 hour	15°
4 minutes	1°
1 minute	15'
4 seconds	1'
1 second	15"

time and hour angle—Both time and hour angle are a measure of the phase of the rotation of the earth, since both indicate the angular distance of a celestial point west of a terrestrial meridian. Hour angles are expressed in arc units and are measured from the upper branch of the celestial meridian. Sidereal time is also measured from the upper branch of the celestial meridian, but solar time is measured from the lower branch. Thus, solar and sidereal times differ by twelve hours; and solar and sidereal hour angles differ by 180°.

time and longitude—The mean sun crosses 360° of longitude in twenty-four hours, moving from east to west. In one hour it passes over 1/24 of the earth's meridians, or 15°. In one minute it covers 1/60 of 15°, or 15 minutes of arc; in four seconds of time it covers 1 minute of arc, and in one second, it covers 0.25' of arc. The time-arc relationship may be summarized in tabular form:

Time	Arc
24 hours	360°
12 hours	180°
1 hour	15°
1 minute	15'
4 seconds	1'
1 second	.25'–(15")

Because of the mean sun's motion from east to west, it is always later at places to the observer's east, and earlier at those to his west. The relationship between time and longitude can be used to determine the difference in local mean time between places in different longitudes.

time diagram—To assist the navigator in visualizing the relationship of the hour circles of the sun, the celestial body being observed, Greenwich, and his assumed position, an aid called the time diagram is frequently utilized. The diagram is a sketch of the earth centered on the North or South Pole, with the hour circles and meridians depicted as radial lines. By convention, the South Pole is generally selected as the center of the diagram. As an example, consider the time diagram shown below. The circumference of the circle represents the equator as seen from the South Pole, P_s, located at the center. East is in a clockwise direction, and west counterclockwise; all celestial bodies, therefore, can be imagined as revolving in a counterclockwise direction about the circle. By convention, the upper branch of the observer's meridian is always drawn as a solid vertical line extended up from the center; it is customarily labeled with a capital M, as shown. The dashed line extending down from the center is the lower branch of the observer's meridian, usually labeled with a lowercase m. After the observer's meridian has been drawn, the Greenwich meridian is located, based on the observer's assumed longitude. For this figure the observer's longitude was assumed to be 135° W, so the upper branch of the Greenwich meridian was drawn 135° clockwise from the observer's meridian (M). The upper branch of the prime meridian is ordinarily labeled with a capital G, while the lower branch, represented by a

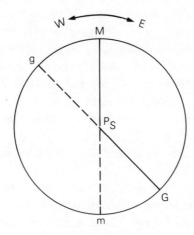

A time diagram

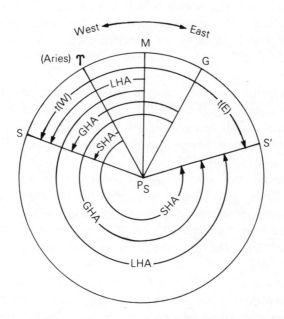

Time diagram. Local hour angle, Greenwich hour angle, and sidereal hour angle are measured westward through 360°. Meridian angle is measured eastward or westward through 180° and labeled E or W to indicate the direction of measurement.

second dashed line, is denoted by a lowercase g. The hour circle of the sun is next located on the diagram by reference to the time of the observation. In positioning the sun's hour circle, one may think of the time diagram as the face of a twenty-four hour clock, with m representing ZT 2400/0000 (midnight) and M 1200 ZT (noon).

time notation—The navigator states time on the basis of a twenty-four-hour rather than a twelve-hour clock; this removes the danger of confusing A.M. and P.M. To simplify writing, hours, minutes, and seconds are expressed in that order and are separated by dashes. Thus, a clock time of 10 hours, 57 minutes, and 17 seconds P.M. is written 22-57-17. If the number of hours, minutes, or seconds is less than 10, an 0 is placed in front of each so that the hour, minutes, and seconds are always expressed by two digits; a time of 4 hours, 9 minutes, and 7 seconds A.M. is written 04-09-07.

time signals—The U.S. National Bureau of Standards maintains two long-range radio stations (WWV and WWVH), which continuously transmit Greenwich time (GMT) by voice. The Canadian government radio station (CHU) transmits Eastern standard time (EST) by tone preceded by voice announcement in both English and French. WWV (Fort Collins, Colorado) transmits on 2.5, 5.0, 10.0, 15.0, 20.0, and 25.0 mHz. WWVH (Maui, Hawaii) transmits GMT on 2.5, 5.0, 10.0, and 20.0 mHz. CHU (Ottawa, Ontario) transmits EST on 3.33, 7.335, and 14.670 mHz.

Other time signals, often called time ticks, are broadcast from many stations throughout the world. Complete information on the time signals of all countries is given in "Radio Navigational Aids," DMAHC (Defense Mapping Agency Hydrographic Center) publications nos. 117A and 117B.

The selection of a frequency for best reception depends on the time of day and on atmospheric conditions. As a general rule, the 15 MHz band is satisfactory during daylight hours, while the 5 MHz band is usually better at night. The time broadcast is called Coordinated Universal Time (UTC), which for normal navigational purposes is GMT.

Universal time (UT) is the mean solar time on the Greenwich meridian reckoned in days of twenty-four mean solar hours, beginning with 0^h at midnight. Universal time, in principle, is determined by the average rate of the apparent daily motion of the sun relative to the meridian of Greenwich; but in practice universal time is computed from sidereal time. UTC is UT adjusted to compensate for tiny, unpredictable changes in the earth's rotational speed.

time zones—The introduction of zone time (ZT) served to straighten out the confusion caused by the multiplicity of different local mean times. In zone time, all the places in a given zone (a 15° band of longitude) keep time based on a specified meridian, usually the central meridian of the zone. Timepieces are reset only when one is moving into an adjoining time zone; they are advanced an hour per zone if travel is to the east and retarded an hour if travel is to the west.

At sea the central meridians selected for time zones are longitudes that are exact multiples of 15°. There are twenty-four of these central, or "standard," meridians, each one an hour apart, and the boundaries of each zone are 7.5° to each side of the zone's standard meridian. The zone description (ZD) of a zone is the correction to be applied to the time of that zone to obtain GMT. For example, between longitude 7.5° east and 7.5° west, the ZD is zero, and GMT will be used throughout the zone. In the zone bordered by longitudes 7°30′E and 22° 30′E, the standard meridian is λ15°E. ZT in this zone will differ from GMT by one hour and, the zone being east of the meridian of Greenwich, will be one hour later. One hour is subtracted from ZT to obtain GMT, and the ZD is (−1). Similarly, in the zone bordered by longitude 7°30′W and 22°30′W, the ZT differs from GMT by one hour, but as this zone is west of Greenwhich it is one hour earlier, and the ZD is (+1), as one hour must be added to obtain GMT. This procedure for determining the sign of time corrections for various zones is valid for any longitude; the sign of the ZD of any zone in east longitude is minus, and that of the ZD of any zone in west longitude is plus. The numerical value of the correction for a zone can be determined by dividing the longitude of its standard meridian by 15°. The ZD at a given position can be similarly determined; the longitude of the place is divided by 15°, and the whole number of the quotient is determined. If the remainder is less than 7°30′, the whole-number quotient establishes the numerical value of the ZD; if it is greater than 7°30′, the ZD is one more than the whole number of the quotient.

track (TR)—The path actually followed by a vessel, or the path of proposed travel. It differs from course (C) and course made good (CMG) by including distance as well as direction. A great circle that a vessel intends to follow is called a great-circle track.

transit, upper and lower—The passage of a celestial body across the upper branch of the observer's meridian is called upper transit. In the figure below, the sun at M is shown at the upper transit. Depending on the observer's latitude and the body's declination, at this instant the body is either due north, due south, or directly overhead of the observer. The passage of a celestial body across the lower branch of an observer's meridian is called the lower transit. In the figure below, the sun is also shown at lower transit, at M. At this instant the body will be either directly to his north, or south, or directly below him, again depending on his latitude and the body's declination. Bodies visible at the observer's position will be above the horizon at upper transit; the majority will be below the horizon at lower transit. Circumpolar stars may be above the horizon for both upper and lower transit for an observer who is not at the equator. At all times, the hemisphere of the earth facing the sun is in sunlight, and the other hemisphere is in darkness. The sun will be in upper transit on the central meridian of the half that is in sunlight, and it will be midday (noon) at that meridian; on the lower branch of the same meridian the sun will be in lower transit, and at that instant it will be midnight. Lower transit of the mean sun simultaneously makes the end of one day (24-00-00) and the beginning of the next (00-00-00). The transits of celestial bodies and the resultant time-arc relationships are, for navigational purposes, generally sketches on a time diagram rather than pictorally.

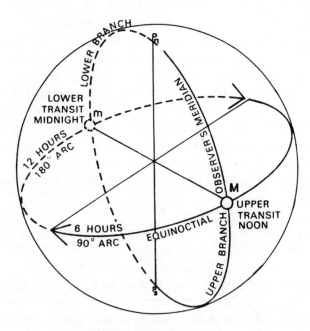

Upper and lower transit

transverse Mercator projection—A conformal cylindrical map projection in which points on the surface of a sphere or spheroid, such as the earth, are projected onto a cylinder tangent along a meridian. This projection is particularly useful for charts of polar regions and for those extending a relatively short distance from the tangent meridian. It is frequently used for star charts.

triangulation—A land-surveying technique that consists of the measurement of the angles of a series of triangles in order to compute latitudes and longitudes. To establish a triangulation between two distant locations, a baseline is measured and longitude and latitude determined for initial points at each end. The end points are then connected by a series of adjoining triangles to the distant location. All angles of the adjoining triangles are measured, and the longitude and latitude are computed of the vertex of each of the triangles, thereby establishing so-called triangulation stations or geodetic control stations.

turning bearing—During conditions when precise piloting is required, the navigator must know at what point the rudder must be put over, so that when allowance has been made for advance and transfer (sideways motion in a turn), the ship will steady on the desired heading at the time the desired track is reached. This is done by selecting an aid to navigation or a landmark ashore and predetermining the bearing at which the appropriate rudder angle should be ordered. Ideally, the object upon which the turning bearing is taken should be abeam at the time of starting the turn; this will give the greatest rate of change of bearing and hence be more precisely determinable. In actual practice, relative bearings from roughly 30° to 150°, port or starboard, can be used if care is exercised at the extremes. Preference is usually given to taking the bearing on the side toward which the turn is to be made. The navigator should commence the turn using a standard rudder. By so doing, a margin for error remains, and the rudder angle can be increased if the turn is commenced too late.

twilight—The period of incomplete darkness occurring just before sunrise and just after sunset. There are two kinds of twilight of concern in celestial navigation, differentiated by the position of the sun below the horizon at the darker limit. Civil twilight is the period extending from sunrise or sunset to the time at which the center of the sun is 6° below the celestial horizon. Nautical twilight is the period extending from sunrise or sunset to the time at which the center of the sun is 12° below the celestial horizon.

U

underwater terrain charting—A vital service a chart can perform is to describe the territory beneath the craft's hull. Using a combination of numbers, color codes, contour lines, abbreviations, and symbols, the chart tells a pilot all he needs to know about an area's undersea topography. Most of the numbers on the chart are the water's depth at mean low tide, taken at the spot by a hydrographic vessel. These soundings may be either in feet or in fathoms (a fathom equals six feet); the chart's legend will indicate which unit is used. Contour lines, which connect points of roughly equal depth, profile the bottom's shape; the lines are either numbered or coded according to depth. Color shadings also indicate depth, with the shallowest areas in the darkest tint. Rocks and reefs, and various other characteristics of the bottom, are marked by either standardized symbols or abbreviations. Cartographers choose from a selection of stylized notations like the ones shown below, to indicate underwater hazards. A sunken wreck, for example, may be shown either by a symbol or by an abbreviation plus a number that gives the wreck's depth. A dotted line around any symbol calls special attention to its hazardous nature. Since slightly different symbols often indicate the same hazard, the boatman should consult the complete list in the pamphlet entitled "Chart No. 1," published by the National Ocean Survey.

A system of cartographer's abbreviations, used alone or in combination, describe the composition of the bottom, allowing a skipper to pick the best holding ground. He should look for hard sand (hrd S), for example, to hold him securely, trying to avoid a rocky (rky) or weed-choked (Wd) bottom that could snag his anchor or allow it to drag.

Dangers

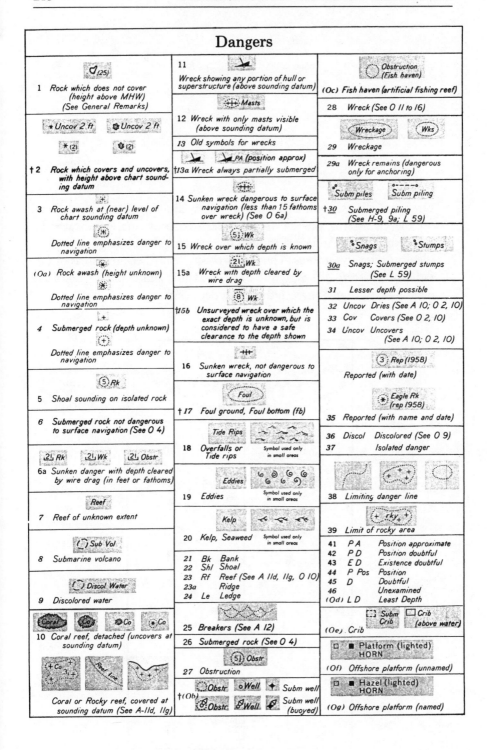

1 Rock which does not cover (height above MHW) (See General Remarks)	**11** Wreck showing any portion of hull or superstructure (above sounding datum)	(Oc) Fish haven (artificial fishing reef)
	12 Wreck with only masts visible (above sounding datum)	**28** Wreck (See O 11 to 16)
†2 Rock which covers and uncovers, with height above chart sounding datum	**13** Old symbols for wrecks	**29** Wreckage
	†13a Wreck always partially submerged	**29a** Wreck remains (dangerous only for anchoring)
3 Rock awash at (near) level of chart sounding datum	**14** Sunken wreck dangerous to surface navigation (less than 15 fathoms over wreck) (See O 6a)	**†30** Submerged piling (See H-9, 9a; L 59)
Dotted line emphasizes danger to navigation	**15** Wreck over which depth is known	
(Oa) Rock awash (height unknown)	**15a** Wreck with depth cleared by wire drag	**30a** Snags; Submerged stumps (See L 59)
Dotted line emphasizes danger to navigation	**†15b** Unsurveyed wreck over which the exact depth is unknown, but is considered to have a safe clearance to the depth shown	**31** Lesser depth possible
4 Submerged rock (depth unknown)		**32** Uncov Dries (See A 10; O 2, 10)
		33 Cov Covers (See O 2, 10)
Dotted line emphasizes danger to navigation	**16** Sunken wreck, not dangerous to surface navigation	**34** Uncov Uncovers (See A 10; O 2, 10)
5 Shoal sounding on isolated rock	**†17** Foul ground, Foul bottom (fb)	Reported (with date)
6 Submerged rock not dangerous to surface navigation (See O 4)	**18** Overfalls or Tide rips · Symbol used only in small areas	**35** Reported (with name and date)
6a Sunken danger with depth cleared by wire drag (in feet or fathoms)	**19** Eddies · Symbol used only in small areas	**36** Discol Discolored (See O 9)
		37 Isolated danger
7 Reef of unknown extent	**20** Kelp, Seaweed · Symbol used only in small areas	**38** Limiting danger line
8 Submarine volcano	**21** Bk Bank	**39** Limit of rocky area
	22 Shl Shoal	**41** P A Position approximate
	23 Rf Reef (See A 11d, 11g, O 10)	**42** P D Position doubtful
9 Discolored water	**23a** Ridge	**43** E D Existence doubtful
	24 Le Ledge	**44** P Pos Position
		45 D Doubtful
10 Coral reef, detached (uncovers at sounding datum)	**25** Breakers (See A 12)	**46** Unexamined
	26 Submerged rock (See O 4)	(Od) L D Least Depth
Coral or Rocky reef, covered at sounding datum (See A-11d, 11g)	**27** Obstruction	(Oe) Crib
	†(Ob) Obstr Well Subm well Obstr Well Subm well (buoyed)	(Of) Offshore platform (unnamed) Platform (lighted) HORN
		(Og) Offshore platform (named) Hazel (lighted) HORN

S	sand	*sft*	soft
M	mud	*hrd*	hard
G	gravel	*stk*	sticky
Sh	shells	*rky*	rocky
Wd	seaweed	*gy*	gray
Grs	grass	*br*	brown

On some charts, as in this excerpt below showing Blackbeard Shoal off the Georgia coast, the depth of each contour line is indicated by a system of dots. And even though the individual soundings are in feet, the dots refer to fathoms. Thus, lines of single dots enclose areas of one fathom (six feet) or less, while lines of double and triple dots indicate depths of two and three fathoms respectively.

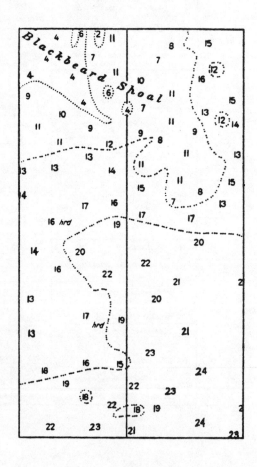

United States Coast Pilot—Modern charts supply enormous amounts of information in highly compressed form. More information still is supplied by the *United States Coast Pilot* series, prepared at intervals by the National Ocean Survey and kept up to date between editions by supplements. Nine volumes of the *Coast Pilot* cover the seacoast of the United States from Eastport, Maine, to Washington State, including Hawaii and Alaska. Written in narrative form, the *Coast Pilot* supplies many miscellaneous bits of information useful for course-planning and effective navigation.

universal drafting machine (parallel motion protractor)—A plotting device that is anchored to the chart table and consists of two parallel links and a drafting arm. Between the two links an elbow permits unrestricted movement. Between the outboard link and the drafting arm a metal disk is graduated as a protractor. It permits orientation of the protractor with the chart. A set screw, usually on the inner edge, is used to set the drafting arm on any given direction. The advantage of the drafting machine over other plotting instruments is speed.

U.S. Coast Guard—Has charge of the inspection of merchant-marine vessels, licensing of merchant-marine officers, and the installation and maintenance of aids to marine navigation (lighthouses, beacons, buoys, etc.). It publishes light lists for the waters of the United States and its possessions, international and inland rules of the road, and pilot rules.

U.S. Coast and Geodetic Survey—Conducts research in hydrography, cartography, tides, currents, geodesy, geomagnetism, and seismology. It publishes coast and harbor charts of the United States and its possessions, aeronautical charts of the United States, tide and tidal-current tables for both United States and foreign waters, coast pilots (Sailing Directions) for coasts of the United States and its possessions (including the Intracoastal Waterway), and a number of special publications covering results of its research.

U.S. Naval Observatory—Conducts research in various branches of astronomy, including measurement and dissemination of time. It furnishes time signals and publishes nautical and air almanacs and an ephemeris, as well as tables of sunrise, sunset, and twilight.

U.S. Navy Hydrographic Office—Maintains liaison with foreign hydrographic departments; makes hydrographic, topographic, oceanographic, and geomagnetic surveys in international waters and along foreign coasts; conducts research in oceanography and in navigational methods (both marine and air); systematically collects data in these fields from public and private institutions and persons in all parts of the world; prepares, prints, and distributes nautical and aeronautical charts.

V

variation (V)—The angle between the geographic and magnetic meridians at any place. The expression "magnetic variation" is used when it is necessary to distinguish this from other forms of variation. This element is measured in angular units and named east or west to indicate the side of true north on which the northerly part of the magnetic meridian lies. For computational purposes, easterly variation is sometimes designated positive (+), and westerly variation negative (−). Grid variation (GV), or grivation, is the angle between the grid and magnetic meridians at any place measured and named in a manner similar to variation.

vertical circle—A great circle on the surface of the celestial sphere passing through the zenith and nadir and through some celestial body. Although it is by definition a complete circle, in actual usage we speak of the 180° through the body and terminating at the zenith and nadir, respectively, as the vertical circle. In practice we make use of the 90° arc from the zenith to the horizon, since the remaining 90° below the horizon is not visible and serves no purpose.

vertical intensity (Z)—The vertical component of the total intensity of the magnetic field. It is zero at the magnetic equator. At the magnetic poles it is the same as the total intensity. While the vertical intensity has no direct effect upon the direction indicated by a magnetic compass, it does induce magnetic fields in vertical soft iron, and this may affect the compass.

virtual PPI reflectoscope (VPR)—The VPR is an attachment that may be used in conjunction with the PPI scope of a radar to show the position of the ship continuously on a navigation chart. It consists of a chart and a set of mirrors to reflect the chart upon the PPI scope. VPR charts must be drawn to a scale that is consistent with the range scale of the PPI scope. Sometimes the VPR chart is a grid chart, thus enabling the operator to read at any time the grid position of the ship.

W

watch time (WT)—Time indicated by a watch. Usually an approximation of zone time, except that for timing celestial observations it is good practice to set a hack or comparing watch to GMT. If the watch has a second-setting hand, the watch can be set exactly to ZT or GMT, and the time is so designated. If the watch is not set exactly to one of these times, the difference is known as watch error (WE), labeled fast (F) or slow (S) to indicate whether the watch is ahead of or behind the correct time. If a watch is to be set exactly to ZT or GMT, it is set to some whole minute slightly ahead of the correct time and stopped. When the set time arrives, the watch is started.

weather maps—The information at each station of the weather network of the world (and of ships at sea), whether surface or upper-air observations, is arranged with a circle drawn at the location of the station (and current position of the ships at sea). The following weather information is plotted for each station and ship on a surface weather chart, with each item plotted in exactly the same position relative to the station/ship circle: wind direction and speed, pressure, temperature, dew point, visibility, ceiling, current weather (rain, snow, fog, etc.), the amount and type of clouds and their heights, pressure changes in the past three hours, weather in the past six hours, and the amount and type of precipitation. The relative position for each weather element around a circle and all the weather symbols and notations are used by weathermen in all countries of the world by international agreement.

weather warnings:

GALE—Two red pennants by day and a white light above a red light at night indicates that winds of 34 to 47 knots (39 to 54 mph) are forecast for the area.

HURRICANE—Two square red flags with black centers displayed by day and a white light between two red lights at night to indicate that winds of 64 knots (74 mph) or higher are forecast for the area.

SMALL-CRAFT—One red pennant displayed by day and a red light over a white light at night indicates that winds up to 33 knots (38 mph) or sea conditions dangerous to small-craft operation are predicted.

STORM—A single square red flag with a black center displayed by day and two red lights at night indicates that winds of 48 knots (55 mph) and above are predicted for the area.

west wind drift—The ocean current with the largest volume transported (approximately 110×10^6 cubic centimeters per second); it flows from west to east around the Antarctic continent and is formed partly by the strong westerly wind in this region and partly by water-density differences.

winds—Varying conditions of topography produce a large variety of local winds throughout the world. Winds tend to follow valleys and to be deflected by high banks and shores. In mountain areas, wind flows in response to temperature distribution and gravity. An anabatic wind is one that blows up an incline, usually as a result of surface heating. A katabatic wind is one that blows down an incline. A wind with a downward component, warm for the season, is called a foehn. In the Rocky Mountains region this wind is known by the name chinook. On the West Coast of the United States, a foehn wind, given the name Santa Ana, blows through a pass and down a valley by that name in southern California. A cold wind blowing down an incline is called a fall wind. Although it is warmed somewhat during descent, as is the foehn, it remains cold relative to the surrounding air. A different name for this type of wind is given at each place it is common. It is the *techauntepecar* of the Mexican and Central American coasts, the *pamero* of the Argentine coast, the *mistral* of the western Mediterranean, and the *bora* of the eastern Mediterranean.

wind, geostrophic—Once a wind is established, Coriolis causes deflection to the right. Because the wind wants to flow inward (left) toward low pressure and the Coriolis force acts away (right) from the low, the wind ends up blowing parallel to the isobars. The wind that results from this balance between forces is called geostrophic wind. Near the ground or water surface, friction slows the wind (thereby decreasing the Coriolis deflection) and the wind crosses the isobars at a small angle, and is not geostrophic. However, at an elevation of a few thousand feet, frictional effects are sufficiently small that maximum Coriolis deflection occurs with a nearly complete balance between the pressure gradient and the deflective force, resulting in the geostrophic wind. The strength of the geostrophic wind is usually determined from graphs based on the isobar spacing and the latitude.

wind, true and apparent—The wind experienced on a ship under way is the result of wind created by the ship's motion and the true wind. The resultant wind is called the apparent wind. The direction and velocity of the apparent wind, as experienced on the deck of a vessel, depends on the force and direction of the true wind and that of the wind caused by the forward motion of the ship. The apparent wind, being the resultant of these forces, must always lie between the true and the ship's wind, except when the true wind is dead ahead or dead astern. It is the true and not the apparent wind that is of significance for weather purposes.

wind direction measurement—Wind direction is most commonly indicated by a wind vane that always points into the wind. Wind vanes are usually constructed so that the fluctuations in wind direction are communicated to some form of indicator or recorder. The wind sock, a typical airport device to show the wind direction, always flies with the wind. To determine the wind direction and speed in the upper air, balloons are utilized. When inflated properly, they have a known rate of ascent. Observations on a balloon are then made at one-minute intervals with a theodolite, which measures the horizontal drift of the balloon and also its vertical angle. Since the drift of a balloon equals the wind speed at the particular elevation, it is a simple matter to compute these values from the observed data. From fixed positions, determination of the wind direction by observation is usually simple. Any object that is bent or swayed or blown by the wind may serve as an indicator. Thus, smoke, flags, or pennants are normally reliable wind guides. On moving vessels, wind direction is best indicated by the surface of the sea. The wind will be nearly perpendicular to the crest line of the waves. The direction of the spume blowing from whitecaps coincides with the wind direction. Clouds are excellent guides to the wind direction prevailing in the upper air.

wind-motion characteristics—Wind is air moving horizontally, or approximately so. Vertically moving air columns are called currents and give the effect known as "bumpy air." An air pocket is simply a current whose descent is rapid enough to create the illusion of an absence of air to support an aircraft. The amount of air moving vertically is negligible compared to that transported as wind. Air motion at low levels is strongly affected by friction with the underlying surface and by thermal convection if the surface is warmer than the air. The smooth, sheetlike flow of air (laminar flow) that prevails aloft is converted into turbulent or eddy motion by these effects, producing gusts and lulls. Wind turbulence increases with the roughness of the terrain as well as with the degree of temperature contrast between the surface and the air above. Turbulence also increases as the wind speed increases. Since wind-eddy action varies with the irregularity in both the relief and the temperature of the surface, it follows that winds should be more uniform over water than over land, owing to greater roughness and temperature variations of the latter. As these effects also reduce the effective wind speed, winds are stronger at sea than on land for the same meteorological conditions. The results of surface friction and convection decrease with altitude, with a consequent decrease of turbulence and an increase in the steadiness and velocity of the wind. Although the wind may be quite variable in direction and speed for short periods as a consequence of eddy action, the main flow of air is usually steady, on the average, from a given direction. Wind shift is a progressive change in direction. A wind may shift in either a clockwise or a counterclockwise manner. Thus a wind whose direction changes from east, through south, to west has shifted clockwise through the compass; such a wind is called a veering wind or is said to veer. A wind that shifts in a counterclockwise manner is said to back and is termed a backing wind.

wind rose—A diagram showing the relative frequency of winds blowing from different directions. It may also show average speed or frequency of occurrence of various speeds from different directions.

wind velocity measurement—Usually wind velocity can be determined quite accurately by means of an anemometer, which consists of three or more hemispherical cups extending on horizontal arms from a vertical shaft or spindle. The higher the wind velocity, the faster the cups rotate. By means of a generator or a gear system, the spinning motion is translated to show the wind speed on remote instruments. When no instruments are available, wind velocities cannot be determined so easily, but a moving mass of air has a certain effect on objects in its path and, once the relation between wind and effect is carefully determined, future estimates of wind velocity may be made by noting the reactions of objects to the wind (*see* Beaufort wind scale).

Z

zenith (Z)—The point on the celestial sphere directly above the observer. A point on the surface of the earth having a star in its zenith is called the star's geographic position, subastral, or ground point.

zenith distance—The angular distance from the zenith to a point on the celestial sphere. It is measured along a vertical circle from $0°$ through $180°$ and is usually considered the complement of altitude. For a body above the celestial horizon it is equal to $90° - H$, and for a body below the celestial horizon it is equal to $90° - (-H)$ or $90° + H$.

zodiac—A belt extending $8°$ to each side of the ecliptic. The apparent paths of all the planets within our solar system fall within this belt except for Venus, which occasionally appears to travel outside the zodiac. The zodiac was divided into twelve sections (signs) by the ancients to correspond to months, each sector being named for the constellation that the sun appeared to be passing through or near at that time. Each sector or sign extends $30°$ in arc.

zone time—At sea, as well as ashore, watches and clocks are normally set to some form of zone time (ZT). At sea the nearest meridian exactly divisible by $15°$ is usually used as the time meridian or zone meridian. Thus, within a time zone extending $7°.5$ on each side of each time meridian, the time is the same, and times in consecutive zones differ by exactly one hour. The time is changed as convenient, usually at a whole hour, near the time of crossing the boundary between zones. Each time zone is identified by the number of times the longitude of its zone meridian is divisible by $15°$ and is positive in west longitudes and negative in east. This number and its sign is called the zone description (ZD) and is added to or subtracted from the zone time to obtain Greenwich mean time (GMT), which is the zone time at the Greenwich ($0°$) meridian, and is often called universal time (UT).

II

WEATHER

air mass—A vast volume of air, often thousands of cubic miles, in which conditions (temperature, moisture, etc.) are much the same at all points in a horizontal direction. An air mass takes on the temperature and moisture of the surface over which it forms. Almost all continents, including the United States, are swept by air masses of large contrast. The North American continent is rather wide at the top, and consequently cold, dry air masses form there continually and travel southward. The southern part of the continent is quite narrow, so the moist, tropical air masses that form over the oceans easily move northward. When a hot, moist air mass traveling northward meets a cold, dry air mass traveling southward, a weather front usually develops where the two bump into each other.

COLD—In the passage of cold air over warmer surfaces, convection and turbulence develop rapidly. Clouds of the cumuliform type tend to form. Visibility is usually good to excellent in such air, owing to the general stirring and turbulence.

EQUATORIAL—When air becomes stagnant in equatorial areas, high temperature and humidity are acquired. Cumulus clouds predominate in such air, with frequent thunderstorms. When equatorial air crosses land areas, solar heating of the ground causes surface air temperatures to be highest in the afternoon. Consequently, towering cumulus and cumulonimbus clouds with showers are common in that part of the day. However, over ocean areas, the cooling occurs during the night and provides the atmospheric instability necessary for thundershowers. Owing to the high humidity of hot equatorial air, precipitation is usually very heavy. On occasions when equatorial air is carried to high latitudes, it is the source of dense fog.

POLAR CONTINENTAL—Polar continental air is characteristically cold, dry air. In the winter it originates over the cold, often frozen areas of central Asia and Canada. During the summer these cold-air bodies

Classification of Air Masses

Name of Mass	Place of Origin	Properties	Symbol
Arctic	Polar regions	Low temperatures; low specific but high summer relative humidity; the cold of the winter masses	A
Polar	Subpolar continental areas	Low temperatures; increasing southward movement; low humidity, remaining constant	cP
Polar maritime	Subpolar and Arctic oceanic areas	Low temperatures, increasing with movement; higher humidity	mP
Tropical continental	Subtropical high-pressure land areas	High temperatures; low moisture content	cT
Tropical	Southern borders of oceanic and subtropical	Moderately high temperatures; high relative and specific humidity	mT
Equatorial	Equatorial and tropical seas	High temperatures and humidity	E

become smaller as their sources retreat northward. In the winter, polar air masses of Asiatic origin flow to the south and east. The air moving southward travels with the northeast Indian monsoon, spreading cold air over the Indian Ocean and even reaching the South Pacific. The air traveling eastward continues into the North Pacific Ocean, where it plays a dominant role in shaping the weather not only of the Pacific but of western North America as well. In the source region, polar continental air is stable and clear, since the cold surface beneath prevents convection. The temperature in such air often increases with altitude, yielding an inversion. This results essentially from the pronounced cooling of the surface air. After it leaves the source region, the nature and amount of modification depend on the underlying surface conditions. Winter continental polar air changes little while crossing cold land surfaces. Upon reaching warmer land areas, local surface heating causes the formation of cumulus clouds, which may join to form stratocumulus. When this air of winter advances over the sea, sea smoke or steam fog may form if the water is warm. With the evaporation of water into it, the dry polar continental air mass undergoes modification to polar maritime air.

TROPICAL CONTINENTAL—In its source region, tropical continental air is warm and very dry. This air occurs over the desert of North Africa, where it affects Mediterranean weather, and over the deserts of the southwestern United States and northern Mexico. Continental tropical air, being dry and warm, has a high moisture capacity and low humidity and will therefore absorb moisture rapidly when traversing water areas. It is thus modified rapidly to tropical maritime air.

TROPICAL MARITIME—Tropical maritime air originates in the subtropical high-pressure zones of the oceans (Azores and Pacific highs in the Northern Hemisphere). The weather here is mostly calm and clear. As maritime tropical air moves outward from its source with either the westerlies or trade winds, its properties are modified. When this air moves with the westerlies, colder water surfaces are encountered. The chilling of the air mass tends to produce fog, stratus clouds, and light rain. With the retreat of the polar air masses in summer, the tropical maritime air extends farther northward. The northward surge of warm, humid air, upon meeting cold Arctic Ocean currents, is responsible for the prevalent summer fogs of the North Atlantic and North Pacific oceans. In moving equatorward with the trades, maritime tropical air becomes warmer and more humid. For the most part, clear skies with scattered cumulus clouds prevail in this air in the poleward portion of the trade-winds belt. The closer the approach to the doldrums, the greater is the tendency for the formation of convection clouds, with associated thunderstorms. The maritime tropical air, moving eastward or westward from the source regions, encounters shore currents of varying temperatures and coastal zones of varying slopes. In California, coastal fog develops when warm, moist, tropical air from the Pacific high moves across the cold California current.

WARM—Usually of tropical origin, moving toward higher latitudes, but may be warm marine-air bodies moving inland over colder land, or warm continental air moving offshore over colder sea surfaces. The effect of the cooler surface beneath is to cool the air slowly from the surface upward. This uniform cooling of the air by a large surface tends to produce stratified conditions within the air, with an absence of vertical air motion, or turbulence. Consequently, any clouds that exist will be of the stratiform type. Any precipitation will be drizzle or light rain. The absence of turbulence produces poor visibility in warm air masses, owing to the settling of dust and other foreign particles in the vertically calm air. Fog will be more common in such air as a result of the surface cooling.

air-mass boundaries—On weather maps, the boundary zones of air masses are drawn as lines, called weather fronts or fronts. The boundaries between air masses are really zones of transition, ranging from about five to sixty miles in width, but because of the small scale of weather maps, this is not apparent. The principal frontal zones around the earth are: (1) Arctic, separating Arctic air masses from either maritime polar or continental polar air masses. (2) Polar, separating continental polar air masses from maritime polar air masses, or separating either continental polar or maritime polar air masses from maritime tropical air masses. (3) Mediterranean, separating the cold air masses over Europe during the winter months from the warmer air masses over North Africa. (4) Intertropical convergence (ITCZ), a bad-weather region in tropical latitudes where the northeast trade winds of the Northern Hemisphere and the southeast trades of the Southern Hemisphere either approach each other at a rather large angle or flow almost parallel to each other. This zone breeds hurricanes and typhoons.

anticyclones—High-pressure areas develop when an air mass is cooled, compressed, and caused to sink toward the earth's surface (a process called subsidence). Because the air is compressed, it is heated (adiabatically) and its relative humidity decreases markedly. Anticyclones show a great deal of variation. They range in size from tiny ones, only 200 miles across, to the huge ones, over 2,000 miles in length. Although the speed of movement of anticyclones varies widely during the summer months, a good average would be 390 nautical miles per day (16 knots). During the winter months, the average movement of highs is somewhat greater, about 565 nautical miles per day (23.5 knots). Surface wind speeds increase considerably from the center toward the periphery of an anticyclone. Anticyclones are usually classified by weathermen as either cold or warm.

In a cold one, the air at the surface and lower layers is colder than the air surrounding the high. The air in the anticyclone is thus denser than the surrounding air, level for level. The high pressure of a cold anticyclone is therefore due primarily to the density of the lower layers' being greater than the density of the same layers in the area surrounding the anticyclone. Although cold anticyclones are of limited vertical extent, seldom exceeding 10,000 feet, they play a very important role in the lower-level atmospheric circulation in winter.

In a warm anticyclone, the air throughout is warmer, level for level, than its environment. Near the surface, the air in a warm anticyclone therefore differs little in density from that of the surrounding air. Since surface pressure depends on the total mass of the air above, the high surface pressure in a warm anticyclone must result from air of greater density than the surrounding air, being present at higher levels in the atmosphere. Also, in warm anticyclones, the pressure at higher levels is greater than in the surrounding air, level for level, since pressure falls more slowly with height through a column of warm air than through a column of cold air. Examples of warm anticyclones are the oceanic subtropical belts of high pressure, for example, the horse latitudes at 30° north and south.

antitrades—A layer of westerly winds in the troposphere above the surface trade winds of the tropics. They constitute the equatorward side of the mid-latitude westerlies but are found at upper levels rather than at the surface. The antitrades are best developed in the winter hemisphere, and also above the eastern extremities of the subtropical highs.

Arctic air—A type of air mass whose characteristics are developed mostly in winter over the Arctic surfaces of ice and snow. Arctic air is cold aloft and extends to great heights, but the surface temperatures are often higher than those of polar air. In summer, Arctic air masses are shallow and rapidly lose their characteristics as they move southward.

Arctic frost smoke—Arctic sea smoke occurs when the air is at least 16°F colder than the sea. If the air temperature is below 32°F, then the Arctic sea smoke is called Arctic frost smoke. This frost smoke is often confined to a layer only a few feet thick, and trawler men in northern waters refer to it as white frost when the top of the layer is below eye level. It is referred to as black frost when it extends above the observer. The small water droplets in frost smoke are supercooled. On contact with the vessel, part of the droplet freezes immediately; the remainder stays liquid for a short time before it, too, freezes. The result is an accretion of opaque, white rime ice with imprisoned air. This rime ice is easier to remove than clear ice, which forms in other circumstances, because it is porous.

Arctic high—A weak high that appears over the Arctic Basin during late spring, summer, and early autumn.

atmosphere—A relatively thin shell of air, water vapor, dust, smoke, etc., surrounding the earth. The air is a mixture of transparent gases and, like any gas, is elastic and compressible. Although extremely light, it has a definite weight, which can be measured. A cubic foot of air at standard sea-level temperature (59°F) and pressure (29.92″) weighs

1.22 ounces, or about 1/817 the weight of an equal volume of water. Because of this weight, the atmosphere exerts a pressure upon the surface of the earth, amounting to about fifteen pounds per square inch. As altitude increases, less atmosphere extends upward and pressure decreases. With less pressure, the density decreases. More than three-fourths of the air is concentrated within a layer averaging about seven statute miles thick, called the troposphere. This is the region of most "weather" as the term is commonly understood. The top of the troposphere is marked by a thin transition zone called the tropopause, immediately above which is the stratosphere. Beyond this lie several other layers, having distinctive characteristics. The average height of the tropopause ranges from about five miles or less, at high latitudes, to about ten miles, at low latitudes. The standard vertical structure of the atmosphere is characterized by a sea-level temperature of 59°F (15°C), a temperature decrease with height (lapse rate) of $3°.6F$ (2°C) per thousand feet to 11 kilometers (36,089 feet), and thereafter a constant temperature of $(-)69°.7F$ $(-56°.5C)$.

DIFFRACTION FEATURES—When rays of light encounter obstacles of very small size, the rays are deflected from their normal path, usually in a straight line. This is the process of diffraction. The various wavelengths composing white light are diffracted somewhat differently, causing dispersion or the separation of white light into its spectral colors. Coronas are the most common example of atmospheric diffraction. They are rings of subdued color caused by the diffraction of sunlight or moonlight by thin clouds. When they are discernible, the colors of shorter wavelengths, blue and green, appear on the inner portion of the corona, with red and orange forming the outer ring.

GENERAL CIRCULATION—The heat required for warming the air is supplied originally by the sun. As radiant energy from the sun arrives at the earth, about 29 percent is reflected back into space by the earth and its atmosphere, 19 percent is absorbed by the atmosphere, and the remaining 52 percent is absorbed by the surface of the earth. Much of this 52 percent is reradiated back into space. The earth's radiation is in comparatively long waves relative to the short-wave radiation from the sun, since it emanates from a cooler body. Long-wave radiation, being readily absorbed by the water vapor in the air, is primarily responsible for the warmth of the atmosphere near the earth's surface. Thus, the atmosphere acts much like the glass on the roof of a greenhouse. It allows part of the incoming solar radiation to reach the surface of the earth but is heated by the terrestrial radiation passing outward. Over time, the total outgoing energy must equal the incoming energy (minus any converted to another form and retained); otherwise the temperature of the earth, including its atmosphere, would steadily increase or decrease. In local areas or over relatively short periods of time, such a balance does not exist, resulting in changes such as those occurring from one year to another in different seasons and in different parts of the day.

DISPERSION—Dispersion can be considered a kind of differential refraction. Visible white light actually consists of light of many colors. When white light is passed through a medium of varying thickness, such as a glass prism, the components of the light are refracted differently, in accordance with their respective wavelengths. The resulting color band is known as the spectrum, consisting of red, orange, yellow, green, blue, and violet regions, which grade into each other. These are the colors commonly observed in rainbows. Dispersion is thus the process whereby white light is separated into its component colors. The wavelength of blue light is about half that of red, and the blue is refracted more than the red.

REFRACTION—Refraction is the process in which rays of light are bent from a straight line in passing through a medium of varying density or from one medium to another of different density. A pencil or rod partly immersed in water appears to bend sharply at the water line and assumes a distorted shape. Light rays are refracted, since they travel with different speeds in media of different density. A ray of light perpendicular to the surface between two media is not refracted. When a ray of light emerges from a dense to a rare (thin) medium, it is bent away from a line perpendicular (normal) to the surface. As the angle of incidence of a ray moving from a dense to a rare medium increases, there comes a situation where the ray is bent so far from the normal as not to enter the rare medium at all but to travel parallel to the surface between the media. The angle of incidence at which this occurs is known as the critical angle and depends on the medium. If the critical angle is exceeded, the ray is bent back into the dense medium, the phenomenon being known as total refraction.

atmospheric pressure—The detectable atmosphere extends many hundreds of miles above the earth's surface, being held by the earth's gravity. Pressure is defined as force per unit area and, in the case of the atmosphere, is determined by the number and speed of the air molecules that strike a square inch or centimeter, depending on the system of units used. When air pressure increases, more molecules are present in a given volume; when air pressure decreases, fewer molecules. Although pressure is given in terms of a force, this force can be equated with length: for example, the height to which it will support a column of mercury in a barometer; or may be given in terms of the mass (weight) of the mercury in the tube.

The sea of air surrounding the earth exerts a pressure of about 14.7 pounds per square inch on the surface of the earth. This atmospheric pressure varies from place to place, and at the same place varies with time. Atmospheric pressure is one of the basic elements of a meteorological observation. When the pressure at each station is plotted on a (synoptic) chart, lines of equal atmospheric pressure, called isobars, are drawn to indicate the areas of high and low pressure and their centers. Atmospheric pressure is measured by a barometer. A mercurial barometer does this by balancing the weight of a column of air against that of a column of mercury. The aneroid barometer has a partly evacuated metal cell, which is compressed by atmospheric pressure, the amount of compression being related to the pressure.

The pressure exerted by the entire atmosphere on one square centimeter is approximately one bar (a bar being defined as a force of one million dynes per square centimeter). Since fluctuations of atmospheric pressure are very small, the millibar, which is a thousandth of a bar, is used in meteorology, thus eliminating pressure expressions involving many decimal places. Although atmospheric pressure varies continuously over a relatively small range, the average of these fluctuations is very close to a value adopted for certain standard conditions, defined as the standard atmosphere. At a temperature of 15°C and a latitude of 45°, the normal pressure is given as 1,013.2 millibars. This latter value is equivalent to 29.92 inches and 760 millimeters. Thus 1 inch is equal to 33.86 millibars and 0.75 millimeter; 1 millibar is about the same as 0.03 inch and 1.33 millibars.

aurora borealis—When visible in the skies of the Northern Hemisphere, this phenomenon is often termed aurora polaris, and, in the southern skies, aurora australis. It is a display of light in the form of streamers, rays, arcs, bands, curtains, draperies, sheets, or patches that shimmer and flit across the sky. Auroras are most common in latitudes around the magnetic poles. The auroral patterns are usually greenish-white, though pronounced reds, yellows, and greens are often observed. Auroras are associated with magnetic storms on the sun, which appear as sunspots and are nearly always attended by magnetic disruptions on earth that impair the normal behavior of communication devices. Auroras are explained as resulting from electrified particles emitted by the magnetic storm areas, which approach the earth and are attracted to the magnetic poles. The effect of the electrical bombardment of the upper, rarefied portions of the atmosphere is to cause excitation of the atoms therein with a consequent emission of radiation.

belt of tropical calms (horse latitudes)—In theory, two belts characterized by high pressure and light winds or calms occur symmetrically about the equator at 30°N and 30°S. The descending air that maintains the high-pressure pattern is warmed adiabatically and therefore develops low relative humidity and clear skies. In the Southern Hemisphere the horse latitudes are mostly over water, so conditions are fairly uniform throughout the year. The annual configuration closely resembles the ideal pattern except for continental breaks in the high-pressure ridge. These breaks become less pronounced in the southern winter (July), owing to the cooling of the land, which increases air subsidence and enhances high pressure. In the Northern Hemisphere, a more drastic annual modification of the idealized pattern occurs following the pronounced temperature variations of the large land areas. During the northern winter, a high-pressure belt roughly encircles the earth, although the position over the continents is displaced to the north and over the oceans, to the south of the thirtieth parallel. In summer there is a partial reversal of pressure over North America and a very strong reversal over Asia. At the same time, an intensification of the high-pressure belt takes place over the oceans, because they become cool relative to the continents. The high-pressure region west of the United States is known as the Pacific high, while that over the Atlantic Ocean is known as the Bermuda high or Azores high.

bora—A fall wind whose source is so cold that, when the air reaches the lowlands or coast, dynamic (adiabatic) warming is insufficient to raise the air temperature to the normal level for the region; hence it appears as a cold wind. The term was originally and is still applied to the cold northeast wind on the Dalmatian coast of Yugoslavia in winter, when cold air from Russia crosses the mountains and descends to the relatively warm coast of the Atlantic. It is very stormy and squally, the squalls sometimes reaching 100 miles per hour or more.

brave west winds—A nautical term for the strong and rather persistent westerly winds over the oceans in temperate latitudes. They occur between 40°N and 65°N in the Northern Hemisphere and 35°S to 65°S in the Southern Hemisphere, where they are more regular, and are strongest between 40°S and 50°S (the roaring forties). They are associated with the strong pressure gradient on the equatorial side of the frequent depressions (lows) passing eastward in subpolar latitudes; hence they fluctuate mainly between southwest and northwest.

ceiling—The height above the ground at which the cloud cover appears broken or overcast. If less than six-tenths of the sky is covered, the ceiling is considered "unlimited," regardless of the cloud heights.

clouds—Clouds form when air at higher altitudes is cooled to the dew point. Nearly all clouds form as a result of air that has cooled adiabatically, that is, air that has risen, expanded, and consequently cooled. Rising air currents tend to keep the clouds from falling, since the droplets composing the clouds are very small and light. If its base falls to an altitude where the temperature is above the dew point, the small droplets evaporate. If the clouds form at sufficiently high altitudes, temperatures are below freezing, and, as in the case of frost, the condensation yields ice crystals.

clouds, classification of—Clouds are classified according to how they are formed, and there are two basic types. The first is clouds formed by rising air currents. These are puffy or piled up and are called cumulus, which means accumulated, or piled up. The second type is clouds formed when a layer of air is cooled below the saturation (dew) point without vertical movement. These clouds are in foglike layers or sheets; they are called stratus, meaning layered or sheetlike. Clouds are further classified by altitude into five families: (1) clouds above the troposphere, (2) high clouds, (3) middle clouds, (4) low clouds, and (5) vertical clouds. The cloud bases of vertical clouds may be as low as the typical low clouds, but the tops may be at or above 65,000 feet. The names of clouds are descriptive of their form. The prefix *fracto,* meaning fragment, is added to the names of windblown clouds that are broken into pieces. The word *nimbus,* meaning rain, is added to the names of clouds that characteristically produce rain or snow. *Alto,* meaning high, is used to indicate clouds of either the cumulus or stratus type.

ALTOCUMULUS—Clouds most often seen as extensive sheets, white or gray, and somewhat rounded. Through altocumulus clouds, the sun often produces a corona, or disk, usually pale blue or yellow inside and reddish outside. The corona's color and spread easily distinguish it from the cirrostratus halo, a larger ring covering much more of the sky. Altocumulus clouds are usually composed of water droplets with ice crystals forming only at very low temperature. Altocumulus clouds, in general, are significant primarily when they are followed by thicker, high-cloud forms or cumulus-type lower clouds. When arranged in parallel bands these clouds are found in advance of warm fronts, with associated steady rain or snow. When altocumulus occurs in the form of turrets rising from a common, flat base, it is usually the forerunner of heavy showers or thunderstorms.

ALTOSTRATUS—Grayish or bluish sheets or striated fibrous clouds that cover part, or all, of the sky. These clouds are composed of water droplets, ice crystals, raindrops, or snowflakes. The sun and moon do not form halos, as with the higher ice-crystal cirrostratus, but appear as if seen through ground glass. Altostratus clouds are the most reliable weather indicators of all the clouds. They almost always indicate warm air flowing up over colder air and rain or snow of the continuous, all-day type, especially if the overcast progresses and thickens. These clouds are also a good indication of a new storm developing at sea. They frequently signal the formation of a stormy low-pressure area long before it is apparent from sea-level pressure or wind. What is important to seafarers is that these clouds are a reliable indication of approaching rain or snow, with associated poor visibility, large waves, and heavy swells.

CIRROCUMULUS—Thin, white, grainy, and rippled patches, sheets, or layers, showing very slight vertical development in the form of turrets and shallow towers. When these clouds are arranged uniformly in ripples, they form what seafarers call a mackerel sky. These clouds are usually too thin to show shadows. Cirrocumulus clouds are quite rare and are of mixed significance. In some areas, these clouds foretell good weather; in others, bad weather. These clouds usually signify good weather along the West Coast of the United States, in New England, and in the British Isles. They signify bad weather in most of southern Europe, particularly in Italy.

CIRROSTRATUS—Transparent, whitish clouds that look like fine veils or torn, windblown patches of gauze. They never obscure the sun to the extent that shadows are not cast by the objects on the ground. Because they are composed of ice crystals, cirrostratus clouds form large halos, or luminous circles, around the sun and moon. Cirrostratus clouds, when in a continuous sheet and increasing, signify the approach of a warm front or an occluded front, with rain or snow and stormy conditions. If these clouds are not increasing and are not continuous, this means that the storm is passing to the south and no bad weather will occur.

CIRRUS—Detached wisps of hairlike (fibrous) clouds, formed of delicate filaments, patches, or narrow bands. Like the other high clouds, they are composed primarily of ice crystals. They are often arranged in bands that cross the sky like meridian lines and, because of the effect of perspective, converge to a point on the horizon. Cirrus clouds, which are scattered and are not increasing, have little weather meaning except to signify that any bad weather is at a great distance. Cirrus clouds in thick patches mean that showery weather is close by. These clouds are associated with, and formed from, the tops of thunderstorms. Cirrus clouds shaped like hooks or commas indicate that a warm front is approaching and that a continuous-type rain will follow, especially if the cirrus is followed by cirrostratus. They also frequently indicate the presence and location of a jet stream.

CUMULONIMBUS—Heavy, dense clouds of considerable vertical extent (often to 45,000 feet and higher) in the form of a mountain or huge tower. These clouds are the familiar thunderheads. The upper part of these clouds is usually smoother, sometimes fibrous with the top flattened to an anvil shape or a vast cirrus plume. These clouds consist of ice crystals in the upper portion and water droplets in the lower portion. Cumulonimbus clouds, or thunderheads, which sometimes reach as high as 65,000 feet, are to be avoided if at all possible. Very gusty surface winds in the vicinity of the thunderstorm, heavy rain, lightning, frequently hail, and in general a bad time can be expected in the immediate vicinity of these clouds.

CUMULUS—Clouds with little vertical development are puffy, cauliflower-like clouds whose shapes constantly change. These clouds are brilliant white in the sunlight, often extending from a relatively dark and nearly horizontal base. Cumulus clouds, when detached and with little vertical development, are termed fair-weather cumulus. The weather is fine, and nothing hazardous is in the offing. However, when cumulus clouds swell to considerable vertical extent, heavy showers are likely, with associated gusty surface winds in the vicinity of the showers. Since cumulus clouds normally cover only about 25 percent of the sky, they can be circumnavigated.

NACREOUS—Observed at altitudes of 70,000 to 100,000 feet, primarily in polar and subpolar regions. These clouds are of unknown origin and are thought to be composed of tiny water particles.

NIMBOSTRATUS—The true rain and/or snow clouds, depending upon the temperature. These clouds are low, amorphous, dark, and usually quite uniform. They are thick enough to blot out the sun, and they have a "wet" look. When these clouds precipitate, the rain or snow is continuous. These clouds are often accompanied by low scud clouds (fractostratus) when the wind is strong. Nimbostratus clouds are of little help as a forecasting tool, since the bad weather is already at hand when these dark clouds, with their associated heavy rain or snow, are overhead. But if they are at some distance and a report states they are coming in your direction, you should take necessary precautions. Once nimbostratus clouds have formed in your area or are heading in your direction, bad weather, wind, and sea conditions will persist.

NOCTILUCENT—The highest clouds of all are observed at altitudes of 250,000 to 300,000 feet, far above the troposphere (average height is above 45,000 feet) and far beyond the realm of weather. They appear brilliant against the background sky, a silvery-white. They move at speeds of 100 to 500 knots, usually from the northeast or east, and are thought to be of fine cosmic dust. They are observed mainly in polar and subpolar regions.

STRATOCUMULUS—Gray and whitish irregular layers with dark patches formed of rounded masses. These clouds frequently look like altocumulus clouds but at a much lower level. They are composed of water droplets, except in extremely cold weather. These clouds do not, as a rule, produce anything but light rain or snow. Stratocumulus clouds that form from degenerating cumulus clouds are usually followed by clearing at night and fair weather. The roll-type stratocumulus is characteristic of the cold seasons over both land and water, where the air is cooled from below and mixed by winds of fifteen knots or more. Stratocumulus will persist for long periods under proper air-to-land or air-to-sea temperatures. Visibility can be seriously reduced in stratocumulus drizzle or snow.

STRATUS—Low, gray layers or sheets, with rather uniform bases and tops. These dull, gray clouds give the sky a heavy, leaden appearance. Only a fine drizzle, ice prisms, or snow grains fall from true stratus clouds, because there is little or no vertical motion in them. Stratus clouds are sometimes formed by the gradual lifting of a fog layer. If the wind speed decreases markedly when stratus clouds are present in large quantity, the base of the cloud can lower to the surface, resulting in a thick fog. Other than light drizzle, no stratus precipitation should be expected except that from higher clouds when stratus forms in advance of a warm front. In this case, the rain supersaturates the colder air below the leading surface of the warm front, and stratus clouds and fog may form.

col—The saddle-backed region between two anticyclones. In all surface pressure systems, the winds blow at varying angles across the isobars from higher toward lower pressure. Winds blow clockwise and spiral outward from the centers of anticyclones (in the Northern Hemisphere), while those of a cyclone blow counterclockwise and spiral in toward the center. In the very center of pressure systems, the pressure gradient vanishes, and there are either calm conditions or light, variable winds. The same is true of a col.

condensation—The process in which water vapor is changed to liquid water. In the process of condensation in the atmosphere, three general conditions must be satisfied: (1) sufficient water vapor must be present, (2) the air must cool to and below the dew point, and (3) nuclei of condensation must exist. These conditions are interrelated. Adequate water vapor is necessary, so that saturation can occur. The air can be brought to saturation through a temperature decrease until the dew point is reached (relative humidity of 100 percent), or by the addition of water vapor. All of the water and ice particles that condense in the atmosphere do so on microscopic- or submicroscopic-sized particles, called nuclei of condensation. The most important of the nuclei are sea salt (sodium chloride), nitric oxide, organic particles, and sulfur trioxide. Without the presence of these nuclei, air can become supersaturated, that is, have a relative humidity greater than 100 percent.

corona—When the sun or moon is seen through altostratus clouds, its outline is indistinct, and it appears surrounded by a glow of light called a corona. This is similar to the corona seen around the sun during an eclipse. When the effect is due to clouds, however, the glow may be accompanied by one or more rainbow-colored rings. These can be distinguished from a halo by their much smaller radii and also by the fact that the order of the colors is reversed, red being on the inside, nearest the body, in the case of the halo, and on the outside away from the body, in the case of the corona. A corona is caused by diffraction of light by tiny droplets of water. The radius of a corona is inversely proportional to the size of the water droplets. A large corona indicates small droplets. If a corona decreases in size (water droplets larger, air more humid), it may be an indication of an approaching rainstorm. The glow of a corona is called an aureole.

cyclone—Extratropical cyclones (lows of nontropical origin) frequently form along fronts. Hence, they occur with the greatest frequency in the higher mid-latitudes, where cold air masses and warm air masses meet. In the Northern Hemisphere, there is a maximum frequency of lows near 50°N and 60°N in summer. In the Atlantic, one of the most favored regions for the development of lows is off the Virginia coast and in the general area to the east of the southern Appalachians. In the Pacific, there is a broad band of frequent cyclone activity extending all the way from Southeast Asia to the Gulf of Alaska. Like anticyclones, cyclones exhibit large variety. The smaller lows may be only a few hundred miles across, whereas the larger ones may extend to 2,000 miles or more. Like highs, lows travel at varying speeds and sometimes remain stationary for a day or two. During the summer months, lows move with an average speed of about 18 knots

(432 nautical miles per day). During the winter months, they travel somewhat faster, at an average speed of about 25 knots (600 nautical miles) per day. Lows are much stormier and more sharply defined in winter than in summer. Low-pressure systems are characterized by many types of clouds, moderate to heavy precipitation, strong winds that shift abruptly, high seas, and generally stormy conditions.

cyclone, occluded—The cold-front portion of a cyclonic wave travels faster than its warm front. Development of the cyclone results in the cold front's overtaking the warm, producing an occluded front. The occlusion begins near the apex of the wave, where the distance between the fronts is least, and gradually extends toward the more open parts of the wave. Ultimately, the warm sector is completely lifted above the surface, producing the fully occluded cyclone. Depending on the density contrast between the cold-air masses on both sides of the occluded front, it develops as either a warm- or cold-front occlusion. The cyclone (low) usually reaches its greatest intensity during the occlusion process, with the maximum weather disturbance extending up to 100 miles north of the point of occlusion. Soon after complete occlusion, the two cold air masses mix across the front, causing dissolution of the occluded front and the weakening and disappearance of the low. The life of a single-wave cyclone is usually five to seven days.

cyclone, tropical—A warm-core nonfrontal cyclone developing over tropical or subtropical waters and having a definite, organized circulation.

dew—On a clear, calm evening, the earth will cool rapidly by radiation and become colder than the air resting on the surface. Consequently, this surface air will cool by contact with the earth. As this process continues, the air will become cooler and cooler until the dew point is reached. This all takes place in a very thin layer of air in contact with the earth, a mere few inches. This cooling is essentially a conduction process and is restricted to a thin layer, since air is a poor conductor. On further cooling, below the dew point, the excess vapor in the air will condense. Dark objects such as vegetation always cool the fastest, as dark objects are good radiators of heat. Clear and calm conditions must prevail. Clouds greatly reduce the cooling of the earth by radiation and the subsequent cooling of the air. Wind prevents the warm air from remaining in contact with the earth or cold objects long enough to cool sufficiently.

dew point—The temperature to which a given parcel of air must be cooled, at constant pressure and constant water-vapor content, in order for saturation to occur. When this temperature is below 32°F, it is sometimes called the frost point. When there is a large difference between temperature and dew point and the difference does not decrease, there will be no fog; when the difference between the temperature and dew point decreases and the two values approach each other or the difference becomes zero, there should be fog. A rise in the dew point is usually accomplished by the evaporation of water from the ground or by the passage of a body of air over a wet surface. A high dew point is characteristic of maritime masses.

doldrums (*see also* equatorial calms)—The belt of low pressure at the surface near the equator; it occupies a position approximately midway between high-pressure belts (horse latitudes) at about latitudes 30° to 35° on each side. Except for diurnal changes, the atmospheric pressure along the equatorial low is almost uniform. With minimal pressure gradient, wind speeds are light and directions are variable. Hot, sultry days are common. The sky is often overcast, and showers and thunderstorms are frequent; in these areas, brief periods of strong winds occur. Both the position and the extent of the belt vary with longitude and season. On the average, the position is at 5°N and is frequently called the meteorological equator.

easterly waves (EWs)—At times, easterly trade winds oscillate in a wavelike manner, and thus weathermen speak of "waves" in the tropical easterlies, or easterly waves. Easterly waves are extremely important phenomena because of their relation to tropical cyclones, hurricanes, and typhoon formation. Basically, these waves are troughs of low pressure that are embedded in the deep easterly currents located on the equator side of the large oceanic high-pressure cells centered near 30° to 35° latitude. Easterly waves occur about every 15° of longitude during the summer season and have lengths of about 15° to 18° of latitude. They extend vertically into the atmosphere from the earth's surface to roughly 26,000 feet and travel from east to west at an average speed of ten to thirteen knots. Rather than being air-mass boundaries (like fronts), easterly waves are zones of transition in which the weather changes gradually.

foehn—A dry wind that is warm for the season; it occurs when horizontally moving air encounters a mountain barrier. As it blows upward to clear the barrier, it is cooled below the dew point; the result is the loss of moisture by cloud formation and rain. As the air continues to rise, its rate of cooling is reduced because the condensing water vapor gives off heat to the surrounding atmosphere. After crossing the mountain barrier, the air flows downward along the leeward slope, being warmed by compression as it descends. It loses less heat on the ascent than it gains during descent, and since it lost moisture during ascent, it arrives at the bottom of the mountain as warm, dry air.

fog—One of the common forms of condensation that occur when the air near the earth's surface falls below its dew-point temperature. Physically, there is very little difference between a fog and a cloud, since they are both composed of minute water droplets suspended in the air. Fog, however, forms in the air near the earth's surface, whereas clouds are features of much higher altitudes. Fog forms through cooling of the air by contact and mixing or, on occasion, through saturation of the air by an increase in the water content. Frequently, a graduation exists from thick fog into low-lying clouds, there being no distinction in appearance. The type of fog that forms depends on existing conditions and falls into four recognized categories: radiation fog, advection fog, frontal fog, and upslope fog. In general, if surface air is close to and is approaching the dew point, fog formation can be anticipated. If the temperature should increase after the fog has formed, the dispersal of the fog may be expected. The thickness of the fog depends on various factors of humidity, temperature, wind, nuclei, and so on. Fogs are usually classified according to their effect on visibility.

ADVECTION—Advection fog may form, day or night, when warm air blows over a colder land or water surface (air is advected). The warmer air gives off heat to the cold underlying surface, and this cools the air to the dew point. As the cool surface chills the warm air flowing over it, the water vapor of the air tends to condense on particles of salt, dust, or smoke before the relative humidity reaches 100 percent. The fog will be light, moderate, or dense, depending on the amount of water vapor. The air in which fog forms tends not to rise, because it is being cooled, thus becoming heavier and more stable. The temperature of the earth's surface (in the Northern Hemisphere) normally decreases as one goes northward. Thus, advection fogs form mainly where the air currents have a direction from the south.

FRONTAL—Fog sometimes forms ahead of warm fronts and occluded fronts and behind cold fronts. This happens when rain falls from warm air above frontal surfaces into the colder air beneath. Evaporation from the warm raindrops causes the dew point of the cold air to rise until condensation on the nuclei present takes place.

INVERSION—Typical of the subtropical coasts of California. The upwelling of cold water is common along west coasts because of the prevailing winds, and the air flowing over this cold water acquires a low temperature and high humidity. Above the cool, moist layer of air is a temperature inversion (increase of temperature with height), which acts as a "lid" and prevents the moist air from rising. Fog forms in a way similar to the advection process and is very frequent offshore. At night, as the land cools, the fog works its way inland.

RADIATION—A nighttime, overland phenomenon that occurs when the sky is clear, the wind is light, and the humidity is high. When the relative humidity is high, just a little cooling will lower the temperature to the dew point. A light wind of three knots is favorable for the formation of fog. The very small amount of turbulence it generates mixes the air particles, which are cooled at the ground upward, thus ensuring a solid fog layer up to 40 to 100 feet. In absolutely calm air, radiation fog will be patchy and may be only waist deep. Because cold air drains downhill, radiation fog is thickest in valley bottoms. Although radiation fog does not occur over water surfaces, it obscures shore-based beacons and landmarks and complicates navigation. Radiation fog normally disappears about one to three hours after sunrise. Autumn and winter are the most favorable seasons for radiation fog. The center of a high-pressure area is a favorite spot for radiation fog because the winds are light and the skies are usually clear.

TROPICAL AIR—A form of advection fog which does not depend upon the flowing of warm air over a cold current but rather on the gradual cooling of the air as it travels from lower to higher latitudes. It occurs over both water and land and is probably the most common type of fog over open sea. In the United States it forms some of the most widespread fogs observed anywhere. Tropical-air fog is more widespread over water than over land because of the smaller frictional effect over water.

UPSLOPE—When air travels upslope for a long time over rising terrain, the decrease in temperature it undergoes because of adiabatic expansion may lead to fog. Across the Great Plains of the United States, the atmospheric pressure decreases by about 130 millibars from the Mississippi to the eastern edge of the Rockies. Surface air traveling this route from east to west undergoes a temperature decrease of about 23°F. This westward motion occurs mainly in late winter and spring. At that time, the difference between temperature and dew point in the lower plains is sufficiently below 23°F that the air traveling over the slowly rising terrain will form upslope (or expansion) fog about 100 to 200 miles to the east of the mountains.

freezing spray—The most dangerous form of icing; occurs when air temperature is below the freezing temperature of the sea water, about 27°F. Spray freezes on exposed surfaces of the vessel, to produce clear ice or glaze.

fronts—Fronts form at the outer boundaries of high-pressure cells (*see* anticyclone), and only between air masses of different temperatures and/or moisture conditions. Warm air always slopes upward over cold air because it is less dense. Fronts are found along low-pressure troughs, with few exceptions. Consequently, the pressure falls as a front approaches and rises after it passes. The winds near the ground always shift clockwise (in the Northern Hemisphere) as a front passes over a position. The isobars at a front are always V-shaped. A front always slopes upward over the cold air either ahead of, or to the rear of, the front's direction of advance.

Although fronts differ, they have many weather properties in common. When cold and warm air masses meet, cold air wedges beneath the warmer air, which in turn rises over the sloping upper surface of the cold mass. The slope of the upper surface of the cold air is actually very gentle, varying from 1:100 to 1:500 with different air masses. By "slope" is meant the ratio of vertical rise to horizontal distance. Thus, a slope of 1:100 indicates a vertical change of 1 unit for each 100 horizontal units. However, this slope is always greatly exaggerated in diagrams, for explanatory purposes. Although treated as such, the frontal surface is not actually a mathematical surface. In reality, a transition zone exists between the two different air masses. The frontal transition zone may vary from a few hundred to a few thousand feet in height, depending on the contrast in properties between the air masses. The greater the temperature and humidity contrast, the less the mixing of the air and the thinner the transition zone. Owing to the gentle slope of the frontal surface, the transition area, even though of small thickness, will cover many miles along the horizontal ground surface.

A pronounced difference in pressure occurs between adjacent points on either side of the front. The nature of this pressure discontinuity depends on the basic temperature and resulting density difference between the air bodies. This pressure discontinuity across fronts is clearly shown by the isobars. Within an air mass, isobars are always smoothly curving lines, but when crossing air-mass boundaries or fronts, they bend sharply in order to conform to the abrupt change in pressure.

The temperature conditions across a front may vary through wide ranges and may take place either abruptly or more or less slowly. Air masses that have strong temperature contrasts will exhibit very abrupt changes across the frontal zone, not only in temperature but in weather conditions as well. The frontal transition zone will be relatively thin when temperature conditions between the air masses differ markedly. In addition, an inversion exists along a vertical line through the front. The temperature in the cold wedge of air will decrease with altitude until the front is reached. Then there will be a rise in temperature in the transition zone, the abruptness and amount depending on the temperature difference between the two masses. With continued increase in altitude, the temperature will again fall in the warm mass.

In many cases, fronts form through the motion and meeting of air masses whose properties are contrasting. The process is known as frontogenesis. Should the air motion in a particular area be such, as a result of the pressure systems, as to cause bodies of air of different temperatures to be brought together, continuation of the process may cause a front to develop along the line of meeting of the different air bodies. Frontolysis is the process in which a front dissolves as the contrasting conditions causing the discontinuity between the air masses disappear. Depending on the motion of the air masses involved, several different types of fronts, each having particular properties, develop. There are four basic types of fronts: cold, warm, occluded, and stationary.

front formation—In many cases, existing fronts form through the motion and meeting of air masses whose original properties are contrasting. Frequently, however, fronts may form where none previously existed or were suspected. The process of formation of a front is known as frontogenesis. Should the air motion in a particular area be such, as a result of the pressure systems, as to cause air of different temperatures to be brought together, continuation of the process may cause a front to develop along the line of meeting of the different air bodies. Frontolysis is the process by which a front dissolves as the contrasting conditions causing the discontinuity between the air masses disappear. Depending on the motion of the air masses involved, several different types of fronts, each having particular properties, develop.

fronts, intertropical—Intertropical fronts require research and explanation. These fronts form as a result of the meeting and convergence of the trade winds of both hemispheres in tropical regions. The position of those boundaries must shift seasonally and geographically in accordance with the migration of the doldrums. The intertropical front of the Atlantic is therefore always north of the equator. The definite identification and evaluation of the intertropical fronts have been uncertain because so much of the equatorial region is over the oceans. Extended regions of storminess in the low latitudes indicates that some structural feature of the air, rather than simple convection, is responsible. When the sun is on or near the equator (during the equinoctial periods), temperature in the air masses on either side of the fronts are very nearly uniform. However, near the middle or end of summer or winter, temperature contrasts reach a maximum, for the temperature difference between the two hemispheres is then most pronounced.

OCCLUDED—Occluded fronts include both the best and the worst features of cold fronts and warm fronts. An occluded front is generated when a cold front following closely on the heels of, and moving faster than, a warm front overtakes the warm front and lifts the warm air mass completely off the ground. Either the cold frontal surface or the warm frontal surface is forced to rise off the ground, depending upon whether the cold air behind the cold front is colder or warmer than the cold air in advance of the warm front.

POLAR—The polar front advances as the polar air advances, and retreats accordingly. In wintertime, polar fronts advance with the polar air masses to much lower latitudes than in summer. An examination of world air-mass maps shows the northwest–southwest trend of the polar front during the winter, which becomes more nearly east–west during the summer.

STATIONARY—The identity of a front depends on its behavior. If the front is moving in the direction of the warm air, it will be a cold front; if in the direction of the cold air, a warm front. If the air masses are not in motion, the front will be stationary and is called a stationary front, represented on weather charts by a combination of the warm- and cold-front symbols. Should the cold air develop a movement toward the warm, the frontal surface, which will be sloping downward in the direction of motion, will buckle and steepen near the ground and develop cold-front characteristics.

UPPER—Those fronts which exist in the upper air but whose effects on the weather may often be experienced at the ground. Most upper fronts occur in connection with, and as the direct result of, occlusions. In the occlusion process, a cold front overtakes a warm one, and, depending on the relative temperatures of the respective cold air masses involved, one of the fronts is forced up over the surface of the other. The front remaining at the ground is the occluded front. The front that is forced up is the upper front. In the case of the warm-front occlusion, the cold front ascends the warm frontal surface and becomes an upper cold front. In the cold-front type of occlusion, the warm front being forced over the cold becomes an upper warm front. On working maps, upper cold fronts are shown by broken blue lines; upper warm fronts, by broken red lines. On printed maps the symbols are the same as those for surface fronts, with the exception that they are not in black.

WARM—Along the leading edge of a frontal wave, warmer air is replacing colder air. This is called a warm front. The approach of a well-developed warm front is usually heralded not only by falling pressure but also by a more or less regular sequence of clouds. First, cirrus appear. These give way successively to cirrostratus, altostratus, altocumulus, and nimbostratus. Brief showers may precede the steady rain accompanying the nimbostratus. As the warm front passes, the temperature rises, the wind shifts clockwise (in the Northern Hemisphere), and the steady rain stops.

WIND SHIFT—The wind shift or wind discontinuity on either side of a front is often one of the best criteria for locating it. There is nearly always some degree of shifting of the wind associated with fronts. This usually shows quite clearly on the synoptic weather chart and enables the proper placing of the front. Consideration of the relationship between winds and fronts shows that in the Northern Hemisphere, if one places one's back to the wind, any associated front will be on the left (*see* Buys Ballot's law).

frost—Frost is formed when water vapor in the air comes in direct contact with a cold surface and changes directly to small, very fine frost crystals, without condensing into water droplets first (this is sublimation, as opposed to condensation). Temperatures must be below freezing. Frost crystals grow on the exposed portions of ships, boats, cars, windows, and so forth and develop feathery patterns as the primary frost melts and recrystallizes.

frost smoke—Foglike clouds owing to the contact of cold air with relatively warm sea water.

hail—A product of the violent convection found in a thunderstorm; occurs only in connection with a thunderstorm. In the thundercloud the strong vertical air swirls the raindrops alternately above and below the freezing level. As a result, the drop grows by accumulation of ice and water until heavy enough to fall free. When a hailstone is cut apart, it shows a series of concentric shells formed by the successive passages above and below the freezing level.

halo—Refraction, or a combination of refraction and reflection, of light by ice crystals in the atmosphere (cirrostratus clouds) may cause a halo to appear. The most common form is a ring of light of radius 22° or 46°, with the sun or moon at the center. Occasionally, a faint white circle with a radius of 90° appears around the sun. This is called a Hevelian haloid. It is probably caused by refraction and internal reflection of the sun's light by bipyramidal ice crystals. A halo formed by refraction is usually faintly colored like a rainbow, with red nearest the celestial body and blue farthest from it.

high—High-pressure cells, or anticyclones. A high is defined as an area within which the pressure is high relative to the surroundings. The wind circulation is clockwise around an anticyclone (in the Northern Hemisphere), with the wind crossing the isobars at an angle and blowing from higher toward lower pressure.

AZORES—The semipermanent subtropical high over the North Atlantic Ocean, so named when it is located over the eastern part of the ocean. The same high when displaced to the western part of the Atlantic, or when it develops a separate cell there, is known as the Bermuda high. This high is one of the principal centers of weather action in northern latitudes.

SIBERIAN—An area of high pressure that forms over Siberia in winter. It is centered near Lake Baikal, where the average sea-level pressure exceeds 1,030 millibars from late November to early March.

horse latitudes—Belts of latitude over the oceans at approximately 30° to 35°N and S where the winds are predominantly calm or very light and the air is hot and dry. These latitudes mark the normal axis of subtropical highs and move north and south by about 5° following the sun. The two calm belts are known as the calms of Cancer and the calms of Capricorn, in the Northern and Southern hemispheres respectively; and in the North Atlantic Ocean they are in the latitudes of the Sargasso Sea. The weather is generally clear, although low clouds are common. In comparison with the doldrums, periods of stagnation in the horse latitudes are less persistent and more intermittent. The difference is due primarily to the fact that rising currents of warm air in the equatorial low carry large amounts of moisture, which condenses as the air cools at higher levels, while in the horse latitudes the air is descending and becoming less humid as it is warmed.

humidity—Water vapor in the air obtained by evaporation from surface waters of the earth. Subsequent condensation and precipitation return this water to the earth, completing a continuous cycle. Evaporation does not take place at a constant rate, regardless of the supply of surface water available. Many factors retard or promote the rate of evaporation: (1) Temperature. The rate of evaporation varies directly with the temperature of the water. (2) Relative humidity. When the air above the water is dry, evaporation will be greater than when air with high humidity overlies the water surface. (3) Wind. An important aid in evaporation in that it replaces the moist air near the water with dry air. (4) Composition of water. Evaporation varies inversely with the salinity of the water, proceeding at a greater rate from fresh water than from saltwater. Under equivalent conditions, ocean water will evaporate about 5 percent more slowly than fresh water. (5) Areas of evaporation. If two volumes of water are equal, evaporation will be greater for the one having the larger exposed surface.

Relative humidity is the ratio of the amount of water vapor in the air to the amount the air can hold at that temperature. The ratio is always expressed as a percentage. If the air has 40 grains of water vapor per pound and can hold at that temperature 50 grains per pound (the capacity), then the relative humidity is 40/50, or 80 percent. Relative humidity varies inversely with temperature.

Absolute humidity is the weight of water vapor per unit volume of air. The unit volume generally used is either the cubic foot or the cubic meter. If the amount of water vapor in one cubic foot of air is extracted and weighed, the result, expressed in grams per cubic foot, is the absolute humidity.

hurricanes and typhoons—Powered by moisture from the sea and driven by the easterly trade winds and their own energy, their winds blow with lethal velocity, and tornadoes frequently descend from the advance thunderclouds. Compared to the great cyclonic storm systems of middle and high latitudes, hurricanes and typhoons are of rather moderate size; their worst winds do not attain tornado velocities. Still, their broad, spiral bases dominate the weather over many thousands of square miles, and they sometimes extend from the earth's surface to over 50,000 feet. Hurricanes and typhoons are tropical cyclones whose wind speeds exceed 64 knots (75 mph). Like all cyclones, they are lows —atmospheric pressure systems in which the barometer pressure decreases progressively to a minimum value at the center and toward which winds blow spirally inward in a counterclockwise direction, in the Northern Hemisphere. In the Southern Hemisphere, winds spiral inward in a clockwise direction. Hurricanes and typhoons are amazingly symmetrical, with central isobars forming almost perfect circles. They develop only over tropical oceans. They break up quickly after moving over land or over an area of very cold water.

hurricane season—That portion of the year having a relatively high incidence of hurricanes. In the North Atlantic it is usually regarded as the period from June through November, and in the East and North Pacific it is usually regarded as the period from June through October.

hygrograph—An instrument that makes a continuous record of humidity. The sensitive element is a bundle of blond human hair which expands or contracts as the humidity increases or decreases. By means of delicate springs and levers, this change in length is communicated to a pen arm, which inscribes a trace on a rotating drum. In appearance the instrument resembles the thermograph. The chart is calibrated vertically in relative humidity from 0 to 100 percent.

hygrometer (psychrometer)—The hygrometer consists of a support to which are attached two ordinary, accurate, mercury thermometers. One of the thermometers has a thin layer of muslin wrapped around the bulb which is kept wet (never with saltwater) when the instrument is in use. This is called the wet-bulb thermometer, and the other the dry-bulb thermometer. The dry-bulb thermometer shows the current air temperature. Tables have been developed to obtain the relative humidity and dew point, given the dry-bulb reading and difference between the wet and dry, known as the depression of the wet bulb.

ice pellets—Transparent or translucent beads of ice, sometimes called sleet, occurring when rain dropping from high-level warm air falls through a layer of freezing air. The raindrops first become freezing rain (supercooled) and, if they strike the ground in this condition, form glaze. Further cooling produces ice pellets, or true sleet.

ice prisms—Ice prisms form hexagonal plates and needles that glitter almost like diamonds as the wind blows them around. Because of their extremely small size, they fall at a very slow rate. Ice needles often make halos around the sun or moon. In very cold climates, ice-needle fogs frequently form at the ground.

insolation—The radiant energy received from the sun is called insolation. This energy is spread over a very broad band of wavelengths known as the solar spectrum, which consists of radio waves, microwaves, infrared waves, visible light (red to violet), ultraviolet waves, X rays, and gamma rays. In addition there are bursts of material in the form of electrons and other ions which occasionally stream out from the sun. About 90 percent of the total energy is concentrated in the visible portion of the spectrum, so it is visible light that indirectly provides most of the heat energy to the atmosphere. As the result of reflection by clouds and other particles in the atmosphere and the irregular reflection by water, ice, and variable ground surfaces, about 43 percent of insolation is returned to space with no appreciable effect on the atmosphere. This is known as the reflectivity of albedo of the earth. Of the remaining portion (57 percent), or the usable insolation, one-quarter is absorbed in the atmosphere and three-quarters penetrates to the earth's surface and is absorbed there.

isallotherm—Lines connecting points in which an equal temperature variation is observed within a three-hour interval.

isobar—Atmospheric-pressure readings are taken simultaneously all over the world. When these are plotted on charts, lines are drawn connecting points of equal pressure. These lines of equal (or constant) pressure, called isobars, resemble equal-altitude contours, which define hills and valleys on a topographic chart. A chart for a particular time, which includes such data as wind, weather, temperature, clouds, isobars, etc., for a large number of stations is called a synoptic chart because it gives a synopsis, or general view, of weather conditions over a large area at a given instant of time. Isobars are usually drawn at intervals of four millibars (mbs) on weather maps. Any synoptic chart will show a distribution of pressure in which there are regions of high pressure and low pressure resembling the mountains, hills, ridges, and valleys found in topographic charts. A typical region of high or low pressure on a weather map has a compact shape and is seldom less than a few hundred miles in width.

In the middle latitudes, isobars display characteristic shapes, indicating areas of alternately high and low pressure. These areas are rudely circular or elliptical in shape and usually cover tens of thousands of square miles. A particular pressure configuration, whether high or low, may cover a few states or one-half the country. There is usually no particular point where the low begins and the high ends (*see* fronts). There is, rather, a continuous increase in pressure from the center of the low to the center of the high and then a steady decrease to the next low, and so on. The highs and lows are not always equally well developed. One may be much stronger than the other, and their circular or elliptical shapes may be considerably distorted at times. Thus, two well-developed low-pressure areas may exist on a map adjacent to each other, in which case they are separated by a narrow ridge of higher pressure. Whatever the case, the uniformity or irregularity of the pressure gradient will be indicated by the shape and spacing of the isobars.

isobaric surface—A surface where the pressure is everywhere the same. This is not necessarily a horizontal surface. If several parallel, equally spaced plane surfaces are used to cut an isobaric surface into horizontal sections, a pattern of isobaric lines is formed. If lines are closely spaced, the pressure gradient is strong.

jet streams—Considered to be tubular ribbons of high-speed winds in the atmosphere, usually found at between 30,000 and 40,000 feet, they tend to form at tropopause overlaps, especially at the Arctic tropopause and the extratropical tropopause, and are at least partially the result of strong temperature contrasts there. On the average, jet streams are about 300 miles wide and 4 miles deep, with wind speeds near the center (core) sometimes reaching 250 knots. The number of jet streams around and over the world and their paths vary from day to day and from season to season. Two places where jet streams occur with great frequency are over Japan and over New England. In winter, over the North American continent there are usually three major jet streams: (1) over northern Canada, (2) over the United States, and (3) over the subtropics.

latent heat—Evaporation is a cooling process because energy is required to transform water from a liquid to a gaseous state. Specifically, 540 calories of heat are required to vaporize 1 gram of water, without any temperature change occurring. Since the earth's surface is close to 71 percent water, evaporation is a very important process. The energy for this comes from the insolation absorbed by the water. When condensation of water occurs in the atmosphere (clouds, fog, etc.), the 540 calories per gram are then released into the atmosphere and provide an important warming process.

Since this heat is used only to bring about the transition to and from a vapor state and has no effect on the temperature of either the liquid or the vapor, it is known as latent heat. When water reaches the boiling point, it remains at a temperature of 100°C (212°F) until all the water has boiled off. The heat absorbed after the liquid has reached 100°C is employed in the change of state, and the resulting steam or water vapor is also at the temperature of 100°C. When water vapor condenses, the latent heat is liberated into the atmosphere.

lows—Areas within which the pressure is low relative to the surroundings. Major lows are formed by horizontal wavelike actions when two different air masses come together (like two highs of different temperatures), coupled with rising air currents. The "wave" grows larger and larger and finally breaks like an ocean wave. The whirling air creates a low-pressure cell, and frequently a storm is born.

A local low may form when the air under a cumulonimbus cloud (thunderhead) is rising very rapidly and the air surrounding the region beneath the cloud spirals horizontally inward, in counterclockwise fashion, because of the earth's rotation. Such lows are quite small in diameter, averaging only twenty to thirty-five miles across.

A heat low develops over deserts and other intensely heated areas. The air heats, then expands, rises, and flows outward (diverges) at higher levels. Thus, there is a net decrease in the air in the vertical air column. The pressure drops and the surrounding air rushes in, spiraling inward in counterclockwise fashion. This type of low lasts most of the summer in southwestern Arizona and southwestern California and in the deserts of the world. Dust devils are very small heat lows.

Semipermanent lows occur in various places, the most prominent ones being west of Iceland and over the Aleutians (in winter only) in the Northern Hemisphere, and near the Ross Sea and Waddell Sea in the Antarctic. The regions occupied by these semipermanent lows are sometimes called the graveyards of the lows, since many lows move directly into these areas and lose their identity as they merge with and reinforce the semipermanent lows. The low pressure in these areas is maintained largely by these migratory lows, which stall there.

monsoon—A name for seasonal winds (derived from Arabic *mausim*, a season). It was first applied to the winds over the Arabian Sea which flow for six months from the northeast and for six months from the southeast, but it has been extended to apply to similar winds in other parts of the world. Winds whose direction reverses with the season require a reversal in the pressure gradient. The most notable and widespread pressure change is that responsible for the Indian monsoon. From winter to summer over Asia there is a reversal of pressure from high to low. This is the direct cause of the Indian monsoon. During the winter, the winds blow normally from the northeast, originating in the high over Asia; but in the summer, pressure is low over Asia, and the winds reverse. The air motion begins in the southern horse latitudes and follows the pressure gradient into central Asia. After blowing across the open tropical ocean, the southwest summer monsoon becomes extremely warm and humid. Upon striking the high plateaus and mountains of India, the air is forced to ascend and cools adiabatically as it does so. This cooling lowers the air temperature beneath the dew point, resulting in the rainy season of the Indian summer. The winter monsoon, blowing from the northeast from central Asia, is cold and dry owing to its continental origin. Monsoon winds become light and variable during the period of change, spring and autumn.

monsoon depressions—Relatively weak cyclones that travel over many portions of the oceanic and continental tropics. Surface temperatures are almost constant through these cyclones, or vortices; wind speeds average 10 to 20 knots. As a rule, these cyclones move toward the west or northwest at ten to twelve knots. These vortices are most prominent over southern Asia during the height of the summer monsoon season, where the intertropical convergence zone (ITCZ) is located. These cyclones, or depressions, as they are called in India, account for much of the precipitation in Southeast Asia.

polar convergence—A line along which cold polar water sinks under warmer water in its movement toward lower latitudes. It is marked by a sharp change in surface temperatures, particularly in the Southern Hemisphere.

pressure gradient—A pressure gradient can be illustrated by reference to a topographic contour map. The steepest slope is at a right angle to the contour lines, and its numerical value is greatest where the contour lines are close together. Similarly, a pressure gradient is spoken of as being at right angles to the isobars, its magnitude being measured by the ratio pressure difference/distance. Thus, if two adjacent isobars (at a 4 millibar interval) are fifty miles apart, the pressure gradient is 4/50 or 0.08 m/mile.

pressure systems—If a weather map is examined, it will be noticed that there is only a limited number of pressure patterns (or systems) occurring in nature. Principal are the highs (high-pressure cells; anticyclones) and the lows (low-pressure cells; cyclones; depressions). The wind circulation is clockwise around an anticyclone (in the Northern Hemisphere), with the wind crossing the isobars at an angle and blowing from higher toward lower pressure. A trough of low pressure is an elongated area of low pressure that extends from the center of a cyclone. A ridge (or wedge) of high pressure is an elongated area of high pressure that extends from the center of an anticyclone. A col is the saddlebacked region between two anticyclones or two cyclones.

prevailing westerlies—In both hemispheres a system of winds is directed poleward from the subtropical high-pressure belt. These winds become southwesterly to westerly in both hemispheres as a result of Coriolis deflection and are known as the prevailing westerlies. In the Southern Hemisphere, conditions are very uniform owing to the broad ocean areas. Because of this, a strong and uniform pressure gradient is normally present in the Southern Hemisphere between the subtropical high and the subpolar low. In the Northern Hemisphere, the prevailing westerlies are very variable and are often masked by the moving low- and high-pressure areas.

ridge—A ridge (or wedge) of high pressure is an elongated area of high pressure that extends from the center of an anticyclone (high). The wind circulation is essentially anticyclonic (clockwise).

rime—A thick, frosty deposit, which forms when objects with subfreezing temperatures encounter a fog.

Saint Elmo's fire—A luminous discharge of electricity from pointed objects such as masts and yardarms of ships, lightning rods, steeples, mountaintops, blades of grass, human hair, arms, and so on, occurring when there is considerable difference in the electrical charge between the object and the air. It appears most frequently during a storm.

sleet—If rain falls into a layer of air at freezing temperature, it solidifies into clear ice pellets. Sleet may also develop from the freezing of melted snow as it falls through a cold layer of air near the ground.

snow—Formed when tiny particles in the air act as nuclei upon which water vapor crystalizes. The air must be supersaturated with water vapor and must be below the freezing point (32°F). Microscopic bits of soil, sand, clay, and smoke are common nuclei. In general, cloud temperatures must be about +10°F to −4°F before snow begins to form. Water vapor changes to snow even without nuclei in supersaturated air at about −38°F.

squall lines—Frequently precede fast-moving cold fronts. They are almost unbroken lines of black clouds, sometimes towering to 40,000 feet or higher, including thunderstorms and, sometimes, tornadoes. From a boat, a squall line looks like a wall of rolling, boiling, black fog. The wind shifts and increases suddenly with the approach of a squall line, and the deluge of rain may carry the cloud right down to the ground. Squall lines occur when winds above a cold front, moving in the same direction in which the front is advancing, prevent the lifting of the warm air mass by the leading edge of the cold air mass.

steam fog—Fog formed when water vapor is added to air that is much colder than the vapor's source, usually when very cold air drifts across relatively warm water. Steam fog is commonly observed over lakes and streams on cold autumn mornings as well as in polar regions. It is sometimes confused with ice fog, but its particles are entirely liquid. At temperatures below −20°F, these may freeze into droxtals (ice crystals) and create a type of fog that is known as frost smoke.

storm surge—A rise above normal water level on the open coast due to the wind. Storm surges resulting from a hurricane or other intense storms also include a rise due to atmospheric-pressure reduction as well as that due to wind. A storm surge is most severe when it occurs in conjunction with a high tide.

storm tides—In relatively tideless seas like the Baltic and the Mediterranean, winds cause the chief fluctuations in sea level. Elsewhere, the astronomical tides usually mask these variations. However, severe extratropical storms or tropical cyclones can produce changes in sea level that exceed the normal range of tide. Like tsunamis, these storm tides are popularly called tidal waves, but are not associated with the tide.

They consist of a single wave crest and hence have no period or wavelength. Three effects in a storm induce a rise in sea level. The first is wind, which results in a piling up of water. The second is convergence of wind-driven currents, which elevates the sea surface along the convergence line. In shallow water, bottom friction and the effects of local topography cause this elevation to persist and may even intensify it. The low atmospheric pressure that accompanies severe storms causes the third effect, which is sometimes referred to as the "inverted barometer"; an inch of mercury is equivalent to about 13.6 inches of water, and the adjustment of the sea surface to the reduced pressure can amount to several feet.

thunder—The noise that accompanies lightning is caused by the heating and ionizing of the air by the lightning, which results in rapid expansion of the air along its path and the sending out of a compression wave. Thunder may be heard at a distance of as much as fifteen miles, but the sound generally does not carry that far. The time between the flash and the thunder is an indication of distance, because of the difference in the speeds of light and sound. Since the former is virtually instantaneous, and the speed of sound is about 1,117 feet per second, the approximate distance from the sound in nautical miles is equal to the elapsed time in seconds divided by 5.5.

thunderstorms—Violent local phenomena produced by cumulonimbus clouds; characterized by squalls, turbulence, gustiness, heavy showers, lightning, thunder, and hail. Visibility is invariably poor in a thunderstorm, and ceilings are low and ragged. Thunderstorms form in a number of ways, but all require warm, unstable air of high moisture content, and some sort of lifting. Parcels must be forced upward to a point where they are warmer than surrounding air, so that they will ascend rapidly until cooled to the temperature of the surrounding air. The air may be lifted in several ways: by heating, by mountains, by fronts. Thunderstorms usually have three stages. First, cumulus clouds develop into thunderheads when the rising air reaches about 25,000 feet. The mature stage commences when the ascending air reaches such a height that precipitation occurs. The final stage occurs when the precipitation becomes light and finally ceases. High-level winds blow the ice crystals at the top of the thunderheads into the characteristic anvil top.

tornadoes and waterspouts—The most destructive storms in the earth's atmosphere; a small funnel with winds up to several hundred knots revolving tightly around a core. Tornadoes travel along paths ranging to seventy miles or more. The funnel cloud usually strikes the ground several times, rising after impacts a few miles long. The funnel does little damage until it actually touches the ground. In the Northern Hemisphere, the frantic winds blow counterclockwise around the vortex. Another destructive force is the 100- to 200-knot updraft at the center of the funnel, which sucks up houses, cars, and animals, often carrying them hundreds of feet. Tornadoes are most common in the spring and early summer, when warm and moist air masses from the Gulf of Mexico encounter cold air masses of the northern part of the continent. Waterspouts are the same phenomenon as tornadoes, except that they form over the sea and are less violent. When they touch the surface, dense spray is drawn upward into the funnel.

trade winds (tropical easterlies)—The winds blowing from the horse latitudes to the doldrums are among the most constant of the planetary system. The name "trade" applied to winds is derived from the expression "to blow trade," which meant to blow constant. These winds are best developed over the Atlantic and Pacific, away from the pressure perturbations of the continents, and tend to follow the pressure gradient toward the equator, but are deflected by Coriolis. The trades have an average speed of ten to fifteen knots and are strongest during the summer, when the subtropical high is strongest.

tropical depression—A tropical depression has one or more closed isobars and some rotary circulation at the surface. The highest sustained surface wind speed is about thirty-three knots.

tropical disturbance—A discrete low-pressure system of organized convection generally 100 to 300 miles in diameter, having a nonfrontal migratory character, and having maintained its identity for twenty-four hours or more. It has no strong winds and no isobars that completely enclose it.

trough—A trough of low pressure is an elongated area of relatively low pressure which extends from the center of a cyclone. The trough may have U-shaped or V-shaped isobars. The V-shaped isobars are associated with weather fronts. The wind circulating around a trough is essentially cyclonic (counterclockwise).

tsunamis—Ocean waves produced by sudden, large-scale motions of the ocean floor or the shore, as by a volcanic eruption, earthquake, or landslide. If they are caused by a submarine earthquake, they are usually called seismic sea waves. The point directly above the disturbance, at which the waves originate, is called the epicenter. A tsunami or a storm tide that overflows the land is known as a tidal wave. If a volcanic eruption occurs below the surface of the sea, the escaping gases cause a quantity of water to be pushed upward in the shape of a dome or mount. The same effect is caused by the sudden rising of a portion of the bottom. As this water settles back, it creates waves that travel at high speed. Near the epicenter, the first wave may be the highest. At great distances, the highest wave usually occurs later in the series, commonly between the third and the eighth wave.

typhoon—A tropical cyclone in the western Pacific west of 180 degrees longitude with sustained surface winds of 64 knots (74 mph) or higher.

weather warnings—*See* entry in Navigation Terms.

III

NAVIGATIONAL
STARS

Acamar—Crosses the celestial meridian near the southern horizon during evening twilight in February and during morning twilight in August. It is part of the constellation Eridanus (the River), which is not a striking configuration. It is the faintest star listed among the fifty-seven in the almanac but is the brightest in its immediate vicinity. The nearest bright star is Achernar, about 20° away in a southerly direction. Dec. 40°S, SHA 316°, mag. 3.1.

Achernar—At the southern end of the inconspicuous constellation Eridanus (the River); is one of the brightest stars of the Southern Hemisphere. It is not visible north of latitude 33°N. It crosses the celestial meridian during evening twilight in January and during morning twilight in early August. Nearly a straight line is formed by Fomalhaut (about 40°WNW), Achernar, and Canopus, about the same distance in the opposite direction (ESE). However, since these stars are widely separated, the relationship is not striking. Dec. 57°S, SHA 336°, mag. 0.6.

Acrux—The brightest and most southerly star in the Southern Cross. It is not visible north of latitude 27°N. It crosses the celestial meridian during evening twilight in early June and during morning twilight in January. It is about 15°WSW of first-magnitude Hadar and Rigil Kentaurus. Dec. 63°S, SHA 174°, mag. 1.1.

Adhara—About 10°S and a little to the east of Sirius is a small triangle of three second-magnitude stars. Adhara is the westernmost and brightest. It crosses the celestial meridian to the south during evening twilight in March and during morning twilight in October. Dec. 29°S, SHA 256°, mag. 1.6.

Aldebaran—If the line formed by the belt of Orion (the Hunter) is extended about 20° to the northwest and curved somewhat toward the

263

north, it leads to first-magnitude Aldebaran, in Taurus (the Bull), a group of stars forming a V. A long, curving line starting at Sirius extends through Procyon, Pollux, Capella, and Aldebaran. Dec. 16°N, SHA 291°, mag. 1.1.

Alioth—The third star from the outer end of the handle of the Big Dipper, and the brightest star of the group. Dec. 56°N, SHA 167°, mag. 1.7.

Alkaid—The star at the outer end of the handle of the Big Dipper, farthest from the bowl. It is the second-brightest star of the group. Dec. 49°N, SHA 153°, mag. 1.9.

Alnair—Westernmost of two second-magnitude stars midway between first-magnitude Fomalhaut, approximately 20° to the northeast, and second-magnitude Peacock, about the same distance in the opposite direction. A curved line extending eastward from the Southern Cross passes through Hadar and Rigil Kentaurus and, if extended with less curvature, leads first to Peacock and then to Alnair. This star forms triangles with Fomalhaut and Ankaa, with Ankaa and Achernar, and with Achernar and Peacock. It is not visible north of latitude 43°N. It crosses the celestial meridian during evening twilight early in December and during morning twilight in June. Dec. 47°S, SHA 28°, mag. 2.2.

Alnilam—The middle star of the belt of Orion (the Hunter). Dec. 1°S, SHA 276°, mag. 1.8.

Alphard—A second-magnitude star, brightest in the inconspicuous constellation Hydra (the Water Monster). The nearest bright star is first-magnitude Regulus, about 20° NNE. It is about midway between the horizon and the zenith when it crosses the celestial meridian to the south during evening twilight in late April and during morning twilight in November. Dec. 9°S, SHA 218°, mag. 2.2.

Alphecca—The brightest star of Corona Borealis, the Northern Crown, about 20°ENE of first-magnitude Arcturus. It forms a triangle with Arcturus and Alkaid. It crosses the celestial meridian near the zenith during evening twilight in July and during morning twilight in February. Dec. 27°N, SHA 127°, mag. 2.3.

Alpheratz—A second-magnitude star, at the northeast corner of the great square of Pegasus (the Winged Horse); is the brightest of the four stars forming the square. It crosses the celestial meridian near the zenith during evening twilight early in January and during morning twilight in July. Dec. 29°N, SHA 358°, mag. 2.2.

Altair—At the southern vertex of a large triangle that is a conspicuous feature of the evening sky in late summer and in autumn. The right angle is at Vega, and the northern vertex is at Deneb. All three are first-magnitude stars. Two fainter stars close to Altair, one on each side in a line through Vega, form a characteristic pattern, making Altair one of the stars easiest to identify. It crosses the celestial meridian during evening twilight in October and during morning twilight in May. Dec. 9°N, SHA 63°, mag. 0.9.

Ankaa—A second-magnitude star, the brightest star in inconspicuous Phoenix. It is surrounded by and forms a series of triangles with Diphda, Fomalhaut, Alnair, Achernar, and Acamar. It crosses the celestial meridian low in the southern sky in January and during morning twilight in July. Dec. 42°S, SHA 354°, mag. 2.4.

Antares—The brightest star in the conspicuous constellation Scorpio (the Scorpion), which is low in the southern sky during evening twilight in late July and during morning twilight in late February. No other first-magnitude star is within 40° of Antares, and none toward the north is within 60°. It has a noticeable reddish hue, like Mars, which is occasionally near it in the sky. Dec. 26°S, SHA 113°, mag. 1.2.

Arcturus—The curved line along the stars forming the handle of the Big Dipper, if continued in a direction away from the bowl, passes through brilliant, first-magnitude Arcturus. The distance from Alkaid, at the end of the Big Dipper, to Arcturus is a little more than the length of the dipper. Arcturus forms a large triangle with Alkaid and Alphecca. Dec. 19°N, SHA 146°, mag. 0.2.

Atria—The brightest of three stars forming a small triangle called Triangulum Australe, the Southern Triangle, not far from the south celestial pole. It is not seen north of latitude 21°N. A line through the east–west arm of the Southern Cross, if continued toward the east and curved somewhat toward the south, leads first to Hadar; then to Rigil Kentaurus; then, by curving more sharply, to the northernmost star of the triangle; and finally to Atria, only about 21° from the south celestial pole. Dec. 69°S, SHA 108°, mag. 1.9.

Avior—The westernmost star of Vela (the Sail, or False Southern Cross), about 30° WNW of the true Southern Cross, about 15° ESE of brilliant Canopus, and nearly enclosed within a large triangle formed by Canopus, Suhail, and Miaplacidus. It is not visible north of latitude 31°N. Below this latitude it crosses the celestial meridian low in November. Dec. 59°S, SHA 234°, mag. 1.7.

Bellatrix—A second-magnitude star north and a little west of the belt of Orion (the Hunter). It is about equidistant from the belt and first-magnitude, red Betelgeuse. Bellatrix is at the northwest corner of a box surrounding the belt of Orion. Dec. 6°N, SHA 279°, mag. 1.7.

Beta Centauri—First-magnitude star in the group Centaurus; one of the pointers to Crux (Southern Cross). Also called Hadar.

Betelgeuse—A conspicuous, reddish star of variable brightness about 10° N and a little east of the belt of Orion (the Hunter). Magnitude varying from .0 to 1.2, SHA 271°, Dec. 7°24'N.

Boötes—Northern constellation whose brightest star is Arcturus, a Latin word meaning "bear guard," star and group having been considered, in ancient times, as guard or ward of the constellation Ursa Major, or Great Bear. Boötes is located about 30°S of Alkaid (or Benetnasch), in Ursa Major.

Canis Major—Constellation lying southeast of Orion and containing the brightest fixed star in the heavens, Sirius, (the Dog Star). Dec. 16.5°S, SHA 259°.

Canis Minor—Constellation located to the east of Orion and north of Canis Major, containing the bright star Procyon. Dec. 5.5°N, SHA 245°, mag. .5.

Canopus—Second-brightest star in the sky; about 35° S of Sirius. A line extending eastward through the belt of Orion and curving toward the south passes first through Sirius, then through the small triangle of which Adhara is the brightest star, and finally to Canopus, which forms a large triangle with Suhail and Miaplacidus. The triangle nearly encloses Vela (the Sail or False Southern Cross), about 20° ESE of Canopus. Canopus is not visible north of latitude 37°N. It is on the edge of the Milky Way; and while many relatively bright stars are nearby, none in the immediate vicinity of Canopus approaches it in brightness. Dec. 53°S, SHA 264°, mag. (−) 0.9.

Capella—A brilliant star about 45° N of the belt of Orion (the Hunter). A curved line starting at Sirius and extending through Procyon, Pollux, Capella, Aldebaran, the belt of Orion, and back to Sirius forms an inverted teardrop figure with Capella at the top and the various stars being about equally spaced along the curve. Capella crosses the celestial meridian near the zenith during evening twilight in early March and during morning twilight in late September. Dec. 46°N, SHA 281°, mag. 0.2.

Cassiopeia—Constellation consisting of five stars, three of which are of second magnitude, in approximately Dec. 60° N. It may be recognized as a distorted W, on the opposite side of the polestar, and at about the same distance from it, as the Great Bear (Big Dipper). Also called Cassiopeia's Chair and the Lady's Chair.

Castor and Pollux—The two brightest stars of the group known as Gemini, the Latin name for "twins"; located in the zodiacal belt between Taurus and Leo and having a declination of about 30° N and SHA 244°.

Centaurus—Southern constellation lying east, north, and west of Crux (Southern Cross). A line joining its two brightest stars, alpha Centauri (Rigil Kentaurus) and beta Centauri (Hadar), and extended westward about 12° enters Crux. Rigil Kentaurus (Centaur's Foot), of mag. 0.3, is said to be nearest to the earth of all the fixed stars.

Cepheus—Constellation located between Cygnus and Polaris. A gentle curve from Deneb (α Cygni) to Polaris passes at halfway mark through Cepheus.

Cetus—Constellation lying near the equator, its greater part in the southern sky, extending through Dec. 5°N to 20°S. It has only two navigational stars, Menkar (α Ceti) and Deneb Kaitos or Diphda (β Ceti).

Columba—Southern constellation adjacent to, and southwest of, Canis Major, containing as its brightest star Phact (α Columbae) in Dec. 34° 6' and SHA 275°, mag. 2.75; called also Columba Noachi, Columba Noae, or Noah's Dove.

Corona Borealis—Northern constellation adjoining and east of Boötes. It contains the bright star Alphecca.

Corvus—Small constellation south of Virgo in about Dec. 20°S, often called the Cutter's Mainsail; also called the Crow and the Raven. A line joining its two northern stars and forming the gaff or head of the "mainsail" extended outward meets, at 10° distance, the bright star Spica (α Virginis).

Crux—Constellation commonly known as the Southern Cross, located in about Dec. 60°S and about 40° due south of Corvus. Four of its stars, suitable for navigational use, mark the extremities of a well-defined cruciform figure and, together with the two brightest stars of Centaurus, lying west of, and pointing toward, the Cross at 9.5° distance, present an imposing sight. Alpha Crucis, a double star of mag. 1.05, is the brightest in the group and marks the Cross's foot, or southernmost limit.

Cygnus—Northern constellation in the Milky Way, adjoining and east of Lyra. Its five principal stars form a well-defined Latin cross 22° in length, with Deneb (α Cygni), the brightest, of mag. 1.3, marking the head or northeastern extremity.

Deneb—A bright star at the northeastern vertex of a large right triangle formed by Altair, Vega, and Deneb, the right angle being at Vega. These three stars are the brightest in the eastern sky during summer evenings. Deneb is not as bright as the other two but is the brightest star in the constellation Cygnus (the Swan). It crosses the celestial meridian near the zenith during evening twilight in November and during morning twilight in late May. Dec. 45°N, SHA 50°, mag. 1.3.

Diphda—Also called Deneb Kaitos, Beta (β) Ceti, brighter of two navigational stars in Cetus (the Whale), of mag. 2.2, Dec. 18.25°S, SHA 349° 40'; located nearly on a line joining the two eastern stars of the square of Pegasus (Alpheratz and Algenib), projected southward about 33°; also written Difda.

Dubhe—Forms the outer rim of the bowl of the Big Dipper. It and Merak (not one of the fifty-seven navigational stars) are the two "pointers" used to locate Polaris, Dubhe being the one nearer the polestar. Dec. 62°N, SHA 194°, mag. 2.0.

El Nath—A second-magnitude star between Capella, about 15° to the north, and Betelgeuse, about 20° to the south. It is a little north of a line connecting Aldebaran and Pollux. It is at the end of the northern fork of V-shaped Taurus (the Bull). Aldebaran is the principal star at the closed end of the V. This constellation is approximately 25° NNW of Orion (the Hunter). Dec. 29° N, SHA 279°, mag. 1.8.

Eltanin—The southernmost and brightest star in the inconspicuous constellation Draco (the Dragon), south and somewhat east of the Little Dipper. A straight line extending northwestward through Altair and its two fainter companions passes first through brilliant Vega, and about 15° beyond, to second-magnitude Eltanin. Eltanin crosses the celestial meridian high in the sky toward the north during evening twilight in early September and during morning twilight in late March. Dec. 15°N, SHA 91°, mag. 2.4.

Enif—A third-magnitude star midway between Altair, and Markab, the southwestern corner of the great square of Pegasus. Enif crosses the celestial meridian to the south during evening twilight in November and during morning twilight in June. Dec. 10°N, SHA 34°, mag. 2.5.

Eridanus—Long, winding constellation extending southward and westward over 53° of declination and 50° of SHA from the west side of the Orion group. The bright star Achernar marks its southern end, about halfway between Canopus and Fomalhaut.

Fomalhaut—A first-magnitude star well separated from stars of comparable brightness and from conspicuous configurations. A line through the western side of the great square of Pegasus, extended about 45° toward the south, passes close to Fomalhaut. Dec. 30°S, SHA 16°, mag. 1.3.

Giena—A third-magnitude star, the brightest in the constellation Corvus (the Crow). A long, sweeping arc starting with the handle of the Big

Dipper and extending successively through Arcturus and Spica leads to this relatively small four-sided figure, made up of third-magnitude stars. Giena is at the northwest corner. It crosses the celestial meridian during evening twilight in late May and during morning twilight in December. Dec. 17°S, SHA 176°, mag. 2.8.

Hadar—A first-magnitude star about 10° E of the Southern Cross and about 5° W of Rigil Kentaurus, the brightest of several bright stars in this part of the sky. Dec. 60°S, SHA 149°, mag. 0.9. (*See* beta Centauri.)

Hamal—The brightest star of the inconspicuous constellation Aries (the Ram). A line through the center of the great square of Pegasus, extended about 25° E and curved slightly toward the north, leads to Hamal. It is on the meridian to the south during evening twilight in January and during morning twilight in August. Dec. 23°N, SHA 329°, mag. 2.2.

Hyades—A V-shaped group of stars in Taurus in which is included Aldebaran (α Tauri).

Hydra—The only navigational star in Hydra (the Water Monster), a long, inconspicuous constellation near Corvus, is the second-magnitude Alphard. This star is more easily identified by its being close to the extension of a line from the pointer of the Big Dipper through Regulus and extending southward.

Kaus Australis—Near the southern end of a group of second- and third-magnitude stars forming the constellation Sagittarius (the Archer), about 25° ESE of Antares. Dec. 34°S, SHA 84°, mag. 2.0.

Kochab—Forms the outer rim of the bowl of the Little Dipper, at the opposite end from Polaris about 15° N. It is directly above the pole during evening twilight in early July and during morning twilight in January, and directly below the pole, low in the northern sky, during evening twilight of early February and morning twilight of late August. Dec. 74°N, SHA 137°, mag. 2.2.

Libra—Southern constellation lying to the northwest of Scorpio and through which the sun passes in November. It contains two navigational stars: Kiffa Australis and Kiffa Borealis.

Lyra—Named for the lyre of Orpheus in Greek mythology; a small northern constellation on the west side of Cygnus (the Swan). It contains the navigational star Vega, or α Lyrae; mag. 0.1, SHA 81° 10′, Dec. 38.75°N. With Deneb (α Cygni) and Altair (α Aquilae), marks out a neat triangle, nearly right-angled at its brightest corner, that occupied by Vega itself.

Markab—α Pegasi, a star of mag. 2.57, situated at the southwest corner of the square of Pegasus. Dec. 15°N, SHA 14°, mag. 2.6.

Menkar—A third-magnitude star at the eastern end of the inconspicuous constellation Cetus (the Whale). No bright stars are nearby. A straight line from Aldebaran extending about 25° in the direction indicated by the point of the V of Taurus (the Bull) leads to Menkar. A long, straight line from Fomalhaut east-northeastward through Diphda, and extended about 40°, leads to Menkar. It crosses the celestial meridian during evening twilight in February and during morning twilight in August. Dec. 4°N, SHA 315°, mag. 2.8.

Menkent—A second-magnitude star about 25° N of Hadar and about 30° NE of the Southern Cross. A line from Giena across the opposite corner of the small, four-sided Corvus (the Crow), and then curving a little toward the east, leads to Menkent. With Antares and Rigil Kentaurus, Menkent forms a large triangle. It crosses the celestial meridian low in the southern sky during evening twilight in late June and during morning twilight in early January. Dec. 36°S, SHA 149°, mag. 2.3.

Miaplacidus—Star of mag. 1.8 in Argo, having SHA 221°50' and Dec. 69.5°S. Southernmost of all stars suitable in magnitude for navigational observation, it may be located southwest and distant about 20° from Acrux, the star marking the lower extremity, or "foot," of the Southern Cross.

Mintaka—Westernmost star of three constituting the belt of Orion. A double star of mag. 2.48, SHA 277°35', Dec. 0°20'S.

Mizar—Second star in tail of the Great Bear (Ursa Major), or handle of the Big Dipper; SHA 159° 29' and Dec. 55° 11'N. It is a binary star of mag. 2.40. The faint companion of this star is called Alcor, from an Arabic word meaning "the weak one."

Nunki—The more northerly of the two brightest stars of a group of second- and third-magnitude stars forming the constellation Sagittarius (the Archer), about 30°E of Antares. It is over the meridian to the south during evening twilight in early October and during morning twilight in April. Dec. 26°S, SHA 77°, mag. 2.1.

Orion—Orion (the Hunter) is probably the best-known constellation in the entire sky, with the exception of the Big Dipper. This figure is well known to observers in both Northern and Southern hemispheres, as the belt of Orion lies almost exactly on the celestial equator. Brilliant Rigel and first-magnitude Betelgeuse lie approximately equal distances below and above the belt, respectively. Several navigational stars may be found by the use of Orion. If the line of the belt is continued to the westward, it leads near first-magnitude, reddish Aldebaran (the

Follower; so named because it follows the Seven Sisters of the Plei-
ades), in the V-shaped head of Taurus (the Bull). If the line of the belt
is followed in the opposite direction, it leads to Sirius, the brightest
of all the stars. This is the principal star in the constellation of Canis
Major (the Hunter's Large Dog). Starting with Sirius, a rough circle
can be drawn through Procyon in Canis Minor (the Little Dog),
Pollux and Castor in Gemini (the Twins), Capella in Auriga (the
Charioteer), Aldebaran, Rigel, and back to Sirius. All of these except
Castor are first-magnitude stars. Several second-magnitude stars in the
general area of Orion are bright enough for navigational purposes but
are seldom used, because there are so many first-magnitude stars nearby.
Four of these second-magnitude stars are listed among the principal
navigational stars of the almanac. These are Bellatrix, just west of
Betelgeuse; Alnilam, the middle star (actually, a spiral nebula) in the
belt; El Nath, in Taurus; and Adhara, part of the triangle in Canis
Major, just south of Sirius. Nearly on the meridian far to the south,
Canopus, the second-brightest star, is visible only to observers in the
United States south of latitude 37.5°. This star is part of the constella-
tion Carina (the Keel).

Peacock—The brightest star in the southern constellation of the same
name. A curved line extending eastward from the Southern Cross
passes through Hadar and Rigil Kentaurus and leads to Peacock, about
30° SE of Scorpio. It crosses the celestial meridian during evening
twilight in early November and during morning twilight in late May
but is not visible north of latitude 33°N. Dec. 57°S, SHA 54°, mag. 2.1.

Pegasus—A little south of the zenith for most observers in the United
States, the great square of Pegasus (the Winged Horse) appears nearly
on the meridian in autumn. The eastern side of this square and Caph,
in Cassiopeia, nearly mark the hour circle of the vernal equinox.
Alpheratz and Markab, second-magnitude stars at opposite corners of
the square, are the principal navigational stars of this constellation.
Second-magnitude Enif is occasionally used. The square of Pegasus is
useful in locating several navigational stars. The line joining the stars
of the eastern side of the square, if continued southward, leads to
second-magnitude Diphda, in Cetus (the Whale). Similarly, a line
joining the stars of the western side of the square, if continued southward, leads to first-magnitude Fomalhaut. A line through the center
of the square, if continued eastward, leads to second-magnitude Hamal,
in Aries (the Ram), the location of the vernal equinox some 2,000
years ago, when it was designated the first point of Aries.

Perseus—Northern constellation lying southeast of Cassiopeia; it contains two navigational stars: Mirfak, or Marfak, of mag. 1.9; and Algol, remarkable for its periodic changes in brilliance from mag. 2.2 to mag. 3.5. A line from Algol westward to the bright Capella forms the base of an isosceles triangle having its apex at reddish Aldebaran 30° SE.

Phecda—The lower inner corner of the bowl in the Big Dipper (or Plow), in Ursa Major. Dec. 54°N, SHA 182°, mag. 2.54.

Pisces—Constellation southward and eastward of the square of Pegasus, containing no navigational stars. The so-called first point of Aries, or vernal equinoctial point, is located in this group.

Piscis Australis—Southern constellation, also sometimes called Piscis Austrinus, containing the navigational star Fomalhaut, of mag. 1.29.

Polaris—Brightest in Ursa Minor (the Little Bear), a constellation also known as the Little Dipper, extremity of the handle of which is marked by this star; also called polestar and North Star, from its close proximity to the north pole of the heavens. Polaris has long been a favorite with navigators for the determination of latitude by its altitude; in lower latitudes for compass observations; and as a ready reference point for showing direction at night.

Pollux—Brighter of two navigational stars in Gemini (the Twins). It lies 23° due north of bright Procyon and 4.5° SE of Castor.

Procyon—Star of mag. 0.48 in the Canis Minor (Little Dog) group, situated next to and east of Orion. It has Dec. 5° 21.5N and SHA 245°. Lines joining Sirius, Betelgeuse, and Procyon form an equilateral triangle.

Ras-Al-Hague (Rasalague)—Brightest star (mag. 2.14) in the group named by the ancients Ophiuchus (the Serpent Holder); Dec. 12° 35'N, and SHA 96°. A line from this star to Spica forms the hypotenuse of an isosceles triangle having its apex at Antares. It also lies at the western corner of a triangle having its apex in Vega, with Altair at its eastern corner.

Regulus—At the opposite end of Leo (the Lion) from Denebola; is the brightest star of the constellation. A line through Dubhe and Merak, the pointers by which Polaris is usually identified, extended about 45° southward and curved slightly toward the west, leads to Regulus, which forms the southern end of the handle of the Sickle (Mane of Leo). Dec. 12°N, SHA 208°, mag. 1.3.

Rigel—A brilliant, bluish star about 10°S and a little to the west of the belt of Orion (the Hunter). A line through the center of the belt and perpendicular to it passes close to Rigel to the south and red Betelgeuse about the same distance north of the belt. Rigel and Betelgeuse are at opposite corners of a box surrounding the belt of Orion. Dec. 8°S, SHA 282°, mag. 0.3.

Rigil Kentaurus—Brightest star in the Centaurus group. Easily recognized as the brightest of a conspicuous couple 4.5° apart called the pointers, because they are in line with about the middle of nearby Southern Cross, to the west. It is a binary star, or one of a pair revolving about a common center and appearing as a single star to the unaided eye.

Ruchbah—Star of mag. 2.80 in Cassiopeia. It is within a minute of inferior transit when Mizar, second from the end of the handle in the Big Dipper, is on the meridian above the pole, and vice versa.

Sabik—Part of the inconspicuous constellation Ophiuchus (the Serpent Holder), about 20°N of Scorpio. Sabik crosses the celestial meridian during evening twilight in August and during morning twilight in March. Dec. 16°S, SHA 103°, mag. 2.6.

Sagittarius—Southern constellation through which the sun passes at about the winter solstice, lying next to and east of Scorpio. The group contains two bright navigational stars, Kaus Australis and Nunki.

Scheat—Probably of Arabic origin, name given the star marking the northwest corner of the square of Pegasus. The star has a magnitude of 2.61 and lies in Dec. 28°N, SHA 14°. Another name for it appears in older usage as Menkhib, from Arabic *mankib,* meaning "a shoulder."

Schedar—Also written Schedir; one of Cassiopeia's brighter stars, having a magnitude varying from 2.1 to 2.6, and southernmost member of the group. When on the meridian below the pole, it is easily recognized as the second star from the western end of this constellation.

Scorpio—Conspicuous southern constellation called by sailors the Chainhook, from its resemblance to that instrument. It extends from northwest to southeast between declinations 20° and 43°. The bright, red Antares lies close to the handle, and another bright member of the group, Shaula, marks the point of the Hook (tail) in 37°S. The sun passes through the northern part of this constellation during the latter part of November.

Sirius—Brightest star in the heavens; of the group Canis Major, located just southeast of Orion. Its magnitude is −1.58; SHA 259.25°; Dec. 16° 39′ S.

Spica—Principal star in Virgo and listed in the *Nautical Almanac* as Alpha Virginis. Has a magnitude of 1.21, SHA 159°, and Dec. 11°S. It may be located by continuing the curve of the Big Dipper's handle through Arcturus, halfway between.

Suhail—One of a number of second-magnitude stars extending along the Milky Way between Sirius and the Southern Cross. It is about 10°N of the False Southern Cross, which is nearly enclosed by a large, equilateral triangle formed by Suhail, Canopus, and Miaplacidus. Canopus and Suhail are on opposite edges of the Milky Way, with a number of second-magnitude stars between them. A straight line extending eastward through the east–west arm of the Southern Cross leads to Suhail, about 35° away. In the southern United States, Suhail crosses the celestial meridian near the southern horizon during evening twilight in April and during morning twilight in November. Dec. 43°S, SHA 223°, mag. 2.2.

Tucana—Also Toucan; a small southern constellation located on the opposite side of the pole from the Southern Cross and having about the same declination. Its brightest star is Alpha Tucanae, of mag. 2.91, SHA 25°, Dec. 60.5°S.

Ursa Major—A conspicuous northern constellation, also known as the Great Bear, Dipper, Plow, and Charles's Wain or Charlie's Wagon; easily recognized by the dipperlike formation of its seven principal stars. The two stars marking the outer limit of the bowl are called the pointers, for their use in locating Polaris, or the polestar. The line of the pointers extended 28°, or about the length of the Great Bear itself, comes close to Polaris, and when the tail star, or end of the Dipper's handle, is directly below or above Polaris, the latter bears very nearly true north, or has arrived at upper or lower culmination. Pointers are named Dubhe and Merak, the former marking the lip of the bowl. Tail-end star is Alkaid, or Benetnasch.

Ursa Minor—Polaris is part of the Little Dipper, as the constellation Ursa Minor (the Little Bear) is popularly known. This constellation is not conspicuous until the sky has become quite dark. Only Polaris, at one end, and Kochab, at the other, both second-magnitude stars, are used by the navigator. The Little Dipper is roughly parallel to the Big Dipper but upside down with respect to it. In the autumn, the Big Dipper is under the Little Dipper, and there is an old saying that liquid spilling out of the little one will be caught in the big one. The handles of the two dippers curve in opposite directions relative to their bowls.

Vega—The brightest star north of the celestial equator, and the third-brightest in the entire sky. It is the western vertex of a large triangle that is a conspicuous feature of the evening sky in late summer and autumn. The other two stars of the triangle are Altair and Deneb, both first-magnitude. Vega passes through the zenith approximately at latitude 38°45'N during evening twilight in September and during morning twilight in April. Dec. 39°N, SHA 81°, mag. 0.1.

Zuben el Genubi—A third-magnitude star, in the southern (or western) base of Libra (the Balance). Libra is about 25° WNW of Antares, in Scorpio. Dec. 16°S, SHA 138°, mag. 2.9.

IV

NAVIGATIONAL

ALPHABET

INTERNATIONAL CODE OF SIGNALS
Allows mariners of different nations
to communicate at sea.

A—International code burgee, or swallowtail flag, white and blue vertically divided, which, hoisted alone, denotes "I am undergoing a speed trial"; shown by towing vessel, "Is the towing hawser fast?" or, by vessel towed, "Towing hawser is fast." When uppermost in a four-flag hoist, distinguishes such signals as that denoting the name of a place. In a two-flag hoist as upper flag, indicates "abandoning vessel," "accident," or "aground."

B—In the International code of signals, a red burgee. Flown by itself, indicates "I am taking on or discharging explosives." In ships' logbooks, "b" is often used for "blue sky" and "B" for "broken sea." "b" corresponds to the Greek letter beta (β), used from ancient times in designating the second-brightest star in a constellation, as β Orionis, or Rigel of Orion.

C—Square flag denoting the letter "C" in International code of signals, horizontal stripes blue-white-red-white-blue. When flown single, indicates "yes" or "affirmative"; in semaphore signaling, letter "C," indicated by the right arm stretched upward at 45°, is given by receiver at end of each word as acknowledgment of receipt. "C" stands for Centigrade thermometer reading. Common abbreviation in ships' logbooks for clouds, or for choppy or cross sea.

D—International code signal flag, horizontal stripes yellow-blue-yellow. Hoisted single, indicates "Keep clear of me—I am maneuvering with difficulty." "d" is often written as an abbreviation for "drilling" in ships' logbooks. Corresponds to Greek delta (δ), denoting the fourth star of a constellation in order of magnitude, usually as observed by ancient astronomers.

E—Corresponds to Greek letter epsilon (ϵ), designating the fifth star (originally in point of brilliancy or magnitude) of a particular group,

279

as ϵ Orionis, fifth in the constellation Orion. Abbreviation for "east" in compass points, as in E by S (east by south); ENE (east-northeast). In International code of signals, flag E (one blue over one red horizontal band) hoisted single, indicates "I am directing my course to starboard"; in Lloyd's classification system, stands for lowest class; in that of American Bureau of Shipping, an encircled "E" annexed to classification symbols signifies that vessel's equipment complies with requirements of the society's rules.

F—Abbreviation for "fog" in logbooks and weather records; for temperature readings by Fahrenheit thermometer, as in 50°F; and for "forward" in recording draft of ship, as in 25′10″F. In International code of signals, flag F (red diamond on white square), hoisted single, or by international Morse code, as a flashing signal, F ($\cdot\, \cdot - \cdot$), indicates "I am disabled. Communicate with me."

G—Abbreviation in ships' logbooks and meteorological records for gloomy appearance of weather; also for ground swell. International code flag G (alternate white and blue vertical stripes) hoisted single, signifies "I require a pilot."

H—Hoisted single, International code flag H (one white and one red vertical band) indicates "I have a pilot on board." As an abbreviation in nautical astronomy, h = hour; h or H = altitude or elevation; H = hack watch. In compass magnetism, H = horizontal component of the earth's total magnetic force. In logbooks and weather recording, H = heavy seas; h = heavy sea; h = hail. H-bar, H-beam, H-girder, H-iron signify structural metal of H-shaped cross-section.

I—In International code of signals, flag I (black ball on yellow), hoisted single, indicates "I am directing my course to port." In mechanics, a symbol of moment of inertia. Descriptive of structural steel, iron, or other metal having cross-sectional shape resembling letter "I," such as used in ship construction, as I-bar, I-iron, I-beam, I-rail.

J—In International code, is called the semaphore flag (blue-white-blue bands), which, hoisted either single or inferior to a group of signal letters, signifies "I am going to send a message by semaphore." It is kept flying while message is being made and is hauled down on completion of message.

K—In International code, denotes, as a single-letter flag (one yellow and blue vertical band) hoist, or as Morse code ($- \cdot -$) flashing signal, "You should stop your vessel instantly." As lowercase letter, abbreviation for knots in expressing speed of vessel, as 14 k.

L—As an International code signal, flag L, (four squares alternately black and yellow) hoisted single, or flashed by Morse code ($\cdot - \cdot\, \cdot$), denotes

"You should stop; I have something important to communicate." In logbooks and weather recording, capital "L" usually signifies long, rolling sea and, sometimes, latitude; a small "l" = lightning. Abbreviation on charts for lake, loch, or lough. On board ship, denotes lower, as in L.H. (lower hold); L.T.D. (lower 'tween deck); L.M.R. (lower mail room).

M—In International code of signals, flag M (white X on blue ground), hoisted single, denotes "I have a doctor on board." "M" or "m" signifies moderate sea or swell and misty, in ships' logbooks or weather-observation records; main, as in main hatch, main topmast, etc.; and minute of time, as in "clocks advanced 17m." In navigation, "M" is often used to denote meridianal parts; "m," for meridianal difference; on charts, "m" indicates mud sea bottom.

N—In International code, denoted by square flag having four horizontal rows of alternate blue and white squares. Hoisted single, signifies "no" (negative). As initial letter in radio-call signs of civil aircraft, indicates nationality, as of United States of America; this five-letter call is painted on the lower surface of a plane and on each side of its fuselage (the "N," or nationality, mark in this case being separated from the rest of the group by a hyphen). As an abbreviation, "N" stands for navy; nimbus (cloud); noon; north or northern. It is signified in Morse code by (– •).

O—Square flag, diagonally halved in red and yellow, hoisted single, or as Morse flashing signal (– – –), denoting letter "O," indicates "Man overboard" in International code of signals. The symbol ö, as that occurring in German and Scandinavian alphabets, in visual and sound signaling by use of international Morse code, is indicated by (– – – •). Overcast sky, in ships' logbooks and weather records, usually is indicated by "O" or "o."

P—In International code, a square blue flag with a white square in its center, popularly known as Blue Peter (a corruption of "blue repeater," as used in a former British naval code). Hoisted single, denotes "All persons are to repair on board, as the vessel is about to proceed to sea." As a Morse code flashing signal at sea (• – – •), denotes "Your lights are out or burning low." By a ship towing, signifies "I must get shelter or anchor as soon as possible"; by a ship towed, "Bring me to shelter or to anchor as soon as possible." As a symbol in a logbook or weather record, "p" = passing showers; in nautical astronomy, denotes polar distance; in navigation, departure.

Q—Denoted in International code of signals by a square yellow flag, or by a flashing or sound signal in international Morse code as (– – • –).

Flag Q, hoisted single by a vessel arriving from a foreign port, signifies "My vessel is healthy and I request free pratique." Displayed by a vessel towing, denotes "Shall we anchor at once?," or, by a towed vessel, "I wish to anchor at once." Abbreviation "Q" or "q," in ships' logbooks and weather records, is used for squalls or squally weather.

R—As an abbreviation in ships' logbooks and weather-observation records "R" or "r" denotes rain; also, rough sea. In U.S. Navy, "R" in records of enlisted men signifies "deserted." International code flag R is a yellow Greek cross on a square red ground. Hoisted single, or as Morse code R (• – •) by flashing, means "The way is off my ship; you may feel your way past me." When shown by ship towed, "Go slower"; by a towing ship, "I will go slower."

S—In freeboard, or Plimsoll, marks on a ship's side, denotes summer-season line, or limit to which a seagoing vessel may be immersed. In ships' logbooks and weather records, abbreviation for snow or snowing; south; smooth sea. International code flag is a white ground with a central blue square. Hoisted single, denotes "My engines are going full speed astern"; displayed by a ship towed, indicates "Go astern"; and by a ship towing, "My engines are going astern." May be indicated by flashing Morse code S (• • •).

T—As an abbreviation, "t" = time or local hour angle; thunder; ton or tons; "T" = tropical, in vessels' load-line marks; true, as in distinguishing a true from a compass or magnetic course or bearing; also = time, as in GCT (Greenwich civil time). The letter is denoted by an International code flag showing red, white, and blue equal vertical divisions. Flown single, it signifies "Do not pass ahead of me"; by a ship towing, means "I am increasing speed"; and, by a ship towed, "Increase speed." In flashing Morse code, "T" is a single dash (-).

U—Abbreviation in the form (U) denotes, on charts and in light lists, that light indicated is unwatched or unattended, thus warning the navigator of possible failure of such light; as "u" in logbooks and meteorological records, signifies ugly, threatening appearance of weather. In International code of signals, flag U is a square showing two white and two red squares of equal size, alternately set. This flag, hoisted single, denotes "You are standing into danger," which signal also may be given by Morse code flashing as (• • –).

V—In the International code signals, V is a square flag having a white ground with an oblique or diagonal red cross. Hoisted single or flashed in Morse code by (• • • –), denotes "I require assistance"; by a ship towing, means "Set sails"; and, by a ship towed, "I will set sails." As a symbol in weather records, "v" equals variable, usually in describing winds.

W—As an abbreviation, stands for compass point west; also winter, in freeboard or load-line markings. In logbooks and weather records, "w" = heavy dew. In International code of signals, flag W is a central red square set to a larger white square with an all-around blue border. Hoisted single, denotes "I require medical assistance." As a towing signal, denotes, by flag or flashing light, "I am paying out the towing hawser." This may be used either by a vessel towing or by a vessel towed.

X—Square flag "X ray" of the International code, showing a white ground with a blue Greek cross extending full breadth and length of flag. Flown uppermost in a four-flag hoist, signifies a true bearing that is indicated by the other three flags, as X 0 0 5; X 3 5 0; or, respectively, true bearings 5° and 350°. Hoisted single, it means "Stop carrying out your intentions and watch for my signals." As a towing signal, hoisted or otherwise exhibited single, by a ship towing, signifies "Get spare towing hawser ready"; by a ship towed, "Spare towing hawser is ready."

Y—In the International code of signals, denoted by square flag, that has a series of diagonal alternating yellow and red bars of equal width, having an upward slant at a 45° angle with the hoist. Displayed single, denotes "I am carrying mails." As a towing signal, the flag, or its Morse code equivalent by flashing light (– • – –), signifies "I cannot carry out your order," as sent by either a vessel towing or a vessel towed.

Z—International code square flag consisting of four colored isosceles triangles having their apexes meeting at flag's center, black triangle being at the hoist, blue at the fly, yellow at the top, and red at the bottom. Flown single, the flag indicates "I wish to address, or am addressing, a shore station"; its equivalent may be indicated by flashing the "Z" character in Morse code (– – • •). As a towing signal, hoisted or otherwise displayed single by a ship towing, flag Z denotes "I am commencing to tow"; by a ship towed, "Commence towing." As an abbreviation, "Z" = azimuth; "z" = zenith distance, and, in weather recording, hazy.

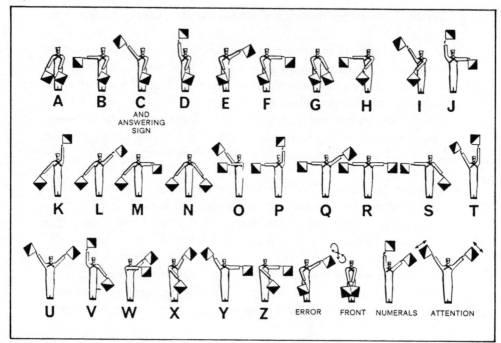

The semaphore signaling code   Courtesy U.S. Navy Training Publications Center

A	• —	J	• — — —	R	• — •
B	— • • •	K	— • —	S	• • •
C	— • — •	L	• — • •	T	—
D	— • •	M	— —	U	• • —
E	•	N	— •	V	• • • —
F	• • — •	O	— — —	W	• — —
G	— — •	P	• — — •	X	— • • —
H	• • • •	Q	— — • —	Y	— • — —
I	• •			Z	— — • •

Period • — • — • —
Comma — — • • — —
Interrogative • • — • • — — • — (RQ)
Distress Call • • • — — — • • • (SOS)
From — • • • (DE)
Invitation to transmit (go ahead) — • — (K)
Wait • — • • • (AS)
Error • • • • • • • • (EEEE etc.)
Received • — • (R)
End of each message • — • — • (AR)

1	• — — — —	2	• • — — —	3	• • • — —
4	• • • • —	5	• • • • •	6	— • • • •
7	— — • • •	8	— — — • •	9	— — — — •
				0	— — — — —

NOTE:
A dash is equal to three dots.
The space between parts of the same letter is equal to one dot.
The space between two letters is equal to three dots.
The space between two words is equal to five dots.

The international Morse code, with certain simple procedure signals.

**Two-letter groups
from the International code of signals.**

(Effective April 1 1969.)

AE	I must abandon my vessel.	**PD**	Your navigation light(s) is (are) not visible.
CJ	Do you require assistance?	**PT**	What is the state of the tide?
CN	I am unable to give assistance.	**QX**	I request permission to anchor.
JI	Are you aground?	**RY**	You should proceed at slow speed while passing me
JL	You are running the risk of going aground.		(or vessels making this signal).
JW	I have sprung a leak.	**UF**	You should follow pilot boat (or vessel indicated).
KN	I cannot take you in tow.	**UO**	You must not enter harbor.
LN	Light (name follows) has been extinguished.	**UT**	Where are you bound ?
LO	I am not in my correct position. (To be used	**YK**	I am unable to answer your signal.
	by a lightship.)	**YX**	I wish to communicate by radiotelephony
LR	Bar is not dangerous.		on frequency indicated.
LS	Bar is dangerous.	**ZM**	You should send (or speak) more slowly.
MF	Course to reach me is . . .	**ZP**	My last signal was incorrect. I will
MG	You should steer course . . .		repeat it correctly.
NF	You are running into danger.	**ZQ**	Your signal appears incorrectly coded. You should
NG	You are in a dangerous position.		check and repeat the whole.

FIG. 2615

How International Code Flags are Used in Signaling

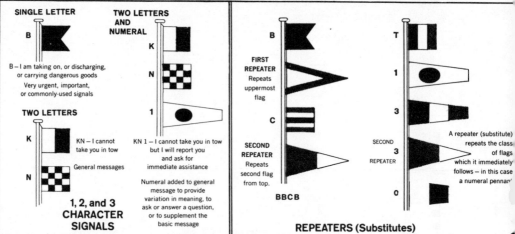

SINGLE LETTER

B – I am taking on, or discharging, or carrying dangerous goods

Very urgent, important, or commonly-used signals

TWO LETTERS AND NUMERAL

KN 1 – I cannot take you in tow but I will report you and ask for immediate assistance

Numeral added to general message to provide variation in meaning, to ask or answer a question, or to supplement the basic message

TWO LETTERS

KN – I cannot take you in tow

General messages

1, 2, and 3 CHARACTER SIGNALS

FIRST REPEATER
Repeats uppermost flag

SECOND REPEATER
Repeats second flag from top.

BBCB

SECOND REPEATER

A repeater (substitute) repeats the class of flags which it immediately follows – in this case a numeral pennant

REPEATERS (Substitutes)

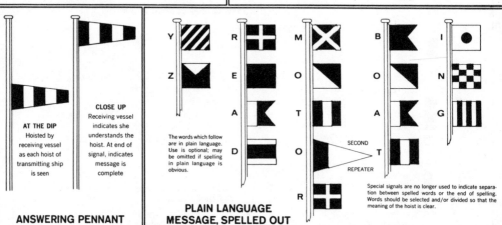

AT THE DIP
Hoisted by receiving vessel as each hoist of transmitting ship is seen

CLOSE UP
Receiving vessel indicates she understands the hoist. At end of signal, indicates message is complete

ANSWERING PENNANT

The words which follow are in plain language. Use is optional; may be omitted if spelling in plain language is obvious.

SECOND REPEATER

Special signals are no longer used to indicate separation between spelled words or the end of spelling. Words should be selected and/or divided so that the meaning of the hoist is clear.

PLAIN LANGUAGE MESSAGE, SPELLED OUT

• SPECIAL NAVY FLAGS AND PENNANTS •
(With spoken and written names)

One 1	Two 2	Three 3	Four 4	Five 5	Six 6	Seven 7
Eight 8	Nine 9	Zero 0	Squad Squad	Div Div	Flot Flot	Port Port
Emergency Emerg	Station Station	Speed Speed	Subdiv Subdiv	Black Pennant Black	Church Church	Starboard
Formation Form	Corpen Corpen	Turn Turn	Desig Desig	Interrogative Int	Negat Negat	Prep Prep
First Sub 1st	Second Sub 2nd	Third Sub 3rd	Fourth Sub 4th			

6-foot length of line with snap and ring

Tack Line ——————— Tack

INTERNATIONAL FLAGS AND PENNANTS

ALPHABET FLAGS			NUMERAL PENNANTS
Alfa *Diver Down; Keep Clear*	**K**ilo *Desire to Communicate*	**U**niform *Standing into Danger*	1
Bravo *Dangerous Cargo*	**L**ima *Stop Instantly*	**V**ictor *Require Assistance*	2
Charlie *Yes*	**M**ike *I Am Stopped*	**W**his-key *Require Medical Assistance*	3
Delta *Keep Clear*	**N**ovem-ber *No*	**X**ray *Stop Your Intention*	4
Echo *Altering Course to Starboard*	**O**scar *Man Overboard*	**Y**ankee *Am Dragging Anchor*	5
Foxtrot *Disabled*	**P**apa *About to Sail*	**Z**ulu *Shore Stations*	6
Golf *Want a Pilot*	**Q**uebec *Request Pratique*	**REPEATERS** 1st Repeat	7
Hotel *Pilot on Board*	**R**omeo *Require a Tug*	2nd Repeat	8
India *Altering Course to Port*	**S**ierra *Engines Going Astern*	3rd Repeat	9
Juliett *On Fire; Keep Clear*	**T**ango *Keep Clear of Me*	**CODE** *Code and Answering Pennant (Decimal Point)*	0

NOTE: From revised International Code of Signals effective 1 April 1969.